The Visio Idea Book

By Debbie Walkowski

alpha books

A Division of Macmillan Computer Publishing
A Prentice Hall Macmillan Company
201 W. 103rd Street, Indianapolis, Indiana 46290 USA

For Frank and Christopher, the two brightest stars in my life.

© 1994 Alpha Books

International Standard Book Number: 1-56761-493-0

Library of Congress Catalog Card Number: 94-70829

96 95 94   8 7 6 5 4 3 2 1

Interpretation of the printing code: the rightmost number of the first series of numbers is the year of the book's printing; the rightmost number of the second series of numbers is the number of the book's printing. For example, a printing code of 94-1 shows that the first printing of the book occurred in 1994.

Printed in the United States of America

Publisher
Marie Butler-Knight

Product Development Manager
Faithe Wempen

Acquisitions Manager
Barry Pruett

Managing Editor
Elizabeth Keaffaber

Senior Development Editor
Seta Frantz

Production Editor
Michelle Shaw

Copy Editor
Audra Gable

Cover Designer
Karen Ruggles

Designer
Barbara Kordesh

Indexer
Chris Cleveland

Production Team
Gary Adair, Dan Caparo,
Brad Chinn, Kim Cofer,
Lisa Daugherty, David Dean,
Cynthia Drouin, Jennifer Eberhardt,
Erika Millen, Angel Perez,
Beth Rago, Bobbi Satterfield,
Karen Walsh, Robert Wolf

Special thanks to C. Herbert Feltner for ensuring the technical accuracy of this book.

Contents

Introduction

Let's face it. Most of us who use personal computers aren't professional graphic artists. We manage to type our letters with a word processor and do some simple calculations with a spreadsheet program, but we shudder at the thought of having to create a drawing on a computer—and with a mouse no less! Many of us have tried using other drawing programs only to find just how difficult it is to draw "freehand" with a mouse. And it's nearly impossible to avoid drawing freehand; any drawing that contains shapes more complex than simple circles or rectangles is likely to require some freehand drawing as well. For most of us artistically incompetent types, we're faced with the options of hiring a professional to do the job or settling for a drawing that looks "homemade."

Well, that's not the case with Visio. The drag-and-drop concept behind Visio is so simple, it's a wonder no one thought of it before now. With Visio, you no longer have to spend tedious hours drawing detailed objects, designs, and symbols. You simply drag a *shape*—a graphic representation of a familiar object—from a stencil and drop it onto your drawing page, then you just connect the shapes and add text where you want it. Drag and drop is the most important feature distinguishing Visio from other drawing programs.

Visio contains literally hundreds of shapes for you to choose from: shapes for designing home and office spaces; shapes for drawing local, city, state, country, and world maps; shapes for creating business and organization flowcharts; shapes for drawing computer networks; and much, much more. But the real power behind Visio is its flexibility. You can bend, stretch, resize, and modify almost any shape, and you can create new shapes by combining or fragmenting other shapes. In addition, some of Visio's shapes are *SmartShapes*—shapes that actually behave differently depending on how you choose to modify them. And, yes, for the very brave, you can even draw using drawing tools. If you're the type of artist who never got past stick-figure drawing, you'll love using Visio.

About Visio Products

Visio 3.0 by Shapeware Corporation includes the Visio program and a set of selected *stencils*. A stencil is a collection of related shapes designed to help you create a particular type of drawing. Shapeware Corporation also produces 15 separate *Visio Shape* add-on packages that do not contain the Visio program itself, but rather provide additional stencils, each containing dozens of shapes, for you to use in your Visio drawings. The add-on Visio Shape packages include:

- Marketing

- Mechanical Engineering

- Advanced Network Diagrams
- Advanced Space Planning
- Advanced Electrical Engineering
- Biotechnology/Medicine
- Advanced Flowcharts
- Chemical Engineering
- Chemistry
- Petroleum Engineering
- Software Diagrams
- Home Planning
- Landscape Planning
- Insurance
- Kids

To introduce you to some of these stencils, this book includes a disk that contains more than 200 of Visio's add-on shapes from the Home Planning, Landscape Planning, Insurance, and Kids packages. Chapter 16 contains several examples of projects created using these add-on shapes.

Who This Book Is For

So, you've purchased Visio 3.0, you've scanned the *Using Visio* manual that came with it, and you've experimented with the program. Now what? What kinds of drawings can you create? What's the best method for creating an organization chart? What tips and tricks will help you draw a map to your home or lay out furniture in your new office?

The Visio Idea Book takes you one step beyond the *Using Visio* manual to show you how you can use the program *productively*. It is designed for users who understand the basic concept behind Visio 3.0, and who grasp the idea of dragging and dropping shapes-but need some ideas for creative drawings. In this book you'll find real-world examples of drawings, maps, floor plans, charts, forms, business drawings, diagrams, and special projects like thank-you cards, certificates, and personal stationery.

If you've never used Visio 3.0 before, this book will teach you how to use it as well as give you ideas for using Visio productively. Although *The Visio Idea Book* is not intended to be a detailed "how to" book, the first three chapters cover the basics of using the Visio program.

What You'll Find Inside

The Visio Idea Book is essentially divided into three parts. The first three chapters cover basic introductory information about starting the program; maneuvering menus, dialog boxes, and toolbars; arranging windows on the screen; and so on. You learn the basics of using the program itself: how to create, move, copy, resize, and rotate shapes. You also learn about connecting, joining, combining, and gluing shapes, and how to add text to your drawings. This is not a heavy-duty "how to" section, but rather a quick reference designed to get you up to speed on the basics of using the program. If you've used Visio before, you might choose to skim Chapters 1–3.

Chapters 4–16 give you examples of real Visio projects for business, home, school, and personal use. Each chapter contains several examples of projects, and ideas for other projects to try on your own. The first project in each chapter describes the drawing in detail and includes illustrations and step-by-step instructions for completing the drawing. Later sections within the chapters describe and illustrate additional projects as needed so that you can create the drawings on your own.

The appendices at the end of the book are a great source of information. Appendix A lists the shapes that come with Visio and their names. Appendix B shows you completed Visio projects to help you generate ideas. Appendix C gives step-by-step instructions for installing Visio.

How to Use This Book

Chapters 4–16 contain step-by-step instructions for creating specific types of drawings. The instructions tell you exactly what to do rather than explaining in detail *why* you should do something. The primary steps in the process are numbered; within each step, substeps are indicated with bullets. You'll also find tips for modifying a drawing, simplifying the creation process, or using the drawing in different ways.

You'll see the following types of examples and explanations in the projects:

When the instructions say:

Align the Manager shape to 6"/1".

this means to position the Manager shape in line with the 6" point on the vertical ruler and the 1" point on the horizontal ruler. When two ruler points are given (as in 6"/1"), *the first number is the point on the vertical ruler; the second number is the point on the horizontal ruler.* You can remember this by remembering to work left to right.

When the instructions say:

Align the Executive shape at 8"/vertical guide.

this means to drag the Executive shape to align with the 8" point on the vertical ruler along the vertical guide.

When the instructions say:

   Align the Assistant shape to horizontal guide/4".

this means to drag the Assistant shape along the horizontal guide to the 4" point on the horizontal ruler.

Now, go have some fun drawing with Visio!

Acknowledgments

My heartfelt appreciation to Barry Pruett, acquisitions manager, and Seta Frantz, senior development editor, who were wonderful to work with on this book. In addition to their creative solutions, both kept their cool—and helped me to keep mine—throughout the myriad of changes this book endured along the way.

A special thanks to all the people at Shapeware—Phil Johanson, Maryann Klustner, Paul Lewis, Michele De William, and a courteous and competent technical support staff—who generously contributed their creative ideas, valuable time, and technical and editorial support. Being able to work so closely with the software vendor contributed greatly to the quality of this book. Shapeware is a topnotch organization, and Visio 3.0 is a fantastic product of which everyone at Shapeware deserves to be proud.

Part 1

Learning the Visio Basics

If you are a new user of Visio, you won't want to skip the first three chapters of this book. Here you get a taste of just what Visio is capable of, and you learn the basics of how to get it to do what you want. You learn about the Visio concept of drawing, which doesn't require you to "draw" anything at all. You learn how to perform basic tasks such as dragging shapes onto a drawing; copying, moving, deleting, and altering shapes; adding text to shapes; and creating new "custom" shapes. You also learn about some of Visio's unique and sophisticated features, such as joining shapes in different ways, creating additional pages in a drawing, and creating a custom stencil or template. Once you've mastered the basics in Part 1, you can have fun creating the useful, timesaving projects in Part 2.

Getting Started with Visio

Visio is the most sensible and easy-to-use drawing program on the market today. It's designed for nonartists who need to create drawings, diagrams, maps, forms, and charts, and it's so easy; if you can click and drag a mouse, you can create a drawing.

Visio's "drag-and-drop" concept lets you drag *shapes* (familiar objects such as chairs or tables) from a Visio drawing stencil and drop them onto a Visio drawing page. You can then size and arrange the shapes as needed, add text where you want, and voilá you've got yourself a drawing. Using Visio shapes, you can create a wide variety of drawings, from landscape plans to pie charts; from kitchen designs to computer network diagrams.

Visio operates in much the same way as other Windows-based programs. For those of you who have never used a Windows-based program, this chapter teaches you the basics of working in a Windows environment and how to work with Visio specifically. If you've used Windows programs before, you might want to quickly skim this chapter or skip it and move on to Chapter 2.

What You Need to Get Started

To run Visio, you must have a 386-based or higher computer running at 20MHz or better and have at least 4MB of RAM (random access memory). You also need a VGA, Super VGA, XGA, 8514/A or other Windows 3.1-compatible graphics card and monitor, as well as a Microsoft Mouse or other Windows 3.1-compatible mouse. Last but not least, you must be running Microsoft Windows 3.1 or later. This may sound like a lot of information to weed through to find out if you can run Visio. However, if you already run Windows and other Windows programs successfully, you probably will not have any trouble running Visio under Windows. If you do have trouble, double check to make sure your system meets all of the above requirements.

When you install Visio, Visio program icons are automatically placed in a Visio group in the Windows Program Manager. If you have not yet installed Visio, refer to Appendix C for instructions.

Starting Visio

Before you start Visio, you need to know about stencils and templates. A *stencil* is a collection of related shapes used to create a specific type of drawing. For instance, the Map stencil contains a variety of shapes, such as roads, road signs, and landmarks, that you can drag and drop onto a drawing page. Stencils are stored Visio files. A *template* is similar to a stencil in that it is a stored Visio file, but it also contains all the proper settings, scale, and stencils required to create a specific type of drawing. The Map template, for example, opens Visio using the Map stencil and sets the drawing page in portrait orientation (8½" wide by 11" high) with a drawing scale in inches. The template also contains stored settings for a specific font and size, selected line style and fill colors for shapes, and so on.

When you want to create a specific type of drawing using predefined settings, you open Visio using a specific template, which automatically opens the proper stencil. Once Visio is open, you can open additional stencils if you want.

Visio templates are represented in the Visio group window in the Windows Program Manager. To open Visio using a specific template, double-click on the template icon. Visio starts, using the template you choose, and automatically opens the corresponding stencil.

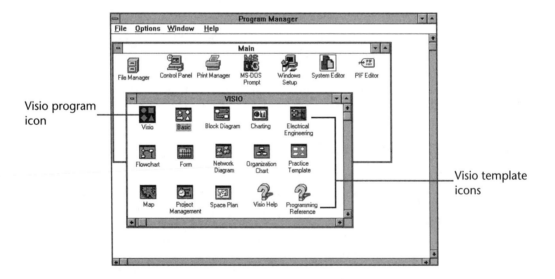

Visio program icon

Visio template icons

If you're not sure which template you want to use, or if you don't want to choose a template at all, you can start Visio by displaying the Visio group in the Program Manager and double-clicking on the Visio icon. Before Visio starts, the New dialog box appears, displaying a list of templates. Highlight the template you want (or No Template), then press Enter or click on the OK button.

If you want to open a Visio drawing that you have previously saved, choose the Open button in the New dialog box. Visio displays an Open dialog box from which you can select the saved file.

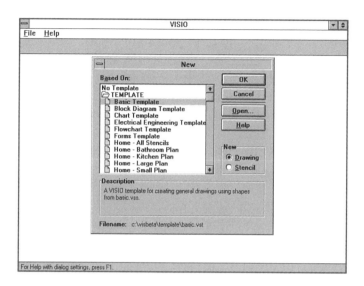

What's on Your Screen?

When you open Visio with a template, a stencil is displayed on the left side of your screen, and a drawing page is displayed on the right. (If you open Visio without a template, the drawing page is displayed by itself.) The figure below shows Visio as it looks when opened with the Basic template.

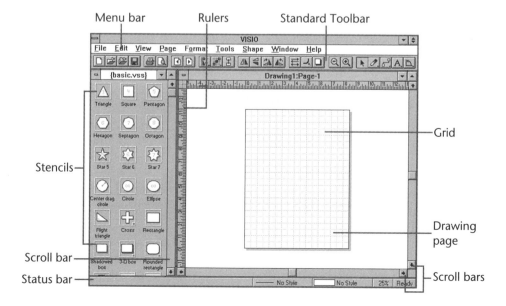

Menu bar   The menu bar contains the commands you use to accomplish specific tasks. You learn how to use the menu bar later in this chapter.

Standard Toolbar   The Standard Toolbar contains buttons with graphical icons that represent frequently used menu commands (such as a printer for the Print command). To activate a command, you simply click on the button in the toolbar. For example, to print your drawing, click on the Print button. (If you are not sure what a button does, simply point at it, and a ToolTip appears telling you about the button.)

Stencil   The stencil contains a collection of shapes that you use to create a drawing. Visio includes a wide variety of stencils designed for creating many different types of drawings.

Drawing page   The white area of the screen that represents a sheet of drawing paper. You place the shapes and text that make up a drawing on the drawing page.

Grid   Faint horizontal and vertical lines that cover the drawing page to help you accurately place shapes where you want them in your drawing.

Rulers   Measurement gauges that run vertically and horizontally along the left and top edges of the drawing page. They can display inches, feet, yards, miles, centimeters, meters, and other units of measure.

Scroll bars   Scroll bars allow you to shift your view of the stencil or drawing page so you can see areas of the drawing that are not visible. The stencil displays a scroll bar only when all master shapes are not visible on the screen at once.

Status bar   The status bar offers useful information as you work. For instance, as you're dragging shapes onto the drawing page, the status bar displays left, right, top, and bottom coordinates. When you point to a stencil without clicking the mouse button, the status bar displays a description of the shape. It's a good idea to get into the habit of checking the status bar for helpful tips as you work.

Opening Saved Visio Drawing Files

Once you have worked with Visio and have saved some drawing files, you'll want to reopen your saved files. To open a saved Visio file, start Visio by double-clicking on the Visio icon in the Visio group in Program Manager. When the New dialog box appears, click the Open button. Visio displays the Open dialog box from which you can select a saved file. Highlight the file name, then click OK or press Enter. You can also open a saved drawing in Visio by selecting the Open command from the File menu or by clicking on the Open button on the toolbar.

Using the Mouse

Because Visio is designed to be used with a mouse, the only way you can place shapes onto the drawing page is by dragging them. You can use either the keyboard or the mouse, however, to select Visio menu commands. If you've never used a mouse before, you should familiarize yourself with the following terms:

Point   Move the mouse pointer to a specific location on the screen.

Click   Press and release the left mouse button once.

Double-click   Press and release the left mouse button twice quickly.

Drag   Point to an object, press and hold the left mouse button, then drag the mouse to a new location and release the mouse button.

Unless otherwise stated, "click" always means to click the left mouse button. However, Visio has shortcut menus that you can access by pressing the right mouse button. So when instructions say to choose a command from the shortcut menu, always click the right mouse button once.

Using Menus, Dialog Boxes, and Toolbars

Like all Windows-based programs, Visio's commands are stored on pull-down *menus*. To open a menu, click on the menu name on the menu bar. When the menu opens, click on the command you want to choose. If the command name on the menu is followed by a *shortcut key*, such as Ctrl+C for Copy, you can bypass the menu by pressing the shortcut key(s) on the keyboard.

Some menu commands take immediate action, some toggle on and off, some are dimmed on the menu, and some open a dialog box. When a toggle command is turned on, a check mark appears to the left of the command name on the menu. When a command doesn't apply to the task you are performing at the time, the command is dimmed on the menu, and you cannot select it. When a command opens a dialog box, the command name is followed by an ellipsis (...) on the menu.

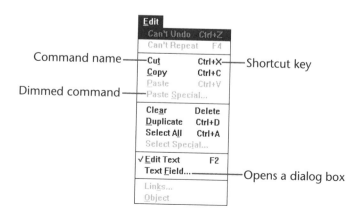

In addition to the standard menus found on the menu bar, Visio also uses *shortcut* menus. Shortcut menus save you the time of choosing and opening a menu on the menu bar because they pop up automatically with a single click and contain the commands you use most often. Shortcut menus are *context sensitive*: the commands on the menu vary depending on the task you are performing at the time. For instance, when a text object is selected, text commands (such as Cut, Copy, and Underline) appear on the shortcut menu. When a shape is selected, the shortcut menu displays commands (such as Rotate Left, Rotate Right, Line, and Fill) that let you change the characteristics of a shape. When nothing on the drawing is selected, the shortcut menu displays commands that let you change your view of the drawing, go to a different page, open a stencil, or insert objects.

To display a shortcut menu, click the right mouse button anywhere on the drawing page. A shortcut menu pops up on-screen near where you click. Select a command from a shortcut menu by clicking on it.

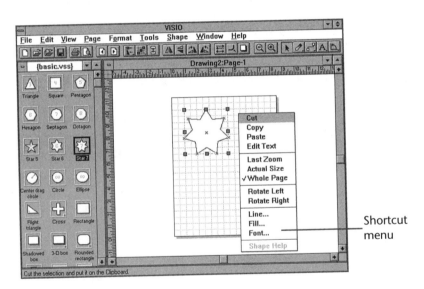

Shortcut menu

Using Dialog Boxes

A dialog box is a separate window that appears when you select a menu command that is followed by an ellipsis (...). In the dialog box, you provide more information about a command you have chosen. Because dialog boxes often contain many different options, they are often divided into sections containing different elements. This list describes the most common dialog box elements.

Text box   A box into which you type the information you are asked to supply.

List box   A box from which you select one item by highlighting it with the mouse or arrow keys.

Check box   A dialog box item preceded by a square check box. When multiple check boxes are displayed, you can select more than one. Each option is turned on or off when you select it. An X in the check box indicates that the option is activated or turned on.

Drop-down box   A box that reveals a list of items when you click on the downward-pointing arrow. You can select only one item in the list.

Option button   A dialog box item preceded by a circle shape. When multiple option buttons are displayed in a group, you can choose only one.

Command button   A button (such as OK or Cancel) that activates a command. Click on the button to choose it. When a command button name is followed by an ellipsis (...), it opens an additional dialog box.

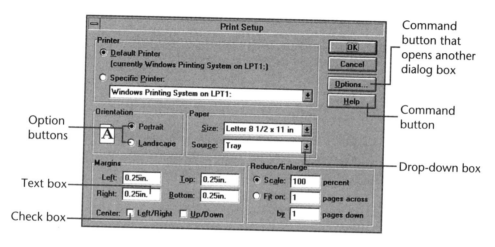

To change dialog box settings, simply click on the item you want to select, or type an entry in a text box. When all settings are correct, choose OK or Close.

Using Visio's Toolbars

The Visio window displays a toolbar just below the menu bar. A toolbar contains buttons with icons that represent frequently used menu commands (such as a printer for the Print command, a disk for the Save command, and so on). Toolbars make it easy for you to bypass menus and activate commands simply by clicking on a toolbar button.

When you click a toolbar button, Visio either takes immediate action, or it displays a drop-down list (as when you click the Align Shapes and Distribute Shapes buttons). When a drop-down list appears, choose a button from the list by dragging the mouse down the list and releasing the mouse on the toolbar button you want to use. Toolbar buttons that contain a drop-down list have a small downward-pointing arrow in the lower right corner of the button.

The buttons that appear on the toolbar vary depending on whether the stencil or drawing window is active. When the drawing window is active, Visio displays the *Standard Toolbar*. The Standard Toolbar contains buttons for working with files and stencils; printing; going to the next page; aligning and distributing shapes; flipping and rotating shapes; changing text, line, and shadow features; using Snap and Glue features; and zooming. The last five buttons are tools you use to draw shapes and create text.

 NOTE: For any toolbar option you choose, the number and location of buttons displayed on the toolbar vary depending on the resolution of your monitor. Monitors set for high resolution display more buttons than monitors set for low resolution.

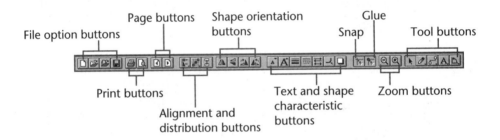

 NOTE: The toolbar in the preceding figure is shown at high resolution. Your toolbar might look different if you are using low resolution.

Visio provides several alternatives to the Standard Toolbar. You can choose the Microsoft Office Toolbar or the Lotus SmartSuite Toolbar, or you can turn the toolbar off. To choose a main toolbar option, choose the View Toolbars command or click the right mouse button on the Standard Toolbar, then choose Toolbars from the drop-down menu. When the Toolbars dialog box appears, click on a toolbar option, then click the OK button.

When you choose the Microsoft Office Toolbar option, Visio displays two toolbars containing all the buttons from the Standard Toolbar along with additional buttons for altering text, lines, and fill. Note that most figures in this book display the Microsoft Office Toolbar option because it displays the most possible buttons.

The Lotus SmartSuite Toolbar contains buttons used by Lotus SmartSuite. Notice that when you choose this toolbar option, pop-up boxes appear at the bottom of the screen on the status bar.

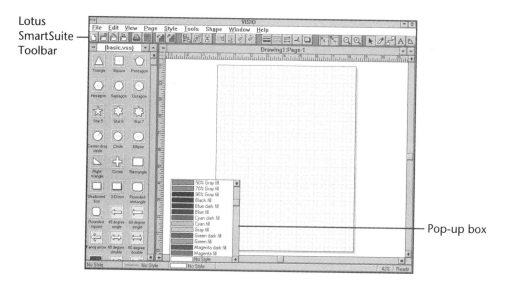

When a text block is selected or you are using the Text tool, the Text Toolbar automatically replaces the previous toolbar. The Text Toolbar contains buttons that let you quickly adjust the font, size, color, style, alignment, and positioning of text. As soon as you deselect a text block, the previous toolbar reappears.

The standard Visio Text Toolbar is shown in the following figure with pop-up boxes on the status bar. Note that the Text Toolbar looks slightly different if you choose the Lotus SmartSuite or Microsoft Office toolbar option.

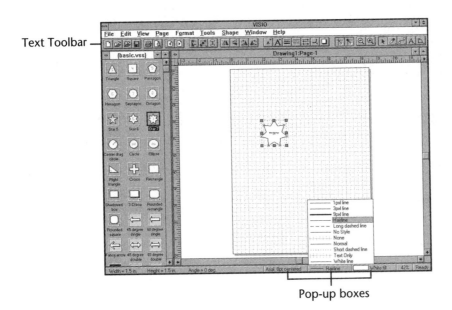

Pop-up boxes

When the stencil window is active, Visio displays the Stencil Toolbar. The tools on this toolbar let you change the way the stencil is displayed. For instance, you can display master shapes and names, master shapes only, or shape names only.

The Stencil Toolbar is shown below. Like the Text Toolbar, the Stencil Toolbar looks slightly different if you choose the Lotus SmartSuite or Microsoft Office toolbar option.

ToolTips

Are you wondering what some of the toolbar buttons do? No need to wonder. When you point to any toolbar button without clicking, the name of the button is displayed just below it. This feature is called *ToolTips*. ToolTips help you to use the buttons more effectively and eliminate the need to memorize the purpose of each button.

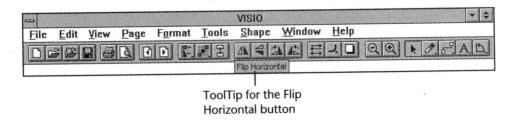

ToolTip for the Flip
Horizontal button

Arranging Visio Windows

As you saw earlier in this chapter, when you start Visio with a template file, a stencil appears on the left side of the screen, and a drawing page appears on the right side of the screen. Notice that the stencil and the drawing page are separate windows; each has its own Control-menu box, Maximize, and Minimize buttons.

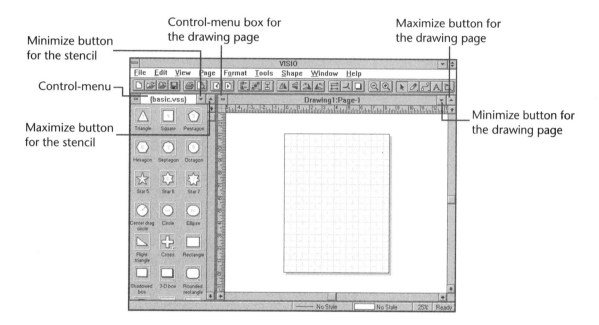

You can close the stencil or drawing page windows by double-clicking on the Control-menu box. When you close a stencil or a drawing page, it is no longer available on-screen.

You can maximize (enlarge to its largest size) either the stencil or drawing page window by clicking on the window's Maximize button. When a drawing you're working on already contains all the shapes you need, you might find it useful to maximize the drawing page window. A maximized window contains a Restore button, which returns the window to its previous size when you click it.

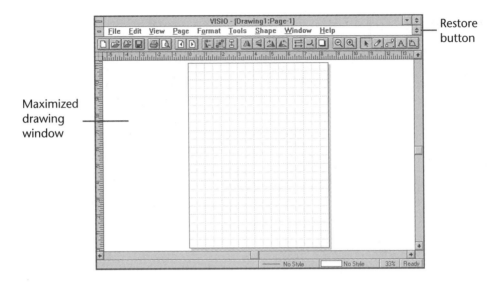

When you click a window's Minimize button, the window is reduced to an icon at the bottom of the screen. To restore a minimized window, double-click on the window icon.

Opening Additional Stencils and Drawing Files

In Visio, you can open more than one stencil or drawing at a time. Opening an additional stencil gives you access to more shapes at one time; opening an additional drawing file enables you to work on one or more drawings at once. To open an additional stencil, click the Open Stencil button on the toolbar, or choose the File Open Stencil command. Visio displays the Open Stencil dialog box. Highlight the stencil you want to open and choose OK. The new stencil appears on top of the previous one. Refer to the next two sections, "Arranging Multiple Windows" and "Switching Between Stencils and Drawing Windows," for information on using a different stencil.

To start a new drawing file (without closing the current one), click the New button on the toolbar or choose the File New command. Visio displays the New dialog box. Highlight the template you want to use and choose OK. You can also open a saved drawing file by clicking the Open button in the New dialog box. The new (or saved) drawing file and any associated stencils appear on-screen.

Arranging Multiple Windows

When you work with two or more stencils, or two or more drawing files at once, you might want to display them all on-screen together. You can do this by choosing the Window Tile command or by pressing Shift+F7. The Tile command displays all open files (stencils and drawing pages) like tiles on the screen, so that all are visible at once. The window with the highlighted title bar is the *active window*. To switch active windows, click anywhere inside the window you want to use.

Tiled stencil windows

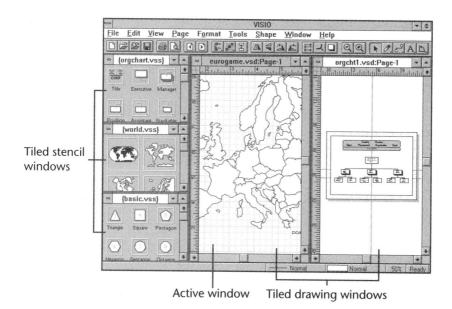

Active window   Tiled drawing windows

An alternative to tiling the open files is to *cascade* them by choosing the Window Cascade command or by pressing Alt+F7. This arrangement lays one window on top of the other, leaving just the title bar of the hidden windows visible. This arrangement makes it easy for you to switch back and forth between drawing pages or stencils by clicking anywhere inside the window you want to use.

Cascaded stencil windows

Cascaded drawing windows

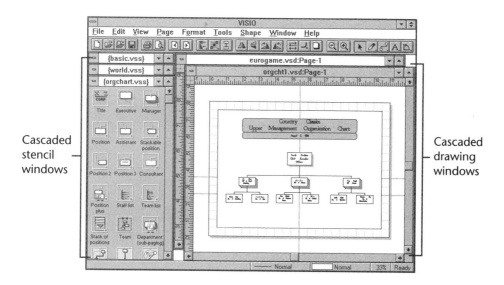

You can also minimize windows by clicking on a window's Minimize button. When you minimize an open window, an icon representing the window appears near the bottom of the screen. To restore a minimized window, double-click on it.

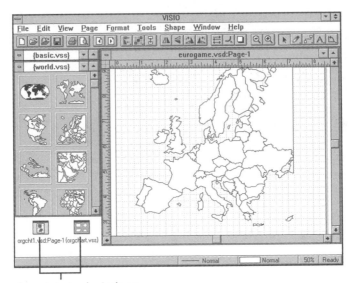

Icons for minimized windows

Switching Between Stencils and Drawing Windows

When you have multiple windows visible on-screen (for example, when windows are tiled or cascaded), it's easy to switch back and forth between windows; you just click anywhere in the window you want to use. However, when multiple drawings and stencils are open and are not all visible on-screen, you must use the Window menu to switch between windows.

Select the Window menu. The names of all open files are listed and numbered at the bottom of the menu. Just click on the file you want to use, or type the number for the file. (The file names of stencils, such as block.vss for the Block stencil, also appear in the Window menu.) A check mark appears to the left of the name of the currently active file.

Currently active file

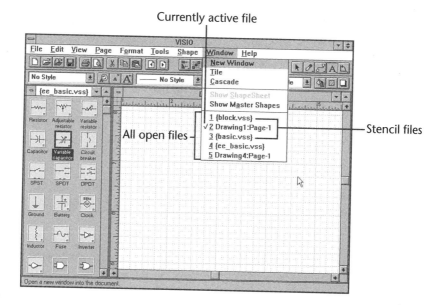

All open files

Stencil files

 TIP: You can also press Ctrl+F6 to cycle through all open windows (stencils and drawings) on-screen.

Adjusting Your View

When you begin a new Visio drawing, Visio displays a full-page view of the drawing page. This view is good for getting an overall picture of a drawing, but it isn't the best to work with as you're creating a drawing. In this view, text is difficult to read, and shapes are relatively small.

To quickly zoom in on the drawing page, press and hold the Shift and Ctrl keys. The mouse pointer changes to a magnifying glass. Drag the mouse pointer to outline the screen area you want to magnify, and Visio gives you a close-up view of that area. Repeat this process to zoom in even closer on a drawing.

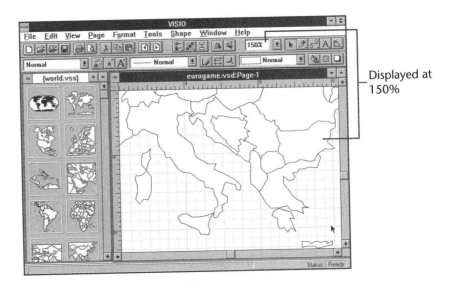

Displayed at 150%

You can also zoom in from a drawing or out from a drawing by clicking the Zoom button on the status bar on the Standard Toolbar. The pop-up list lets you choose 50%, 75%, 100%, 150%, 200%, and 400%, or you can type in a custom percentage such as 65%. Also from the pop-up list, the Page option switches you back to the original view, which fits a view of the entire page in the drawing page window.

TIP: As you are labeling a shape, Visio automatically zooms in so the text is readable as you type. When you finish typing, Visio returns to the previous zoom percentage. Refer to Chapter 2 for instructions on entering text.

The Width option fits the drawing to the width of the window, and the last Zoom option returns to the last zoom percentage you used. If you're using the Standard Toolbar, you can use the Zoom In and Zoom Out buttons to change your view. Zoom, percentage, and custom percentage options are also available on the View menu.

Saving Visio Drawing Files

Each new drawing you create in Visio is a *file*. Visio gives each new file you create a temporary name such as Drawing1, Drawing2, Drawing3, and so on. Each time you create a new file, the number in the file name is incremented. When you save a drawing file, you give it a unique file name, and Visio automatically adds the .VSD (for

Visio drawing) file extension to the name. (Template file extensions are .VST for Visio template, and stencil file extensions are .VSS for Visio stencil.) To save a drawing, click the Save button on the toolbar or choose the File Save command. The first time you save a file, the Save As dialog box appears.

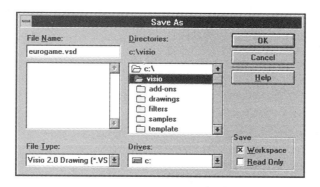

To save a file to a drive other than Drive C, choose a disk drive from the Drives drop-down list. In the Directories list, select the directory where you want to store the file on your disk. In the File Name box, type a unique file name. If you omit the file extension from the file name, Visio adds it for you automatically. When all settings are correct, choose OK.

Once you have saved a file with a permanent file name, the Save As dialog box does not appear when you click the Save button or choose the File Save command. You only need to display the Save As dialog box if you want to save the current file under a different name, with a different file type, or in a different directory or drive. To do this, choose the File Save As command.

There are two Visio Save options in the lower right corner of the Save As dialog box. The first, Workspace, allows you to save the configuration of your screen along with the file. The next time you open the file, the file and the current screen configuration are opened together. For instance, suppose you have a drawing and three stencils open on your screen, and two of the stencils are minimized. If you save the current file using the Workspace option, the next time you open the file, Visio opens the file and all stencils exactly as you had them arranged on your screen when you saved the drawing file.

The other Visio Save option in the lower right corner of the Save As dialog box lets you save a file as Read Only. This means that when the file is opened again, it can be read but it can't be altered. This is a good way to protect a drawing if you are loaning a file to another user or using a file for demonstration purposes.

Printing Visio Files

You can print a Visio drawing at any point as you're creating it. To print a drawing, choose the File Print command. In the Print dialog box that appears, choose the All Pages or Current Page option. To print selected pages, choose the Pages option and enter the correct page numbers in the From and To boxes. Choose other printing options (number of copies, collated copies, print color as black, and so on) in the Options box. To print high-quality graphics, choose 300 dpi in the Print Quality box. To print more quickly but at a lower quality, choose the 150 dpi setting. When all settings are correct, click OK. To print all pages of a drawing quickly without selecting any special print options, click the Print toolbar button.

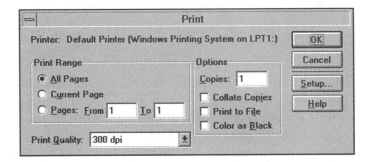

NOTE: If the print orientation does not match the orientation of your drawing—that is, if both are not landscape or both portrait—Visio displays an error message when you try to print. To match the print setup to the orientation of your drawing, choose the File Print Setup command. In the Print Setup dialog box, choose the correct page orientation, then click OK. Then select the File Print command again to print your file.

Closing Files and Exiting Visio

To close a file when you are finished working (a drawing *or* a stencil file), double-click the window's Control-menu box. If the file contains changes that have not yet been saved, Visio displays a message asking if you want to save the changes. Click Yes to save, No to discard the changes, or Cancel to return to the drawing without saving changes.

To close Visio, double-click on the Visio window's Control-menu box. For all open drawing files that contain changes, Visio displays a message asking if you want to save the changes. Click Yes to save, No to discard the changes, or Cancel to return to the drawing without saving changes.

Chapter Summary

In this chapter, you learned the basics of getting around in Visio; opening and closing files; working with menus, dialog boxes, and toolbars; arranging windows; and so on. In Chapter 2, you begin to learn about creating drawings in Visio.

A Quick Reference for Using Visio

Many first-time users will jump right into the projects in this book and begin creating real Visio drawings. If you're one of those users, you'll find Visio extremely easy to use, both in concept and in practice. In fact, you can't do much wrong by simply starting up the program and experimenting with it a bit.

As easy as Visio is to use, however, it's not a toy program. Like most programs that are worth the money you pay for them, Visio has some slick and sophisticated features—in addition to the basic ones—that you might not stumble across simply by accident. So if you're new to Visio, this chapter will help you quickly learn the basic concepts for creating a drawing—everything from adding, moving, copying, resizing, and deleting shapes to creating unique shapes and adding text to a drawing. If you've used Visio and feel confident performing basic tasks, you might want to skip this chapter and move directly to Chapter 4 where the specific project examples begin. You can come back and refer to the material in this chapter when you need further explanation or help on a task.

How Visio Works

Before you jump right into Visio, it's helpful if you have a basic understanding of how Visio works and how to create a drawing. The *drag and drop* technique employed by many Windows programs is a key feature in Visio. Instead of tediously drawing shapes with unwieldy drawing tools, you create drawings by dragging shapes from a stencil and dropping them onto the drawing page.

What is a *stencil*? A stencil is a collection of related shapes designed to help you create a particular type of drawing. For instance, the Flowchart stencil contains a collection of shapes you are most likely to need when creating a flowchart. Each shape in a stencil is called a *master shape* because dragging a master shape onto the drawing page creates a copy, or *instance*, of the master shape in your drawing. The master shape itself remains in the stencil so you can use it over and over again. For clarity, *master shapes* are often referred to simply as *shapes*.

On a typical Visio screen, a stencil appears on the left side of the screen. On the right side of the screen is the drawing page. To create a drawing, you drag a master shape from the stencil onto the drawing page and release the mouse button. The master shape remains in the stencil and a copy of the shape appears on the drawing page. Once you have the shape in the drawing, you can move, size, copy, reshape, rotate, or make a variety of other changes to the shape to complete your drawing.

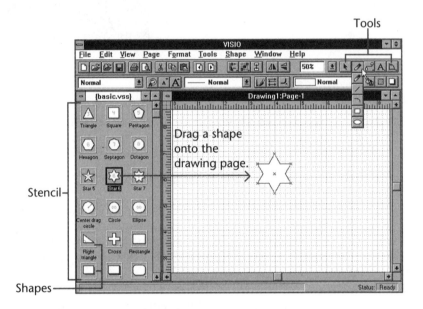

In Visio, you use a *tool* to drag shapes and accomplish other tasks. When doing routine tasks such as dragging, moving, or copying a shape, you use the pointer tool, a large black arrow. Visio has a variety of other tools (such as the Pencil tool, Line tool, Arc tool, Rotation tool, and Text tool, to name a few) that you use instead of the pointer tool for particular tasks. All Visio tools are located at the right end of the toolbar. Some are located on drop-down menus under the toolbar buttons.

The table below describes Visio's tools:

Icon	Tool	Use
	Pointer	For selecting, moving, sizing, and dragging shapes.
	Pencil	For drawing lines or arc segments.
	Line	For drawing straight lines.
	Arc	For drawing elliptical arcs.

Icon	Tool	Use
□	Rectangle	For drawing rectangular shapes.
○	Ellipse	For drawing elliptical shapes.
🔲	Connector	For drawing connectors between shapes.
×	Connection Point	For adding connection points to a shape.
⊥	Rubber stamp	For stamping multiple instances of a master shape in a drawing.
A	Text	For typing and editing text in text blocks.
🔲	Text block	For selecting text blocks to move or rotate independently of a shape.
◳	Rotation	For rotating a shape.
◳	Crop	For sizing the border around an imported object.

Working with Visio's Stencil Shapes

Visio contains literally hundreds of shapes available in more than twenty stencils. Aside from just dragging and dropping shapes onto the drawing page, you need to know how to "manipulate" shapes: that is, to move, size, reshape, copy, and rotate them. In this section, you learn the basic techniques for working with Visio's stencil shapes.

Shape Descriptions

Some stencils contain literally dozens of shapes. Just by looking at a shape icon, it's often not clear what the shape is for or how it can be used or modified. If you point to a shape on a stencil without clicking the mouse button, the status bar displays a description and tips. For instance, when you point to the Rounded Square shape on the Basic stencil, the status bar reads **Move control handle to change roundness of corners on square.** When you point to the Roadway Break shape on the Map stencil, the status bar reads **Place on top of roadway to indicate not-to-scale distances.** Be sure to check the status bar for these descriptions and hints, especially when you work with stencils you're not yet familiar with.

Placing a Shape on a Drawing

To place a stencil shape on your drawing, click on the Pointer tool, click on a master stencil shape, then drag the shape onto the drawing page. When the shape is positioned approximately where you want it, release the mouse button. As you drag the mouse over the drawing page, a rectangular box representing the shape tracks your mouse movements. To see an outline of the actual shape (such as a circle or arrow), pause for two or three seconds without releasing the mouse button, then continue dragging the mouse. Seeing the actual shape helps you position the shape more accurately in a drawing.

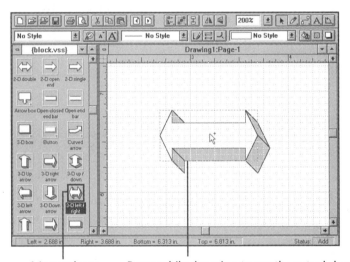

Master shape   Pause while dragging to see the actual shape.

Selecting Shapes for Editing

Before you can make changes (such as moving, deleting, and so on) to any shape in a drawing, you must first select the shape. Selecting a shape is easy: just click on the Pointer tool and click on the shape you want to select. When the shape is selected, selection handles appear in green around the shape. See the following section for more information on selection handles.

To select more than one shape at a time, select the first shape, then press and hold the Shift key as you click on additional shapes. The selection handles for the first shape appear in green; selection handles for subsequent shapes appear in blue.

Click in any blank area of the drawing to deselect a shape. To remove one shape from a multiple selection, continue to hold the Shift key and click on the shape again to deselect it.

Identifying and Using Shape Handles

Depending on the tool you use when you select a shape, shapes display different *handles* on the drawing page. Handles are control points that appear around a shape when the shape is selected. They can appear along the outline of a shape, or along a rectangular frame that surrounds the shape. The type of handle that's displayed varies depending on the tool used to select the shape.

Handles allow you to alter a shape in a number of ways, whether you want to resize the entire shape, change the curve of a line or arc segment, rotate the shape, or adjust an angle formed by two segments. The following list describes the various types of handles that appear when you select a shape.

 NOTE: A segment is a line or arc that is part of a more complex shape.

- **Selection handles**   Small, square-shaped handles that appear at the four corners of a shape and on each side of a shape when you select a shape with the Pointer tool. Drag a corner selection handle to resize a shape in two dimensions at once. Drag a top, bottom, or side handle to resize a shape in only one direction.

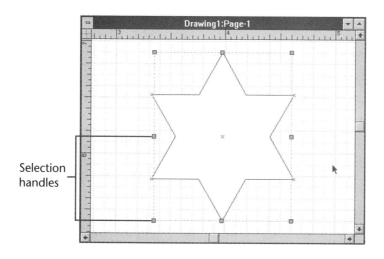

Selection handles

- **Control handle**   A square, shaded handle that enables you to change a special characteristic of a shape that you have selected with the Pointer tool. For instance, a control handle lets you change the depth of a 3-dimensional cube shape or the width of the point of an arrow shape. (Note that not all shapes contain control handles.)

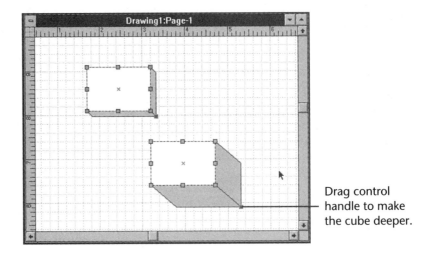

Drag control handle to make the cube deeper.

- **Control point**   A circle-shaped handle that appears on a line segment or arc when you select a shape with the Pencil tool. Drag a control point to change the shape of a line or arc.

Drag a control point to change the shape of a line.

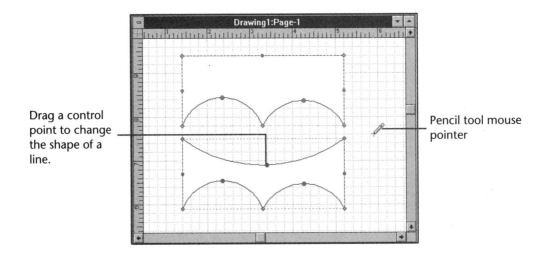

Pencil tool mouse pointer

- **Vertex**   A diamond-shaped handle that appears at the point where two line segments meet. Vertices are visible when you select a shape using the Pencil tool, Line tool, or Arc tool. Drag a vertex to change the shape or depth of an angle formed by two line segments.

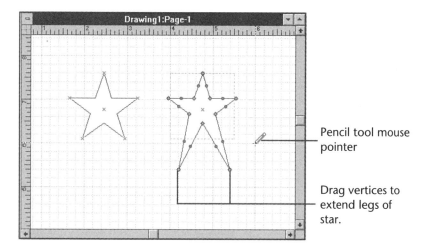

Pencil tool mouse pointer

Drag vertices to extend legs of star.

- **Rotation handle**   A circle-shaped handle that appears at the corners of a shape you have selected with the Rotation tool. Drag a rotation handle clockwise or counterclockwise to rotate a shape around its center of rotation.

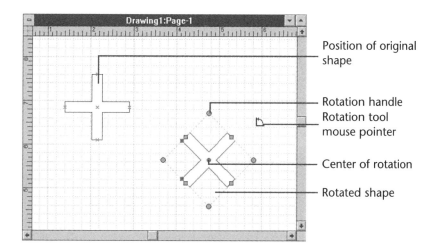

Position of original shape

Rotation handle
Rotation tool mouse pointer

Center of rotation

Rotated shape

- **Endpoints**   Line segments and arcs display a beginning point (indicated by a square with an X inside) and an ending point (indicated by a square with a + inside). They are often collectively referred to as *endpoints*. Use endpoints to shrink, extend, or change the direction of a line or arc.

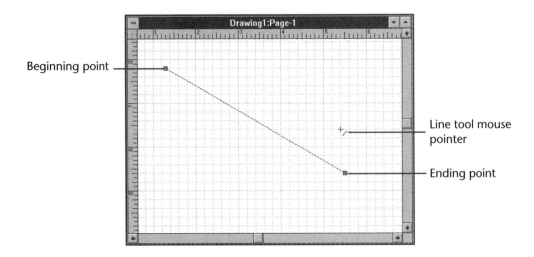

Beginning point

Line tool mouse pointer

Ending point

- **Connection point**   Although connection points don't actually let you alter a shape like other handles do, they are important markers on shapes because they represent the points at which you can connect connectors. (Connectors are lines that connect two shapes, such as in a flow chart or organization chart. You learn more about connectors later in this chapter.) Connection points are visible on all shapes when the View Connection Points command is selected.

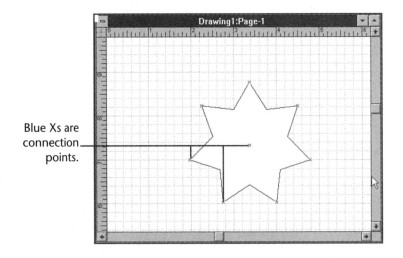

Blue Xs are connection points.

TIP: You can add a connection point anywhere on a shape. Select the Connection Point Tool, then select the shape. Point to the location where you want to add a connection point, then hold the Ctrl key as you click. You can also delete a connection point by selecting it with the Connection Point Tool and pressing the Delete key.

Moving a Shape

To move a shape, click on the Pointer tool, click anywhere inside of the shape (it isn't necessary to select the shape first), and drag it to a new location. As you drag the shape, the selected shape remains in its original location, and a rectangle follows your mouse movements. To see an outline of the actual shape, pause for two or three seconds as you're dragging the shape to its new location. When you release the mouse button, the shape moves to its new location.

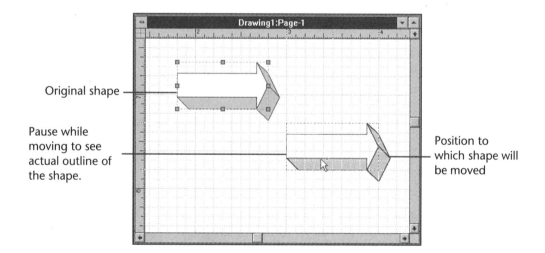

Original shape

Pause while moving to see actual outline of the shape.

Position to which shape will be moved

Duplicating a Shape

Often as you create and edit a drawing, you'll find that you need to repeat a shape. For example, if you were drawing a house with four doors, you would need to repeat the door shape four times. It's easier to drag one door shape onto the drawing and copy it three times than it is to drag four instances of the door from the stencil onto the drawing.

You can easily copy a shape by dragging the shape onto the drawing page (or selecting a shape already on the drawing page), then holding down the Ctrl key as you drag the mouse to a new location. When you press the Ctrl key, a plus sign (+)

appears next to the mouse pointer, indicating that a shape will be added to the drawing. When you release the mouse button, the original shape remains in its location, and the duplicate shape appears in its new location.

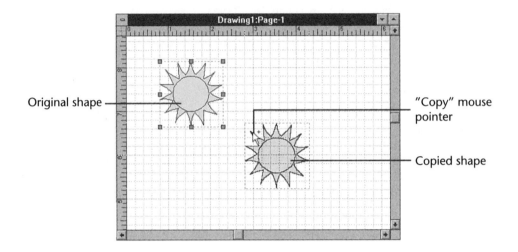

Original shape ⎯⎯⎯⎯⎯⎯

"Copy" mouse pointer

Copied shape

Resizing a Shape

You use a shape's selection handles to resize a shape. Display a shape's selection handles by clicking on a shape using the Pointer tool. To size a shape in one direction only, point to a selection handle until the mouse pointer changes to a double-headed arrow. Then drag a side, top, or bottom handle in the direction you want to size. To size a shape in two dimensions at once while maintaining the shape's height-to-width ratio, drag a corner selection handle. You can alter a shape's height-to-width ratio by holding the Shift key as you drag a corner handle.

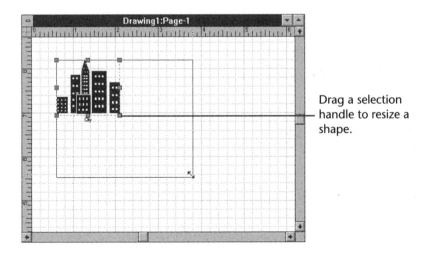

Drag a selection handle to resize a shape.

Reshaping a Shape

To change the curve or angle of a shape, select the shape using the Pencil tool. The shape's vertices and control points are visible on the outline of the shape. To change the angle between two lines, drag a vertex in any direction. To change the shape of a line or arc, drag the line or arc's control point (see the section titled "Identifying and Using Shape Handles" earlier in the chapter for more information on shape handles).

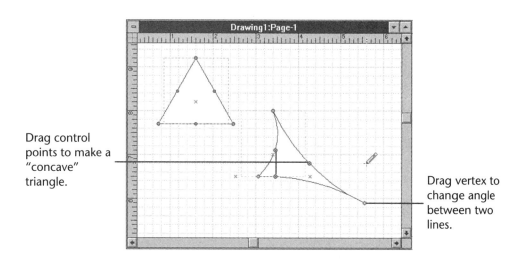

Drag control points to make a "concave" triangle.

Drag vertex to change angle between two lines.

TIP: You can add a vertex anywhere on a shape by pointing with the Pencil tool anywhere on the outline of the shape, holding the Ctrl key, and clicking on the shape.

Rotating, Flipping, and Reversing Shapes

Rotating, flipping, or reversing a shape can come in very handy when you're creating a drawing. When you rotate a shape, you move it clockwise or counterclockwise around a center point of rotation. Select the Rotation tool, then select the shape you want to rotate. Rotation handles appear at the corners, and a center of rotation handle appears somewhere inside the shape. When you move the mouse pointer over a rotation handle, the mouse pointer changes to two circular arrows. Drag the shape in a clockwise or counterclockwise direction, then release the mouse button. You can also adjust a shape's center of rotation by dragging the center of rotation handle.

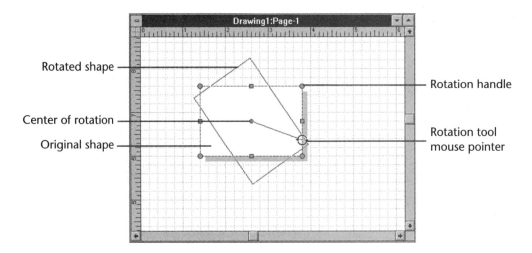

A quick way to rotate a shape exactly 90 degrees to the right or left is to choose the Rotate Left or Rotate Right command from the shortcut menu. To display the shortcut menu, click the right mouse button when a shape is selected.

NOTE: If you are using high resolution (600 x 800), the toolbar displays Rotate Right and Rotate Left buttons. You can simply click on these toolbar buttons to rotate a shape 90 degrees in either direction.

In Visio, you can also flip a shape vertically, horizontally, or both. To flip a shape vertically, select the shape, then click the Flip Vertical button on the toolbar. To flip a shape horizontally, click the Flip Horizontal button on the toolbar. To flip a shape both horizontally and vertically at once, select the shape, choose the Shape menu, and select the Reverse Ends command.

Deleting Shapes

To delete a shape from a drawing, select the shape you want to delete using the Pointer tool, then press the Delete key on the keyboard or choose the Edit Clear command. You can delete more than one shape at once by selecting all the shapes you want to delete and pressing Delete or choosing Edit Clear. When you want to completely clear a drawing page of all shapes and start over, the fastest way is to select all shapes on the page at once by pressing Ctrl+A or choosing Edit Select All, then press Delete or choose Edit Clear.

Gluing and Snapping Shapes

Gluing is the technique by which Visio enables you to stick shapes together and keep them together, even when one shape is moved or altered in some way. Being able to glue shapes greatly simplifies your task of creating drawings. Organization charts offer the perfect example. Imagine how tedious it would be to create an organization chart if you had to move every connecting line each time you shifted a box. With Visio's Glue feature, boxes that are connected remain connected, no matter where you move a box.

NOTE: One-dimensional shape   A shape that has no corner selection handles and can be resized only by its endpoints.

Two-dimensional shape   A shape that has corner selection handles and can be resized by its corner or side selection handles.

You can glue an endpoint of any one-dimensional shape to the endpoint of another one-dimensional shape, or to a selection handle, connection point, or vertex of a two-dimensional shape. You can also glue selection handles of one- and two-dimensional shapes to guides. (Guides are described in the next section of this chapter.)

You turn Visio's Glue feature on and off by clicking the Glue button on the toolbar, or by choosing the Tools Snap and Glue Setup command to display the Snap and Glue Setup dialog box. You also use this dialog box to determine the points at which you want Glue to be active. For instance, you might want Glue to be active at guides and connection points, but not at shape handles and shape vertices.

NOTE: The Glue toolbar button is visible only when your monitor is set for high resolution (600 x 800).

Turn Snap and Glue on or off here.

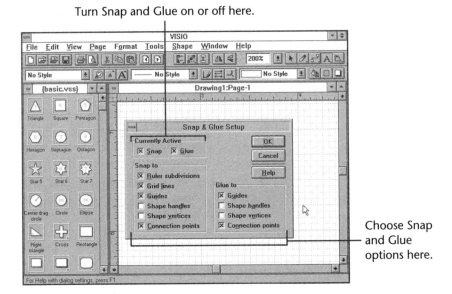

Choose Snap
and Glue
options here.

To glue an endpoint of a one-dimensional shape to a selection handle, connection point, or vertex of a two-dimensional shape, drag the endpoint to the proper point and release the mouse button. The red selection handle indicates the shapes are glued.

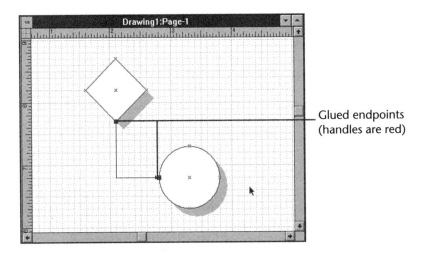

Glued endpoints
(handles are red)

Like the Glue feature, the Snap feature can be turned on or off. To toggle it on or off, click on the Snap button on the Standard Toolbar, or choose the Tools Snap and Glue Setup command to display the Snap and Glue Setup dialog box. As with Glue, you can choose the points at which you want Snap to be active. For instance, you might want shapes to snap into place only when near a guide. In this case, you choose the Guides option and turn off all other Snap options.

NOTE: The Snap toolbar button is visible only when your monitor is set for high resolution (600 x 800).

Working with Rulers and Guides

Visio displays a horizontal ruler across the top of the drawing page and a vertical ruler along the left side of the drawing page. *Rulers* help you find your place on the drawing page and help you position shapes. The scale shown on the ruler depends on the template you choose. For instance, if you choose the Basic template, the rulers display inches. However, if you choose the Space Planning template to design a room, the rulers display feet at a scale of ¼" = 1'. You change the scale shown on the ruler by choosing the Page Page Setup command and choosing the Size/Scale button.

When you start a new Visio drawing, the zero point of the horizontal ruler aligns with the left edge of the drawing page, and the zero point of the vertical ruler aligns with the lower edge of the drawing page. For some drawings, it's helpful to move the rulers' zero points. For instance, if you want a 1" left margin and a 1" top margin for your drawing, you might want to move the rulers' zero points so that you can begin measuring from the margins.

To move the zero points, press Ctrl and drag the square in the upper left corner where the rulers intersect. As you drag the square toward the drawing page, two black intersecting lines follow your mouse movements. Place the intersecting lines on the grid lines where you want the ruler's zero points to appear.

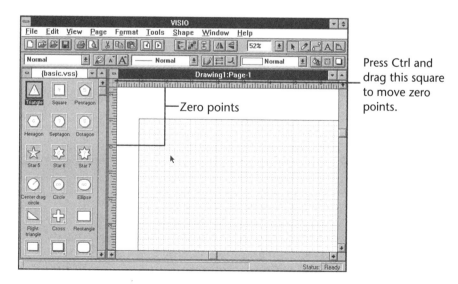

Guides are vertical or horizontal lines you can draw anywhere on the drawing page to help you position and align shapes accurately. They are especially helpful when the Glue feature is turned on because you can glue shapes to guides. To draw a guide that runs horizontally on the drawing page, place your mouse anywhere on the horizontal ruler. When the mouse pointer changes to a double-headed arrow, click and drag the mouse toward the drawing page, releasing the mouse button when the guide is correctly placed. To draw a guide that runs vertically on the drawing page, use the same method, dragging the guide from the vertical ruler.

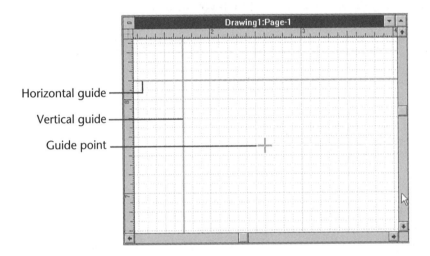

A *guide point* consists of two ½" lines that intersect perpendicular to one another. You use a guide point the same way you use a guide: to help you position shapes or glue shapes in place. To create a guide point, hold the Shift key as you drag the square in the upper left corner where the two rulers intersect. As you drag the square toward the drawing page, two blue intersecting lines follow your mouse movements. Place the intersecting lines on the drawing page where you want the guide point to appear.

You can move, add, or delete guides and guide points at any time. Guides and guide points appear only on-screen; they do not print when you print a drawing.

Connecting Shapes

Connectors are special shapes—usually lines or arcs—that are designed to form connections between two shapes. For instance, in a flow chart or technical drawing, you might want to connect two boxes with a line. You *could* do this by simply drawing a line between the two boxes using the Line tool, but then if you have to move one of the shapes, your line will be pointing to the wrong spot. SmartConnectors work much better than hand drawn lines: If you move one shape, the connector is automatically moved or resized as necessary. In some cases, the connector actually changes its path to avoid crossing over the shapes it connects. This behavior is what makes the connectors "smart."

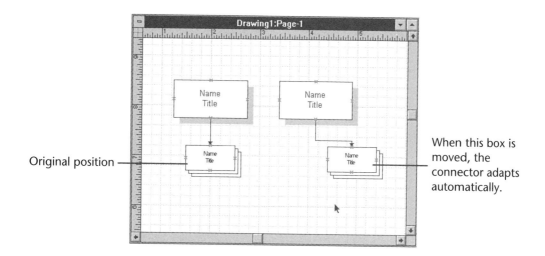

Original position ——

When this box is moved, the connector adapts automatically.

Using Shape Connectors

All connectors have two endpoints: you drag one endpoint to a connection point on the first shape, and you drag the other endpoint to a connection point on the other shape. The endpoints are automatically glued to the connection points on both shapes. (Recall that connection points are marked by light blue Xs on the screen.) The red endpoints with the X inside indicate the endpoints are glued to connection points on the respective shapes.

NOTE: Visio's Glue feature must be turned on in order for connectors to be glued and function properly. If Glue isn't turned on, click the Glue button on the toolbar.

In the Visio window, there are a number of different ways to create connectors. The following list describes five ways to create connectors.

- **Built-in connectors** Some shapes have built-in connectors, indicated by yellow lines on the master shape icon shown in the stencil. To connect a shape that has a built-in connector, you use the shape's control handle, which is visible when the shape is selected. Drag the control handle to a connection point on the shape to which you are connecting. The endpoints turn into red boxes with an X, indicating the connector is glued to the connection points.

Control handle for
built-in connector

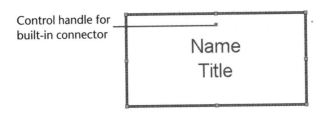

Name
Title

- **Stencil connector shapes**   Most stencils contain at least one connector shape, indicated by a yellow background on the master shape. To use a connector shape from a stencil, drag the connector shape onto the drawing page near the shapes you want to connect, then drag each endpoint to the connection points on each shape.

Connector shapes in the orgchart stencil

- **The Connector tool**   If the stencil you're using doesn't contain any connector shapes, you can connect two shapes by using the Connector tool located at the right end of the toolbar. To connect shapes using the Connector tool, click on the tool, then drag the mouse pointer over one of the connection points on the first shape. (Notice that the mouse pointer shows a connector tool icon next to the arrow.) Click on the connection point of the first shape, then drag the mouse to a connection point on the second shape and release the mouse button. The Connector tool automatically draws a SmartConnector between the two shapes and glues each endpoint.

   You can also use the Connector tool to automatically connect all new shapes that you add to a drawing. Click on the Connector tool on the toolbar, then drag shapes from the stencil onto the drawing page. Each time you add a shape, it is automatically connected to the previous shape. When you want to stop connecting new shapes, click on the Pointer tool.

- **The Universal Connector shape**   Some stencils contain a Universal Connector shape, identical to the shape that you draw using the Connector tool. Drag the shape onto the drawing, then drag each endpoint to a connection point on a shape.

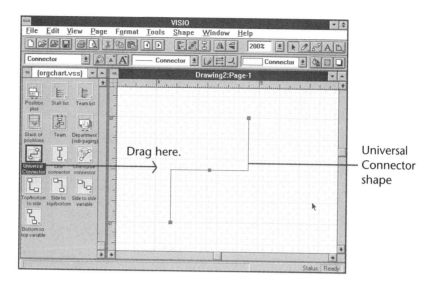

- **The Connect Shapes button**   This button 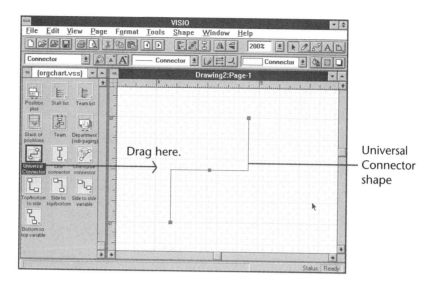 enables you to quickly connect two or more existing shapes without dragging any connector shapes onto the drawing. First, select the shapes you want to connect, in the order in which you want to connect them, then click on the Connect Shapes tool on the toolbar. Visio automatically draws SmartConnectors from shape to shape in the order you selected them.

Working with Text

For most drawings, you need to include some type of text, whether it's a title, caption, or label. Visio makes it easy to add text to drawings because any shape in the drawing page can contain text. In this section, you learn how to work with text in a drawing.

Adding Text to a Shape

Most shapes that you drag onto the drawing page or create using a drawing tool have a corresponding text block—whether you add text to it or not (see the section called "Creating New Shapes" for more information on drawing tools). The text block is a rectangular box outlined by a green dotted line. To add text to a shape, select the shape and begin typing. When you begin typing, the text block becomes visible. When the text you type is too wide for the text block, Visio automatically wraps the text to the next line. When you're finished entering text, press Esc or click anywhere outside the text block.

NOTE: When you type text in a text block, Visio automatically zooms in on the text block so the text is readable as you type. When you're finished, Visio returns to the previous zoom percentage.

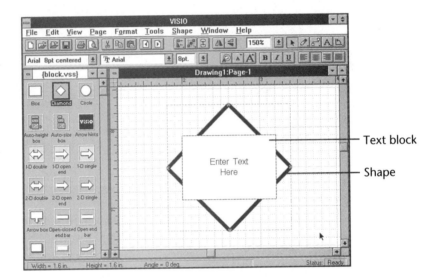

TIP: To display the text block associated with a shape, select the shape and press F2.

Rotating and Resizing Text Independently of a Shape

Earlier in this chapter, you learned how to rotate a shape. When you rotate a shape that contains text, the text automatically rotates in the same direction along with the shape. But suppose you want to rotate just the text and not the shape. Or, maybe you want to rotate a shape without rotating the text.

You can control the rotation of a shape's text by using the Text Block tool on the toolbar. When you select this tool, the mouse pointer changes to a text block icon. When you click on a shape, the text block of the shape automatically becomes selected instead of the shape itself. Rotation handles appear at the corners of the text block, and selection handles appear on all four sides, as shown in the following figure.

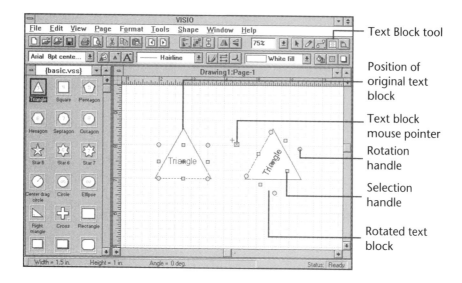

Text Block tool

Position of original text block

Text block mouse pointer

Rotation handle

Selection handle

Rotated text block

To rotate a text block, point to one of the four rotation handles. The mouse pointer changes to two circular arrows. Click and drag the rotation handle clockwise or counterclockwise to rotate the text block. Release the mouse button when the text is positioned where you want it.

You can also change the position and size of the text block using the Text Block tool. In this figure, the text block is moved to the right side of the triangle, and the size is reduced so that just the word "Triangle" fits in the text block. Notice, also, that the mouse pointer is now a shadowed text block. This mouse pointer appears when you point the mouse anywhere on a text block except on the rotation handles.

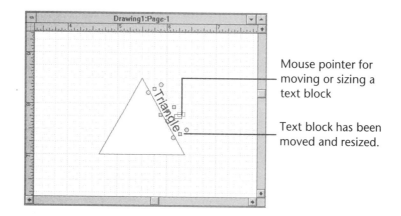

Mouse pointer for moving or sizing a text block

Text block has been moved and resized.

To move the text block, point to it until the mouse pointer shown in the preceding figure appears, then click and drag the text block to a new location. To size the text block, point to a selection handle on the text block until the shadowed text block mouse pointer appears, then click and drag the handle just as you would to size any other shape.

Adding Freestanding Text

Some Visio shapes don't have associate text blocks. For instance, if you add a shape from the Clipart Stencil to your drawing, you can't add text to it directly, but you can add a freestanding text block next to it.

To add a freestanding text block, choose the Text tool. The mouse pointer changes to a + symbol with a document. Click the mouse where you want text to appear, and begin typing. The text block becomes visible and contains the text you type. When you're finished entering text, click anywhere outside the text block or press Esc. You can move or resize the text block as necessary by selecting the text block with the Pointer tool.

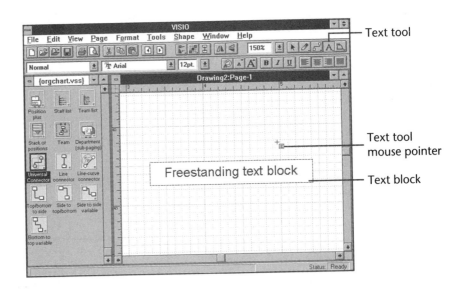

Changing Text

You can change or edit the text in a text block in one of two ways. You can replace it entirely, or you can edit it.

To replace text entirely, select the shape or freestanding text block (you aren't replacing the shape or the block, just the text inside), then begin typing. The new text you type automatically replaces all of the previous text. Click anywhere outside the text block when you're finished replacing text.

When you edit text, you can delete individual characters or add new ones. To edit text, select the shape or text block and press F2 to display the shape's text block. Visio highlights all the text in the text block. Click on the character you want to change. The text is no longer highlighted, and the insertion point blinks where you clicked the mouse. To add new characters, begin typing. Press Delete to delete characters to the right of the insertion point, or press Backspace to delete characters to the left of the insertion point. If necessary, click the mouse or use the arrow keys to reposition the insertion point. When you're finished changing text, click anywhere outside of the text block.

Choosing a Text Font and Size

When you add text to a shape, Visio automatically uses the Arial font in 8-point for most shapes. When you create freestanding text, Visio uses Arial 12-point. You can change the text's font to convey a different feeling or attitude, and you can change the size of text to make it easier to read or small enough to fit inside of small shapes.

To change the font in a text block, select the shape or text block, press F2, then click and drag the mouse over the characters you want to change. The characters are highlighted. Click on the Font button on the toolbar and choose a new font from the drop-down list that appears, or choose the Format Font command and choose a font in the Font dialog box.

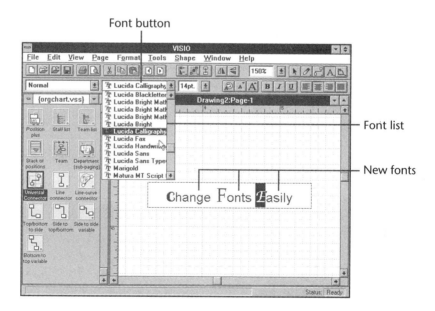

TIP: If you choose the Format Font command to change a font, you can also change the color of text and add special styles such as bold or underline.

You can change the size of text for all the text in a shape or for selected characters. To change the size of all text, select the shape or text block, then click the Decrease Font Size or Increase Font Size toolbar button. With each click, Visio decreases or increases the size of characters from their current size. To choose a specific size, choose the Font command from the shortcut menu, choose a font size from the Font dialog box, and click OK.

To change the size of text for selected characters, select the shape or text block, press F2, then click and drag the mouse over the characters you want to change. When the characters are highlighted, change the font size using either the Decrease Font Size or Increase Font Size toolbar button or by choosing the Font command from the shortcut menu.

Creating New Shapes

Even though Visio's stencils contain literally hundreds of different shapes, there will be times when you'll want to create unique shapes using Visio's drawing tools. Visio's Line tool lets you draw straight lines, the Arc tool lets you draw curved lines, and the Pencil tool lets you draw either lines or arcs.

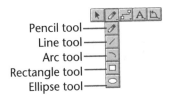

Using the Pencil, Line, and Arc tools, you can create open or closed shapes. Let your imagination fly. For drawing symmetrical, fully-enclosed shapes, use Visio's rectangle and ellipse tools.

Using the Line and Arc Tools

With the Line tool, you can draw a straight line at any angle. When you select the Line tool, the mouse pointer changes to a line with a + symbol. Click in the drawing page where you want the line to begin, then drag the mouse in any direction. Release the mouse button when the line is the angle and length you want. To draw a line at 45 degree increments from the starting point, hold the Shift key as you drag the mouse in a clockwise or counterclockwise direction.

With the Arc tool, you can draw an elliptical arc. When you select the Arc tool, the mouse pointer change to an arc shape with a + symbol. Drag the mouse in the direction you want the arc to curve, then release the mouse button.

To draw shapes that consist of a series of lines or arcs, draw the first line or arc and release the mouse button. Without moving the mouse, draw another line or arc. The first segment is automatically connected to the second at the vertex. Repeat this process until you're finished drawing. To create a closed shape, connect the endpoint of the last line or arc to the beginning point of the first line or arc.

Using the Pencil Tool

When you need to draw a shape that is a combination of lines and arcs, use the Pencil tool. When you use the Pencil tool, Visio "senses" the types of movements you make with the mouse and knows whether to draw a line or an arc. If you move the mouse along a straight path in any direction, Visio draws a line. If you move the mouse in a circular or curving motion, Visio draws a circular arc. (To draw an elliptical arc, hold the Shift key as you move the mouse along a curved path.)

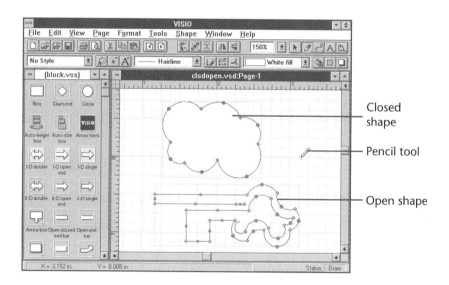

Using the Rectangle and Ellipse Tools

To create rectangles and ellipses, use the Rectangle and Ellipse tools. When you choose the Rectangle tool, the mouse pointer changes to a small rectangle with a + symbol; the Ellipse tool displays a small ellipse with a + symbol as its mouse pointer. Using either tool, establish a starting point, then click and drag the mouse pointer in any direction, releasing the mouse button when the shape is the size you want. To draw a square or circle using these tools, hold the Shift key down as you drag the mouse.

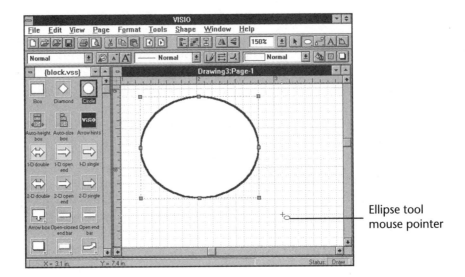

Ellipse tool
mouse pointer

Summary

In this chapter, you learned the basic skills for creating drawings: dragging shapes; moving, copying, deleting, and resizing shapes; and working with text in shapes. You also learned how to use Visio's drawing tools (such as the Pencil, Line, Arc, Ellipse, and Rectangle tools) to create new shapes. You discovered how Visio's Snap and Glue features can help you align and place shapes on a drawing, and you learned about connectors, which enable you to draw connecting lines between shapes. In the next chapter, you learn how to use the drawing features unique to Visio.

Using Visio's Unique Features

Already you can see that Visio isn't like any other computer drawing program. Its drag-and-drop concept makes creating drawings easier than ever. In addition to the features you've already learned about, some unique features distinguish Visio from other drawing programs. These features, such as joining shapes, fragmenting shapes, and layering drawings, add a level of sophistication to Visio that other drawing programs lack. You learn each of these techniques in this chapter, as well as how to create a custom Visio stencil and a custom Visio template. You might not need these features for every drawing, but when you do need them, it's nice to know they're at your fingertips.

Joining Shapes

In Chapter 2, you learned how to create special shapes using the drawing tools in Visio. You can also create new shapes by joining multiple shapes. Visio offers some creative ways for joining shapes using the Shape Union and Shape Combine commands. With each of these commands you can create new shapes from existing shapes or from shapes that you draw. By using the Shape Group command, you can also group shapes so that they behave as a single shape.

Uniting Shapes

Visio's Union feature blends two or more overlapping shapes to become one shape. The points at which the shapes overlap are erased, and the outer silhouette of all of the shapes defines the new shape. This feature is especially helpful for creating irregular or asymmetrical shapes.

Suppose you wanted to create an L-shaped object. Without Visio's Union feature, you would have to draw the L-shaped object freehand using the Line tool. With the Union feature, however, you simply overlap two rectangles at right angles to one another, then unite the two shapes. This may not sound like such an impressive feat for a simple L-shaped object, but when the shape you want to create is more complex, you'll find this feature very useful. The following figure shows the grid-like shape from overlapping vertical and horizontal rectangles as it was created using the Union feature. Imagine how difficult this shape would be to draw freehand.

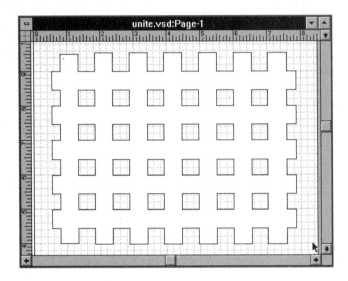

To unite shapes, select all the shapes on the drawing that you want to unite, then choose the Shape Union command. The points at which the shapes previously overlapped one another are now blended together into a single shape. The selection handles of the original shapes are replaced by one set of selection handles for the new united shape.

Combining Shapes

Visio's Combine feature is useful for creating shapes that have openings in them. In fact, without this feature you wouldn't be able to create these types of shapes. When you choose the Combine feature, Visio creates "cutouts" in a shape where other shapes overlap it. Whatever is below the cutouts (which could be the blank drawing page or another shape) shows through. The following figure shows combined objects with another shape showing through and with the drawing page showing through.

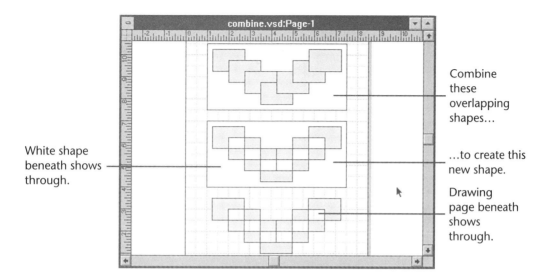

Combine these overlapping shapes...

White shape beneath shows through.

...to create this new shape.

Drawing page beneath shows through.

To create cutouts in a shape, select all the overlapping shapes and choose the Shape Combine command. The individual shapes become one shape with cutouts at the points where shapes overlap.

Grouping Shapes

By grouping shapes, you can treat several shapes as if they were a single shape. This feature is most useful when you're drawing or creating component parts of a shape, as in the clock shown in the following figure. Once grouped, you can move, copy, size, delete, or change all components of the shape as a group. To group shapes, select the shapes you want to include, then choose the Shape Group command or press Ctrl+G.

When you group selected shapes, the selection handles of the individual shapes are replaced by selection handles that encompass the new grouped shape. You no longer select the shapes individually, instead you select the grouped shape. If you click on an individual component of a grouped shape, its selection handles are displayed in gray, indicating the component is part of a group. This is called *subselecting*.

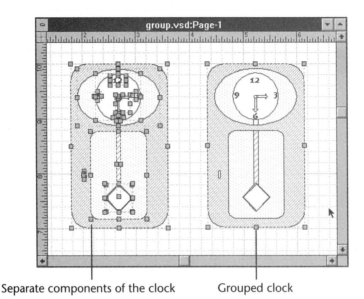

Separate components of the clock   Grouped clock

Occasionally, you might want to modify a shape that's part of a group. You can do so without ungrouping the shapes. Simply select the group and choose the Edit Open Group command, or double-click on that group. Visio opens a special *group window* on top of the drawing page window in which you can edit individual shapes. Select the shape you want to modify (green selection handles appear) and change the shape as necessary. The changes you make appear in the group window as well as in the drawing page window. When you're finished modifying the shape, double-click the Control-menu box in the upper left corner of the group window. The group window closes, and the changes you make are reflected in the drawing window.

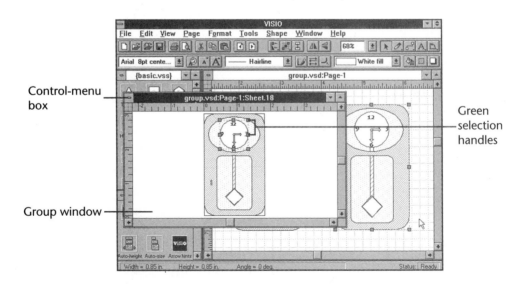

TIP: If you select a shape on the drawing page and its selection handles are gray instead of green, you have subselected a shape in a group. To modify the shape, you must open the group.

When you no longer want shapes to be grouped, you can ungroup them just as easily as you group them. Select the group, then choose the Shape Ungroup command or press Ctrl+U. The selection handles of the original shapes are visible again, and each shape can be selected or manipulated separately in the drawing window.

Fragmenting Shapes

When you fragment shapes, you break overlapping shapes into individual pieces. The points at which shapes overlap become the dividing lines between shapes. Each shape can then be moved, deleted, sized, filled, or changed in some other way, separate from the other shapes.

Visio's Fragment feature can be used in a variety of creative ways. For instance, fragmenting is often the easiest way to create irregular shapes such as a half-circle, a rectangle with an odd-angled side, or a polygon. It can also be used to "explode" the components of a shape, similar to the way the slices of a pie chart are exploded (see the next figure). To fragment shapes, select the overlapping shapes and choose Shape Fragment.

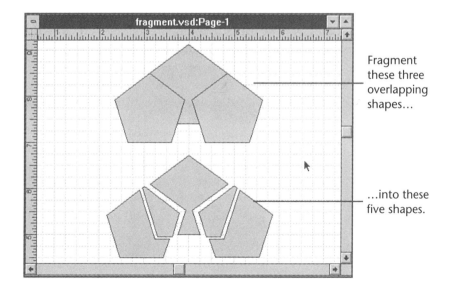

Fragment these three overlapping shapes...

...into these five shapes.

Working with Drawing Pages

One of Visio's most sophisticated features is its capability to create background and foreground pages. This feature gives you a great deal of flexibility because it enables you to create layered drawings. If you were designing the furniture layout of a room, for example, you could draw the walls on a background page and then create several foreground pages showing different furniture arrangements. If you were designing a home, you could draw the wall frame on a background page and overlay the plumbing, heating and air conditioning, and electrical wiring on three separate foreground pages. The walls you draw on the background page appear automatically on each foreground page—you don't need to draw them again and again. For a sample project that uses layered pages, refer to the project "Creating a Cubicle Design," in Chapter 10.

In a single drawing, you can create multiple foreground and background pages. A foreground page can have only one background page, but a background page can have more than one foreground page.

To use the furniture arrangement example again, the background page—which shows the walls—can have one or more foreground pages (furniture arrangements A, B, C, and D, for example). And if you had several possible wall arrangements, you could create multiple background pages (walls A, B, and C), each with associated foreground pages.

When you start a new Visio drawing, Visio defaults to the Foreground page setting. To specify a drawing as a background page, choose Page Page Setup to display the Page Setup dialog box. Choose the Background option, type a name in the Name box, then choose OK. If you want to use a different measurement scale on the background page, choose an item from the Measurements list before you close the dialog box.

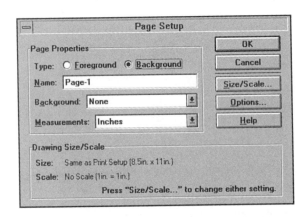

After your background page is completed, create a foreground page by choosing Page New Page. In the New Page dialog box, choose Foreground and type a name in the Name box. From the Background list, choose the named background page you want to assign to the foreground page, then choose a scale from the Measurements list, if necessary, and choose OK. To create additional foreground pages, repeat these steps.

Creating a Custom Visio Stencil

When you go to the trouble of creating a custom shape (or a whole collection of custom shapes), you would like to store them in a safe place. If you could store them only in the drawing in which they were created, they would be vulnerable to change or accidental deletion. It would also make it difficult, if not tedious, to share or reuse the shape in other drawings.

To ensure that your custom shapes are protected, you can create a custom stencil in which you store the shapes. The shapes are stored as *master shapes* just like the master shapes that appear in Visio stencils. Creating a custom stencil also enables you to organize your custom shapes in a logical way. For example, if you have custom furniture shapes, custom business chart shapes, and custom border shapes, you would probably want to store them in three separate custom stencils. You can create your custom shapes in the drawing window at the time you create a custom stencil, or you can copy existing custom shapes into the stencil when you create it.

To create a custom stencil, click the New (File) toolbar button and choose the Stencil option (instead of the Drawing option) in the New dialog box. If you want the stencil to contain only your custom shapes, choose No Stencil in the Based On list. If you want to include a Visio stencil along with your custom shapes, highlight the appropriate stencil name in the Based On list.

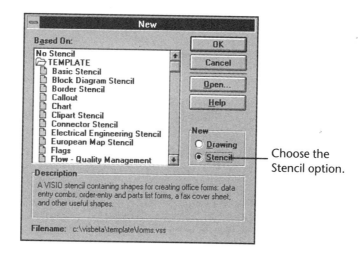

Choose the Stencil option.

If you choose No Stencil in the New dialog box, Visio opens with a blank stencil window on the left side of the screen labeled "Stencil1." If you choose a stencil name in the New dialog box, Visio opens the same way but the stencil's master shapes will appear in the Stencil1 window. To display the drawing page, choose the Window Show Drawing Page command.

If you choose a stencil name, master shapes appear here. If you don't, you will see an empty stencil window.

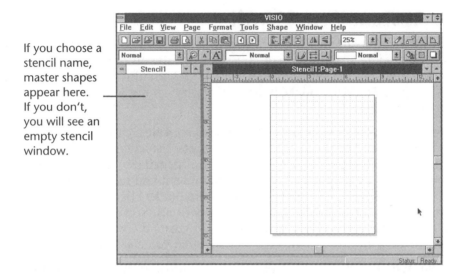

Now create your custom shape in the drawing window. When the shape is complete, use the Pointer tool to drag the shape onto the stencil window. (Hold the Ctrl key as you drag if you want the shape to be copied and not moved.) Your shape now appears in the stencil and is labeled "Master .*x*" where .*x* is a number.

To give the master shape a name and specify its characteristics, use these steps:

1. Select the stencil window so that it is active.

2. Select the shape you want to name.

3. Choose the Master Properties command to display the Properties dialog box.

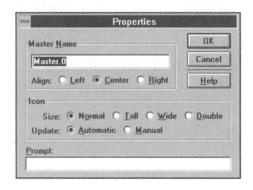

4. Type a name for the shape in the Master Name box.

5. Choose Left, Center, or Right alignment.

6. Choose Normal, Tall, Wide, or Double for the icon size.

7. Choose Automatic or Manual for the Update option. (Choose Automatic if you want the icon to reflect changes you make to the master shape. Choose Manual if you want the icon to remain the same, even if you change the master shape.)

8. In the Prompt box, type the message you want to appear in the status bar when the master shape is selected.

9. Click OK.

To add a shape from another drawing to your custom stencil, follow these steps:

1. Click the Open button, select the drawing file to open, and choose OK.

2. Make sure the custom stencil is still visible on-screen. (Use the Window Tile or Window Cascade command if necessary.)

3. Drag the shape from the drawing to the stencil. Hold the Ctrl key as you drag if you want the shape to be copied and not moved.

Your shape now appears in the stencil and is labeled "Master *.x*" where *.x* is a number. Use the previous steps to name the shape and define its characteristics.

Once all your custom shapes are copied to your custom stencil, you must save your stencil file using the following steps:

1. Click the Save button or choose File Save. The Save As dialog box is displayed.

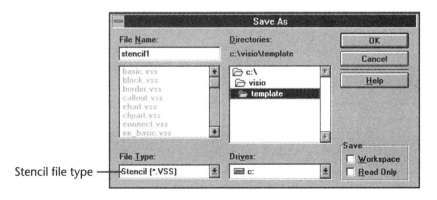

Stencil file type

2. Type a name for the stencil in the File Name text box. Don't type a file extension. The Stencil file extension (*.VSS) shown in the File Type box is used automatically.

3. To store your stencil where other Visio stencils are stored, choose the C:\VISIO\TEMPLATE directory in the Directories listing.

4. To protect your stencil from changes, check the Read Only option in the Save box. Choose Workspace only if you want to save your custom stencil with all other files that are currently open.

5. Choose OK.

Now you can open your custom stencil anytime you use Visio by clicking the Open Stencil toolbar button and choosing the stencil name. If you saved your custom stencil in the C:\VISIO\TEMPLATE directory, the stencil name appears in the Open Stencil dialog box along with other Visio stencils. If you save your stencil in a different directory, you'll have to click the Browse button in the Open Stencil dialog box in order to open your stencil file.

Modifying a Visio Stencil

In the previous section, you learned how to create your own custom stencils. An alternative to creating a custom stencil is to modify a Visio stencil. This includes adding shapes, changing shapes, or deleting master shapes. For instance, if you only use a portion of the master shapes in a particular stencil, you could delete the shapes you never use. Or, if you use a particular stencil frequently along with some custom shapes, you might want to add your custom shapes to the Visio stencil.

 TIP: Be careful when modifying a Visio stencil. When you save changes to a Visio stencil, the original stencil is permanently changed. The only way to restore it is to reinstall the original Visio stencil file.

When you open a stencil in Visio, it is automatically opened as a Read Only file. The read only condition is indicated by the braces that appear around the stencil name in the stencil window's title bar. In order to modify a stencil, you must choose the Original option from the Open Stencil dialog box (click the Open Stencil toolbar button to display this dialog box). When you open the stencil using this option, the stencil name is not enclosed in braces in the stencil window's title bar.

Braces
indicate
the stencil
can't be
modified.

No braces
indicate
the stencil
can be
modified.

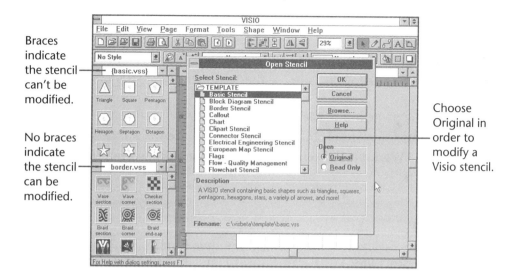

Choose
Original in
order to
modify a
Visio stencil.

You can add new shapes to the stencil using the same methods you learned in the previous section. If you want to delete any existing master shapes, select the shape in the stencil, then click the Cut toolbar button, press Ctrl+X, or choose Edit Cut.

You can edit a master shape by selecting the shape and choosing the Master Edit Master command. Visio displays the shape in a separate stencil window (similar to the group window). Make whatever changes you want to the shape, then double-click the stencil window's Control-menu box. Visio asks if you want to update the master shape. Choose Yes, No, or Cancel.

Creating a Custom Visio Template

Stencils and templates are both types of Visio files. A stencil file contains only master shapes, whereas a template contains print and page settings; drawing pages; styles and colors for lines, text, and fills; snap and glue settings; and links that open stencil files. The advantage to having a custom template is that when you create a new file using that template, all the special settings you specified are already made, and the stencils you want to use are opened automatically.

If you have a drawing file that already contains the special settings you want to save, you can save it as a template by following the steps below. If you don't have a drawing file, use the same steps but choose all the special page, printer, and style settings after step 3.

1. Open the drawing file.

2. Open all stencils you want to save with the template.

3. Arrange all open windows as you want them to appear when you create a new drawing.
4. Choose the File Save As command.
5. In the Save As dialog box, choose the Template (*.VST) item in the File Type box.
6. Enter a file name in the File Name box.
7. Choose the C:\VISIO\TEMPLATE directory in the Directories box.
8. Check the Workspace check box in the lower right corner of the dialog box.
9. Choose OK.

Summary

In this chapter, you learned some of Visio's unique features that distinguish it from other drawing programs. You learned how to join shapes in different ways, how to fragment shapes, and how to group shapes. You also discovered how to create layered drawings with drawing pages, and how to create custom stencils and templates.

Part 2

Visio Projects

The remaining chapters constitute the "ideas" section of this book. These chapters include over 100 examples and ideas for a wide variety of projects. Each chapter covers a particular type of drawing, such as a flow chart, map, or business form. In general, you work with one particular Visio stencil per chapter, although in some chapters you open additional stencils when necessary. In Chapter 15 you use a wide variety of stencils for what can only be called "special projects." This chapter gets you thinking creatively about the many different uses for Visio.

As the introduction to this book describes, many "add-on" packages are available from Shapeware Corporation for Visio. Each add-on package includes a set of stencils designed for a particular type of drawing. For instance, the Landscape Planning package includes realistic shapes for flowers, shrubs, trees, and other landscape items such as bricks, fences, and paving stones.

To introduce you to some of the shapes in Visio's add-on packages, the bonus disk at the back of this book includes a valuable sampling of Visio master shapes worth over $100.00. Chapter 16 includes sample projects that utilize these additional shapes. Here you'll find special projects for a master bathroom, kitchen, landscape plan, auto accident scene, and a "dinosaurscape" your kids will flip over.

Organization Charts

Without Visio, creating a standard business organization chart on a computer is a nightmare. About the time you get all the boxes spaced and aligned correctly and draw all the connecting lines, you realize you forgot a box or you need to delete a box. Suddenly every box and every connecting line must be moved, respaced, re-aligned, and reconnected. Making these adjustments could take as much time as it took to create the original chart.

Visio's organization chart stencil takes all the pain out of creating organization charts. Each shape has a built-in connector that you drag to a box at a higher level. If you need to move a box, the built-in connector automatically adjusts to the correct position. And if you decide not to use a shape's built-in connector, seven more "self-adjusting" connectors are included in the stencil. In addition, Visio's alignment and distribution features make it easy to determine spacing and alignment of boxes, and you can glue shapes to vertical and horizontal guides as well.

In this chapter, you learn how to create several different kinds of organization charts using the organization chart template shown in the following figure. When you open Visio or create a new file using this template, Visio displays a landscape-style drawing page (11" wide by 8½" high), and the vertical and horizontal rulers display inches. To change either of these default settings, choose the Page Setup command from the Page menu.

Take a minute now to review the shapes in the organization chart stencil. Use your mouse to point to each shape, then read the description of the shape on the status bar. At a glance, many of the shapes look similar, if not identical; but each is slightly different. For example, although it isn't visible in the stencil, the Executive shape is slightly larger than other shapes and is shadowed. The Manager shape is slightly smaller than the Executive shape and is shadowed by boxes depicting layers of management. The Consultant shape is outlined with a dotted line as opposed to a solid line.

Side-to-bottom connector
(on Assistant shape)

Bottom-to-top connector
(on Manager shape)

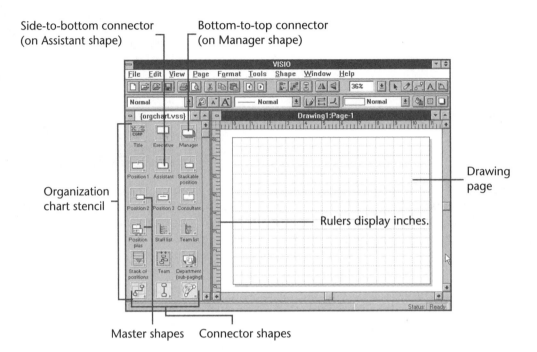

Organization
chart stencil

Drawing
page

Rulers display inches.

Master shapes   Connector shapes

Connectors vary from one shape to another as well. Notice that the Executive shape doesn't include a built-in connector as most other shapes do. This is because other shapes—typically Manager shapes—are connected from lower levels upward to the Executive shape, not vice versa. Notice also that the shapes of connectors are different from one master shape to another. For instance, the Assistant shape has a *side-to-bottom* connector, whereas the Manager shape has a *bottom-to-top* connector. Because each connector is self-adjusting, the actual path it takes is slightly different from that of other connectors.

To use built-in connectors in an organization chart, drag a shape's control handle to a connection point on a shape. (Recall that a control handle is a shaded square handle on a shape.) For instance, to connect a Manager shape to an Executive shape, drag the Manager's control handle to the lower middle connection point on the Executive shape. To connect an Assistant to the Executive shape, drag the Assistant's control handle to a middle side connection point on the Executive shape.

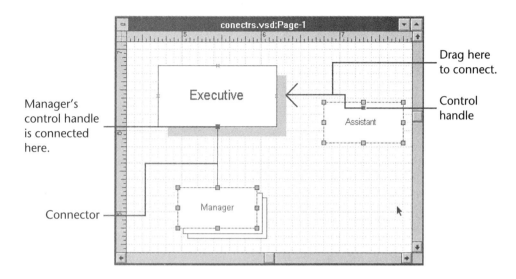

Manager's control handle is connected here.

Connector

Drag here to connect.

Control handle

Creating a Simple Organization Chart

A standard business organization chart usually depicts an organization (or a single group within an organization) beginning with the top manager at the highest level of the chart and including all other positions in the group at successive levels. A simple organization chart like the one shown below includes only a few levels of positions and simple connecting lines.

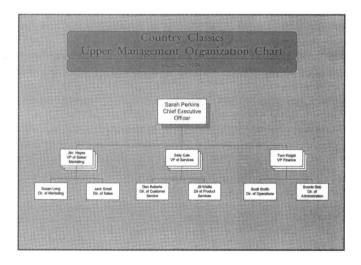

To create this organization chart, use the following steps. (For this example, it's best to align boxes with horizontal and vertical guides instead of with the Align Shapes toolbar button.)

1. Open Visio using the Organization Chart template.

2. Click the Snap and Glue buttons on the toolbar to turn these features on. Or, choose the Tools Snap & Glue Setup command to display the Snap & Glue Setup dialog box, then click both the Snap and Glue check boxes.

3. From the horizontal ruler, drag two horizontal guides onto the drawing page at 2½" and 3½". • From the vertical ruler, drag one vertical guide onto the drawing page at 5½".

4. Drag a Title shape onto the drawing. • Size the shape to 7" wide by 1¼" high. • Align the shape at 7" and glue its center to the vertical guide (at 5½").

5. With the Title shape still selected, type the title of the organization chart on the two available lines (press Enter after the first line). • With the text still selected, click the Font toolbar button and choose Garamond or a similar font from the drop-down list. Note: In the Title shape, the current date is supplied automatically. • With the Title shape selected, click the Line toolbar button and click on the 3-pixel line option in the drop-down menu. • Click the Corner Rounding toolbar button once. • Click the down arrow to the right of the Fill Style toolbar button, then click on the 30% gray option in the drop-down menu.

6. Drag an Executive shape onto the drawing. • Align the Executive at 5" and glue its center to the vertical guide (at 5½").

7. Drag three Manager shapes onto the drawing, gluing each to the horizontal guide at 3½". • Align the first and third shapes at 1¾" and 8¼" on the horizontal ruler. Glue the second shape to the vertical guide at 5½". • Drag the connector shape from each Manager shape to the bottom connection point of the Executive shape.

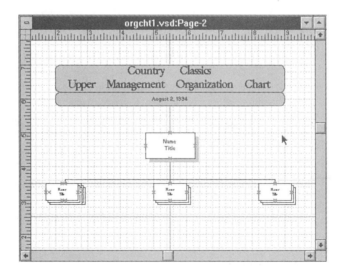

8. Drag a Position shape onto the drawing page. • Align the shape at 1" and glue it to the horizontal guide at 2½".

9. Copy the Position shape, aligning it at 9" and gluing it to the horizontal guide at 2½".

10. Make four more copies of the Position shape and glue them to the 2½" horizontal guide anywhere between the first two shapes.

11. Select all six Position shapes using the Pointer tool. • Click the second button under the Distribute Shapes toolbar button.

12. Drag the control handles of the first two Position shapes upward and connect them to the bottom middle connection point of the first Manager shape.

13. Repeat step 12 for the remaining four Position shapes, connecting them to the middle and right Manager shapes.

14. Enter names and titles for each position by clicking on a shape and then typing.

15. To create a background for the organization chart, choose the Rectangle tool from the toolbar.

16. Draw a rectangle approximately 10" by 7" and center it on the page. • Click the Send to Back toolbar button or choose the Shape Send to Back command. • Click the down arrow to the right of the Fill Style toolbar button, then choose the 10% Gray option.

Complex Organization Chart

Organization charts are often more complex than the one just described. Your organization might include consultants, staff lists, teams of workers, and so on. If so, you can easily create these types of charts with the additional master shapes available on the organization chart stencil.

The following organization chart shows an independent consultant (Consultant) reporting to the Regional Sales Manager. Under the consultant is a staff list of researchers (Staff List). Under the Regional Sales Manager are two managers of sales teams depicted by dotted lines from the Team shape. Salespeople are shown using the Stack of positions shape.

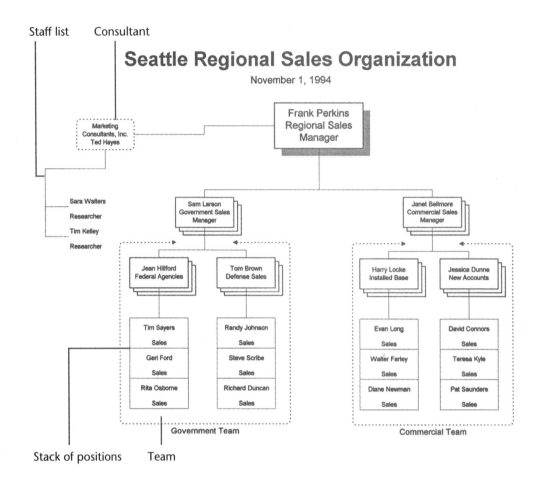

Multi-Page Organization Chart

The Department (sub-paging) shape is a special shape that lets you create a multi-page organization chart. Suppose, for example, you want your organization chart to show nine major departments in a corporation. Instead of including the detail for each department on the original organization chart, you want to include the detail for individual departments on separate pages. Think of the original chart as a *summary* chart and the additional pages as *detail* charts.

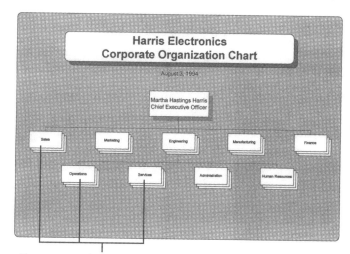

Department (sub-paging) shape was used for these boxes.

When you use the Department (sub-paging) shape for your departments in the orga-nization chart, Visio helps you automatically create the supporting charts. For ex-ample, to create a supporting chart for the Sales department box, drag a Department (sub-paging) shape onto your drawing and type **Sales** as the text label. Double-click on the Sales box, and the Sub Maker dialog box appears, displaying the label Sales in the Sub-Page Name text box. When you click OK, Visio automatically creates a sub-page to the original chart and displays it on-screen. (Note that the title bar for the drawing window now says **Drawing 1:Sales**.) At the top of the sub-page, Visio in-serts a shaded text block labeled Sales that acts as a title for the page. You then drag other shapes from the organization chart stencil onto the drawing to build the orga-nization chart for the Sales department.

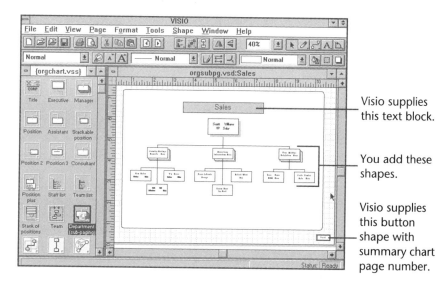

Visio supplies this text block.

You add these shapes.

Visio supplies this button shape with summary chart page number.

In the lower right corner of the sub-page, Visio automatically inserts a button shape that contains the page number of the original (summary) organization chart. You can double-click on this button at any time to return to the original summary chart on page 1. The button is not a page number for the detail chart, and it doesn't print when you print the detail chart. It simply provides a reference to the page number of the summary chart and is a quick "clicking point" you can use to return to the summary chart. To return to a detail organization chart from a summary chart, double-click on the Department (sub-paging) shape in the summary chart, or choose the Page Go to Page command and double-click on the name of the summary chart you want. You can create a sub-page for each Department (sub-paging) shape you use in the summary chart. When you save your drawing, all pages are saved under one file name.

Special Notes in Organization Charts

The Position plus shape is a unique and useful shape that's found in the organization chart stencil. This shape lets you add information about a specific person or position. The shape looks like a regular organization chart box, but it has a down arrow in the lower right corner. When you double-click the arrow, a drop-down box opens, and the down arrow changes to an up arrow.

In the drop-down box, you can add information about the position or the person named in the Position Plus box. To add information in the drop-down box, click on the drop-down box until the gray selection handles appear. Then press F2 to select all of the sample text. When you begin typing your text, the sample text is removed. To close the drop-down box, double-click on the up arrow on the Position plus shape.

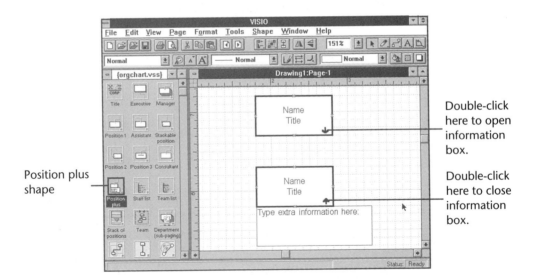

Other Ideas

Although the organization chart stencil is designed to create typical business organization charts, you certainly are not limited to this type of chart. You can use the shapes in the stencil to illustrate other types of information as well. For example, you can illustrate any type of hierarchical structure using these shapes.

Disk Directory Organization Chart

A disk directory is a typical hierarchical structure that many of us work with each day. You can create the disk directory shown here using the Executive, Manager, Stack of positions, and Team shapes from the organization chart stencil. It has the look of a typical organization chart, but depicts entirely different information.

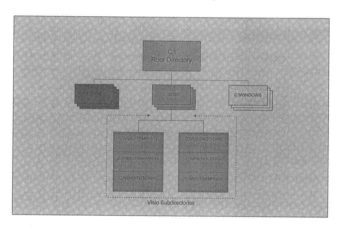

Disk Directory

Tournament Chart

Many organized sports end their seasons with a championship or tournament. You can easily create a chart showing the competitors for your tournament using the organization chart stencil and the Connector stencil. To create a chart like the one below, create the final, semifinal, and quarterfinal boxes using resized Executive and Position shapes, and connect the boxes using their built-in connectors. Add the shadow to each box by clicking the Shadow toolbar button.

Create the tree structure where the names are listed using three Double tree square shapes from the Connector stencil. Group the shapes, rotate them to the right, and add names using the Text tool. The tennis player is a clip art design from another program. Add any appropriate clip art image to your tournament chart using the Page Insert Clip Art command.

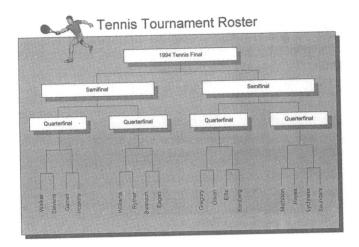

Family Tree

Another creative way you can use the organization chart stencil is to make a family tree. To create a family tree like the example here, use the Position shape for the names and birthdates of each family member. If your family tree is very large (as most are), reduce the size of the Position shapes and use an 8-point font for the text.

You can also use the Position shape to illustrate marriage dates. For these shapes, change the shape line to None or White so that a box does not appear around the text. The next step is to round the connecting lines that connect spouses (which you draw using the Connector tool) to make the marriage dates easy to identify in the chart. To round the connecting lines, select all marriage connectors, then click the Corner Rounding toolbar button once. To represent the children near the bottom of the chart, use the Staff list shape. If you need to delete unwanted names, shrink the Staff list shape; if you need to add more names to the list, stretch the shape.

Hendricks Family Tree
1884 - 1994

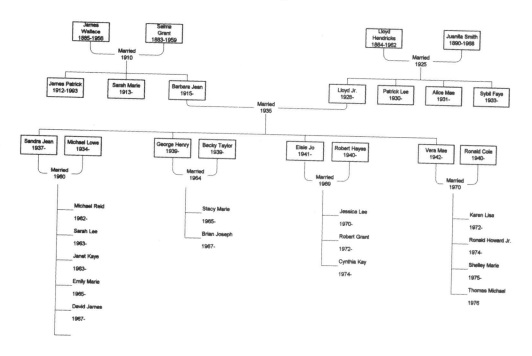

Creating Flowcharts

A *flowchart* is a graphical representation of a procedure or process, which contains various standardized symbols for each step. Connecting lines between the symbols guide you on a specific path through the chart based on responses to certain questions. Although flowcharts have traditionally been used by technicians, scientists, and analysts to represent complex, scientific, or technical processes, flowcharts can also be used to represent the simplest of processes.

To create flowchart drawings, you use the shapes in Visio's Flowchart stencil shown in the following figure. You don't need to be familiar with the standardized flow-charting symbols to use the Flowchart stencil. The status bar in Visio displays an explanation of each shape when you point to it on the stencil. For instance, when you point to the Document shape, the status bar reads **This symbol represents human readable data, such as printed output.**

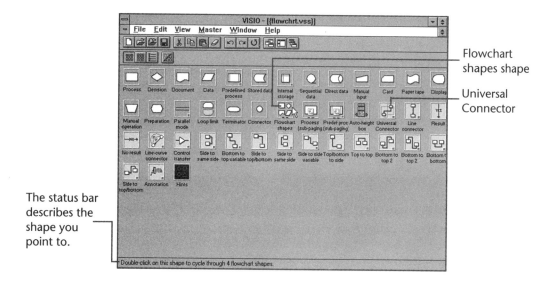

Flowchart shapes shape

Universal Connector

The status bar describes the shape you point to.

Most of the flowchart symbol shapes don't contain built-in connectors because the way in which you connect symbols varies depending on the process you are documenting. The stencil, therefore, contains a wide variety of connector shapes, such as Side to same side, Bottom to top, Top to top, and so on. Notice that one of the connector shapes is the Universal Connector, a smart shape that you can use to form almost any type of connection. Refer to Chapter 2 for a discussion of how to use the Universal Connector.

If you're in a hurry to create a flowchart, however, you can connect shapes automatically by using the Connector Tool. Click on the Connector Tool button on the toolbar, then drag shapes onto your drawing. Each new shape you drag onto the drawing is automatically connected to the previous shape by a connector. The endpoints of the connector are glued to the shapes. If you don't like the path of the connector, you can move the endpoints to different connection points on a shape, or you can delete the connector entirely and draw a new one.

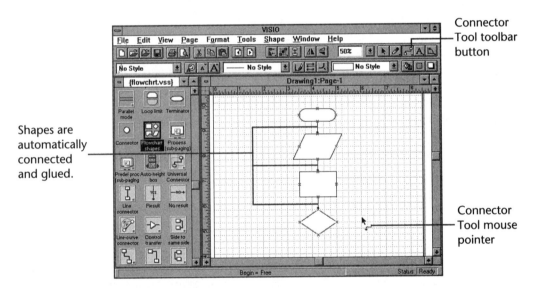

Connector Tool toolbar button

Shapes are automatically connected and glued.

Connector Tool mouse pointer

One of the most important shapes in the Flowchart stencil is the Flowchart shapes shape. This shape not only enables you to draw a flowchart quickly, but also makes it easy for you to change your mind and your drawing easily, when necessary. Just drag a Flowchart shapes shape onto the drawing, then double-click on the shape. When you double-click, the Flowchart shapes shape cycles through four of the most commonly used shapes: the Process, Decision, Document, and Data shapes. Continue double-clicking until the shape you want to use is displayed. If you choose the wrong shape, you can change it at any time just by double-clicking on it again (even after you've typed a text label).

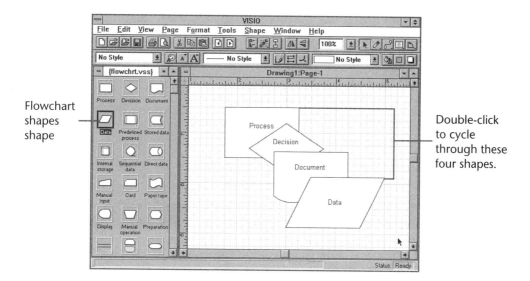

Flowchart
shapes
shape

Double-click
to cycle
through these
four shapes.

Creating a Computer Program Flowchart

Flowcharts have been used for many years to depict the logic used to develop computer programs. In the simple example shown below, the Terminator, Data, and Decision shapes are used to show how a customer invoice is read and printed.

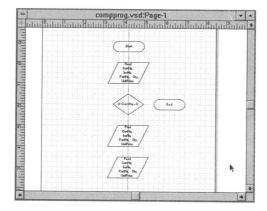

To create this flowchart, follow the steps below. Notice that the Connector Tool is not used in these steps so that you can learn how to connect shapes manually.

1. Open Visio using the Flowchart template.

2. Choose Tools Snap & Glue Setup to confirm that Snap and Glue are both turned on (an X appears in each check box). • Click OK.

3. Drag a vertical guide from the left ruler to 4¼". All shapes except one in the flowchart are glued to the guide.

4. Drag a Terminator shape onto the drawing and glue it near the top of the guide. • Type **Start** to label the shape.

5. Drag a Data shape onto the drawing and glue it to the guide ¼" below the Terminator shape.

6. Type **Read CustNo, InvNo, PartNo, Qty, UnitPrice** to label the shape.

7. Drag a Decision shape onto the drawing and glue it to the guide ¼" below the Data shape.

8. Label the shape **If CustNo = 0**.

9. Drag a Terminator shape onto the drawing and place it about 1" to the right of the Decision shape.

10. Drag a Data shape onto the drawing and glue it to the guide ¼" below the Decision shape. • Type **Print CustNo, InvNo, PartNo, Qty, UnitPrice** to label the shape.

11. Hold the Ctrl key and drag a copy of the previous Data shape ¼" below the shape in step 9. • Type **Read CustNo, InvNo, PartNo, Qty, UnitPrice** to label the shape. Your chart should now look like this:

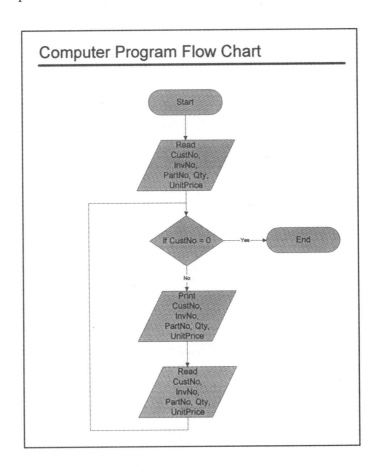

12. Drag a Line connector shape onto the drawing, and connect the bottom of the Start shape and the top of the first Data shape, gluing the Line Connector's endpoints to the connection points on each shape.

13. Repeat step 12 to connect the second and third shapes and the fourth and fifth shapes.

14. Drag a (Yes) Result shape onto the drawing and connect its upper endpoint to the right connection point on the Decision shape. • Connect its lower endpoint to the left connection point on the Terminator (End) shape.

15. Drag a No result shape onto the drawing and connect its upper endpoint to the bottom of the Decision shape. • Connect its lower endpoint to the top of the Print CustNo... data shape.

16. Drag a Bottom to top 1 shape onto the drawing, and glue the lower endpoint to the bottom connection point on the Read CustNo... data shape. • Glue the upper endpoint to the top connection point on the Decision shape. Drag the Bottom to top 1 shape's control handle to the left until it aligns approximately with the 2" point on the horizontal ruler.

17. Use the Text tool to add a title to the chart.

Other Ideas

You can use flowcharts to illustrate processes as well as computer programs. In the following sections, you see how to draw a flowchart that depicts the editing process of a manuscript. You also see how to create multipage flowcharts, which enable you to add greater detail to specific areas on sub-pages.

Drawing a Process Flowchart

The same shapes and techniques used to draw a computer program flowchart can be used to illustrate a process. This figure illustrates the manuscript review process between editor and author. Other than the Predefined process shape used in this flowchart, the shapes and connectors are the same as those used in the computer program flowchart, and the method for creating the chart is the same.

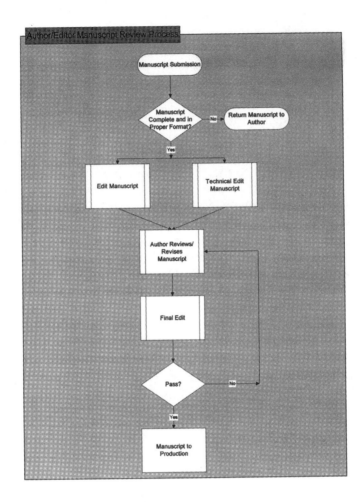

Creating a Multi-Page Flowchart

Some flowcharts illustrate processes that are detailed and complex. However, if you tried to include all the detail, it would defeat the purpose of the flowchart, which is to convey information clearly and simply at a glance. When it's important to include the detail, Visio provides a way for you to add the detail on *sub-pages*. A sub-page is a supplemental page to your flowchart and is displayed when you double-click on a particular shape in the chart. The following figure illustrates how a sub-page is used to provide the details of a technical edit in the Author/Editor Manuscript Review Process flowchart.

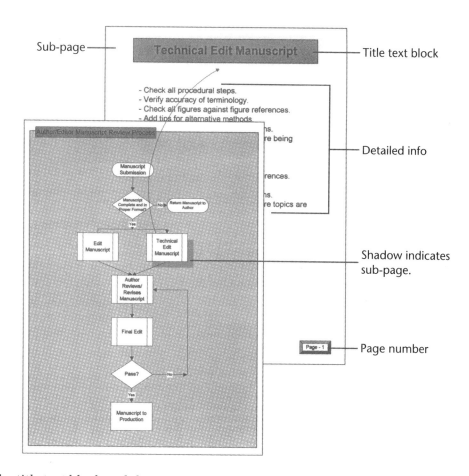

Sub-page

Technical Edit Manuscript

Title text block

- Check all procedural steps.
- Verify accuracy of terminology.
- Check all figures against figure references.
- Add tips for alternative methods.

Detailed info

Author/Editor Manuscript Review Process

Manuscript
Submission

Manuscript
Complete and in
Proper Format?

No

Return Manuscript to
Author

Yes

Edit
Manuscript

Technical
Edit
Manuscript

Shadow indicates
sub-page.

Author
Reviews/
Revises
Manuscript

Final Edit

Pass?

No

Yes

Page - 1

Page number

Manuscript to
Production

The title text block and the page number in the previous figure automatically appear on the sub-page when Visio creates the page. The title reflects the label given to the shape in the original flowchart—in this case, *Technical Edit Manuscript*. You can have text on the sub-page, as shown above, or perhaps another flowchart that illustrates the details of the process shown.

The Flowchart stencil contains two shapes that enable you to create sub-paging: the Process (sub-paging) and the Predefined process (sub-paging) shapes. To create a sub-page, you must include at least one of these shapes in your drawing. When you double-click on the shape, Visio automatically creates the sub-page and displays it on-screen. To return to the original flowchart, choose Page Go To Page. In the Go to Page dialog box, double-click on the Page-1 option.

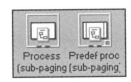

To create a sub-page, follow these steps:

1. Drag the Process (sub-paging) or the Predefined process (sub-paging) shape onto your drawing.

2. Position the shape, size it, and label it the way you want it.

3. Double-click on the shape. Visio displays the Sub Maker dialog box, which displays the shape's label.

4. Click OK. Visio creates a sub-page using the shape label as the page title. The page includes a title block at the top of the page and a page number at the bottom of the page.

5. Enter the detailed information you want to include on this page.

6. When you are finished with the sub-page, choose Page Go to Page, then double-click on Page-1. Visio returns to your original flowchart.

Idea List

Use the principles you learned in this chapter to create these additional types of flowcharts:

- Manufacturing process flowchart
- Customer service flowchart
- Sales and service flowchart
- Technical support flowchart

Business Charts

Visio's Chart stencil contains shapes designed for creating the most common types of business charts, such as pie, bar, and line. For creating custom charts, the stencil also contains unique shapes such as stretchable dollars, an extend-o-hand, unit people, and a divided bar. When you open Visio using the Chart template, the Chart stencil automatically opens, and the drawing page is 8½ " wide by 11" high.

In addition to shapes that represent specific types of charts, the Chart stencil (shown in the following figure) also includes supplemental shapes designed to enhance a chart. Data points, graph scales, axis tick marks, text blocks, and word balloons give your charts visual impact and make them more readable. Some typical business charts and chart enhancements are described in the following chart examples.

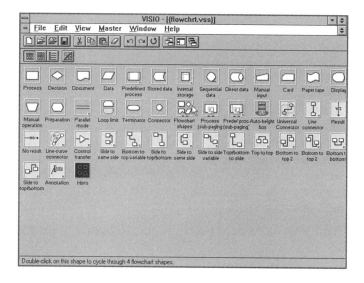

Creating a Pie Chart

Pie charts are used to emphasize how individual parts contribute to the whole. For instance, you would use a pie chart to show how a particular industry's market share is divided among several competitors.

Visio's Chart stencil contains three pie chart slice shapes: Pie chart slice 1, Pie chart slice 2, and the Super smart slice. Each slice is 25%, or ¼, of a circle when you drag it onto the drawing.

NOTE: The different colors of the shapes on the stencil are used to distinguish their different features, not to create different colored slices. You can change the color of any pie slice by choosing a different fill color for the shape.

When creating a pie chart, you can use any of these three pie chart slice shapes. The one you choose depends on how you want to create the chart. Use Pie chart slice 1 when you want to adjust the size of the slice by dragging a control handle. When you release the control handle in a new position, the percentage label on the slice automatically changes accordingly. The + endpoint enables you to adjust the length of the slice from the pie's center point.

Use Pie chart slice 2 when you want to adjust the size of a slice by selecting the slice and then typing a new percentage as the slice label. For instance, if you replace the default 25% label with 34%, the slice automatically changes to a size that represents 34% of the whole, and 34% appears as the slice label. (Be sure to include the % symbol when you type the new percentage.)

NOTE: The Pie chart slice 2 shape contains no control handles.

Use the Super smart slice to glue slices together at their center points, then adjust the size of each slice by dragging a control handle. When you release the control handle in a new position, the percentage label on the slice automatically changes accordingly, and the size and label of the bordering slice changes automatically as well. Use the + endpoint to move adjacent slices into position and to change the length of the slice from the pie's center point.

The following figure shows each of these pie slice shapes and their control handles and endpoints.

For Slice 1, drag control handle to change slice size; drag endpoint to change length of slice from pie's center point.

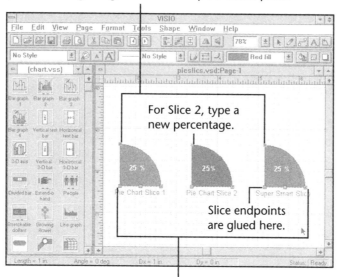

For Super smart slice, drag control handle to change slice size; drag endpoint to change length of slice from pie's center point.

To create a pie chart, choose only one type of pie chart slice shape to work with, then build the pie in a counterclockwise direction. The following steps describe how to create a pie chart using the Super Smart Slice.

1. Open Visio using the Chart template.
2. Drag a Super smart slice shape onto the drawing.
3. Hold the Ctrl key and drag the slice to make a copy of it.
4. Align the second slice directly on top of the first slice.

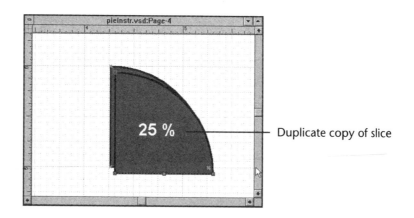

Duplicate copy of slice

TIP: Remember that the most recent shapes you draw appear on top of previous shapes. So when you place pie slices directly on top of one another, the most recent slice is on top, and you can't see the slice beneath.

5. Drag the slice's + endpoint counterclockwise around the edge of the pie slice until it glues itself to the control point on the previous slice.

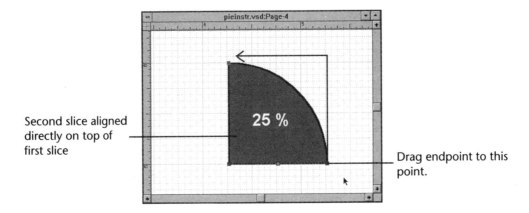

Second slice aligned directly on top of first slice

Drag endpoint to this point.

6. Release the mouse button. The second slice is glued to the first at the point shown in this figure.

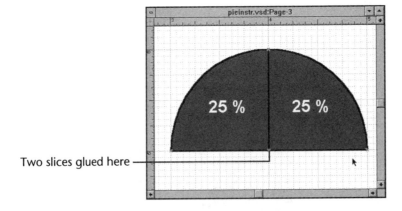

Two slices glued here

7. Drag the control handle on the second slice clockwise to approximately 15%, then release the mouse button. (You can't tell the exact percentage until after you release the mouse button.)

TIP: Drag clockwise to make the slice larger; drag counterclockwise to make the slice smaller.

8. Hold the Ctrl key and drag a copy of the second slice, placing the new slice directly on top of the second slice.

9. Drag the third slice's + endpoint counterclockwise around the edge of the pie slice until it glues itself to the control point on the previous slice. Then release the mouse button.

10. Drag the control handle on the third slice to change its size, then release the mouse button. (Remember, drag clockwise to make the slice larger; drag counterclockwise to make the slice smaller.)

11. To complete the pie, repeat the process of copying the previous slice, gluing the new slice to the previous slice, then adjusting its size. Your pie should resemble the one shown here.

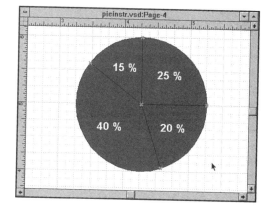

TIP: To change the color of a pie's slices, click on a slice, click on the Fill Style toolbar button, then choose a color from the drop-down menu. To add a pattern to a pie slice, click on the slice, then click on the Fill Pattern toolbar button until you find a pattern you like. For a larger selection of patterns and colors, choose the Format Fill command and choose a pattern, foreground color, and background color from the Fill dialog box.

Experiment with the other pie chart slice shapes in the Chart stencil to create pie charts using other methods. A common means of emphasizing a particular slice in a pie is to *explode* one slice from the rest of the pie, as shown in the following figure. Visio gives you two ways to create an exploded pie chart. The first is to create the pie without using Visio's Glue feature. When Glue is turned off, you can move any slice without disturbing other slices. (To turn Glue off, click the Glue toolbar button. Or choose the Tools Snap & Glue Setup command, and in the dialog box that appears, click on the Glue check box to remove the X and click OK.) Then create your pie, and move the slice you want to explode slightly away from the center of the pie.

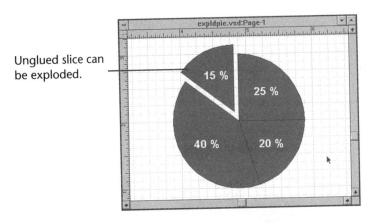

Unglued slice can be exploded.

You use the second method of exploding a pie slice when you've created a pie chart using the Glue feature, and all the slices are glued together. You must break the glued points on a pie chart before you can explode a slice. To do so, click the Glue toolbar button or choose the Tools Snap & Glue Setup command, then click on the Glue check box to remove the X. (Don't turn off Snap; you'll need it to help realign slices.) Return to your pie chart, select each slice individually, move it slightly, then let Snap draw each slice back into its proper position in the pie. As you do this for each slice, the endpoints change from red to green, indicating the slices are no longer glued. Then you can move the slice you want to explode away from the other slices.

Line Graphs

A line graph is most often used to depict trends in a series of data, so the X axis (the lower axis) usually represents time, such as days, months, or years. Creating a line graph couldn't be easier than it is with Visio's Line graph shape, shown in the following figure. The shape contains 12 control handles that mark data points on the graph. Drag the control handles up or down to change the location of data points and, therefore, the trend indicated in the graph. At the uppermost left corner and the lowermost right corner are two additional control handles that enable you to change the length of the black border along the X and Y axes. Use the shape's selection handles to change the height or width of the graph.

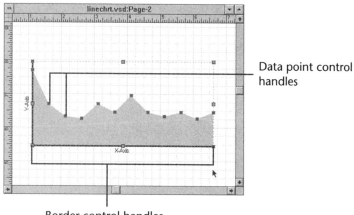

Data point control handles

Border control handles

There are many ways to enhance a line graph. To add text along the x-axis at each data point, subselect the x-axis text block (click until the gray selection handles appear), then type the text for each data point, pressing Tab between entries. For example, in the following figure, the months of the year represent data points along the x-axis. Use the same technique to add text entries to the y-axis.

TIP: *Subselecting* is selecting a shape that's part of a grouped shape. To subselect a shape that's part of a group, click on the grouped shape first (green selection handles appear). Then click on the shape within the group (gray selection handles appear). Refer to Chapter 3 for more information on subselecting.

You can add horizontal or vertical gridlines to the graph by using the Line tool to draw a line and then copying and aligning each line with the axis text labels. The following figure shows a line graph with gridlines and other enhancements added.

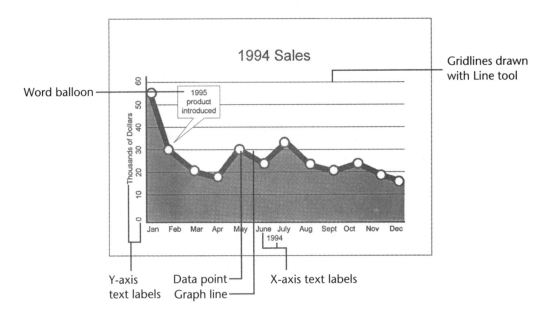

To emphasize the line itself, drag a Graph line shape onto the drawing for each line segment, aligning the Graph line endpoints with each data point. You can also call attention to each data point on the line by dragging the Data point shape onto the drawing and placing it on top of each data point.

TIP: Be sure all data points are accurate before you add Graph line and Data point shapes to the graph. If you need to change a data point afterward, you'll have to move graph lines and data point markers as well.

To complete the graph, add a title and use either the 1-D or 2-D word balloon shape to add a note about a particular data point. Using the 1-D word balloon shape, you can adjust the width of the column of text in the balloon by stretching or shrinking the balloon's width. Using the 2-D balloon, you can drag the control point to aim the balloon pointer in any direction.

TIP: To show more than 12 data points on a line graph, align two Line graph shapes side by side and flip the second shape horizontally.

Bar Graphs

Bar graphs enable you to compare distinct items or emphasize the relationship of items to one another over a period of time. They emphasize comparisons and relationships among items instead of the flow of time, as a line graph does. Visio's Chart stencil contains several shapes for creating bar graphs. Two of the shapes (Bar graph 1 and Bar graph 2) express bars in terms of numbers; the other two shapes (Bar graph 3 and Bar graph 4) express bars in terms of percentages. To create a monochrome graph, choose Bar graph 1 or Bar graph 3. To create a color graph, choose Bar graph 2 or Bar graph 4.

Bar graph 1   Bar graph 2   Bar graph 3   Bar graph 4

All four bar graph shapes have typical selection handles at each of the four corners and four sides of the shape. Each shape also has two control handles. The control handle along the bottom of the shape controls the width of bars. Drag the control handle to the right to make wide bars; drag it to the left to make narrow bars.

The control handle along the left side of the shape controls the relative height of the bars. For instance, if you want your graph to be taller than the standard size of the shape, drag the left control handle up. You can also change the relative height of the bars by subselecting the non-printing bar at the far left of the graph (it contains the number 10) and typing a new number. This has the same effect as dragging the left control handle up or down.

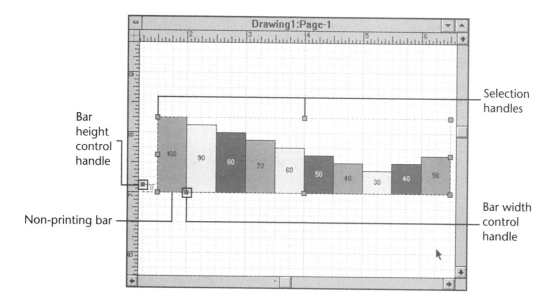

When you use the Bar graph 1 or Bar graph 2 shapes, change the height of each bar by subselecting a bar and typing a new number as the bar label. To enter a negative number, precede the number by a minus sign (–). To adjust percentage bars in the Bar graph 3 or Bar graph 4 shapes, use the same method but include the % sign after the number. In both cases, the bars adjust to the correct height automatically.

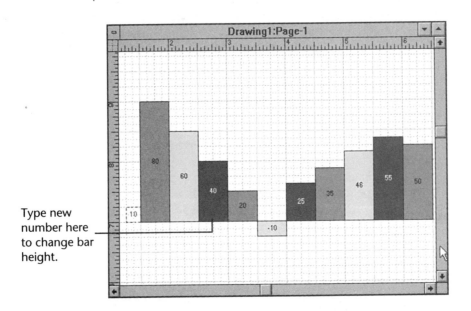

Type new number here to change bar height.

All four bar graph shapes include ten bars when you drag the shape onto the drawing page. You can add or delete bars from a graph in one of two ways. The first method is to adjust the bar width. When you increase the individual bar width, the number of bars in the graph decreases; when you decrease the individual bar width, the number of bars in the graph increases. To add or delete bars in this way, select the graph shape, then drag the control handle on the bottom of the graph shape to the right or left.

The second way to delete bars is to edit the graph shape in the group window. To do this, click on the graph shape, then choose the Edit Open Bar graph command. When the group window opens, click on the bar you want to delete and press the Delete key. (If you delete bars from the middle of the graph, you'll have to move remaining bars to the left to fill in the blank space.) If you delete a bar by mistake, you can choose Edit Undo to restore it if you haven't made other changes already. Or, you can re-store a bar by copying another bar and typing the correct number or percentage in it. When you're finished deleting bars, click the group window's Control-menu box to return to the regular drawing page.

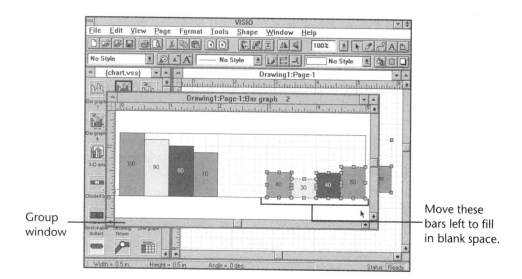

Group window

Move these bars left to fill in blank space.

You can enhance bar graphs (like line graphs) by using various supplemental shapes in the Chart stencil. Because bar graphs don't have built-in labels along the x and y axes, you can add text labels here by using the Vertical text bar and Horizontal text bar shapes. To add a graph title or add a pointer note to the graph, use one of the text block or word balloon shapes. You can also add a scale to the x and y axes of the graph by choosing one of the graph scale shapes. Align the shapes end-to-end and type the correct text labels for each. The following figure illustrates these graph enhancements.

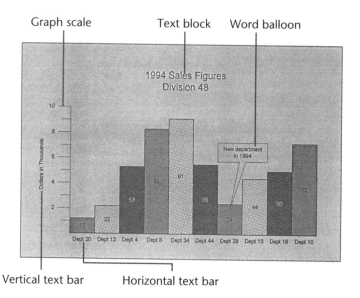

Creating Custom Charts

Visio's Chart stencil contains four shapes (People, Stretchable dollars, Extend-o-hand, and Divided bar) designed for creating custom charts for those times when pie, bar, and line charts don't meet your needs. Three of the four shapes are used as a substitute for bars in a bar chart. The fourth shape is a 100% bar divided into three color categories. To use these shapes, you must build a chart "from scratch."

The People shape is often used in business charts that convey statistics about numbers of people. When you drag the People shape onto the drawing, it contains a monochrome figure of one person. By dragging the right selection handle to the right, you can extend the shape to include four people. To create a bar that includes ten people, then, you would copy the four-person shape once, create a two-person shape, and align the three shapes side by side. The following "bar" chart shows a chart made with the People shape.

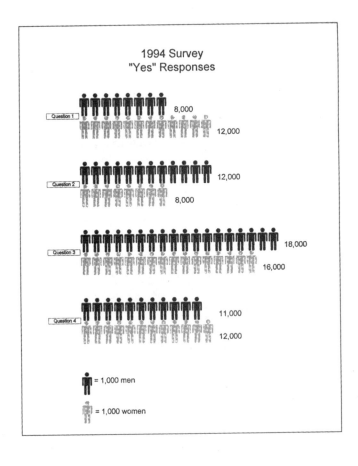

The Stretchable dollars shape works the same way the People shape does and is good for depicting monetary growth. When you drag the shape onto the drawing, it displays one dollar bill. You can stretch the shape to display up to four dollar bills. To display a "bar" that contains more than four bills, align multiple Stretchable dollars shapes side by side. The following chart illustrates the use of this shape.

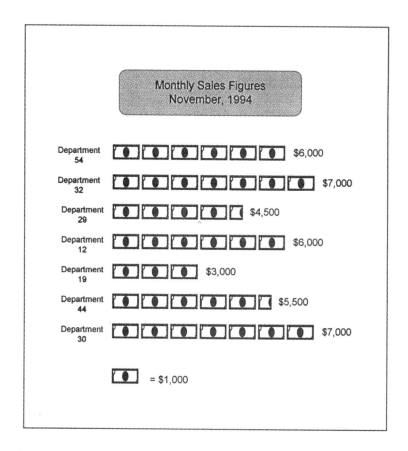

The Extend-o-hand and Growing flower shapes are similar to the People and Stretchable dollars shapes in that they can all be stretched or shrunk. However, when you change the size of these shapes, only one image is still displayed—that is, one Extend-o-hand or one growing flower—not multiple images. Use the Extend-o-hand shape to display horizontal bars; use the Growing flower shape to display vertical bars.

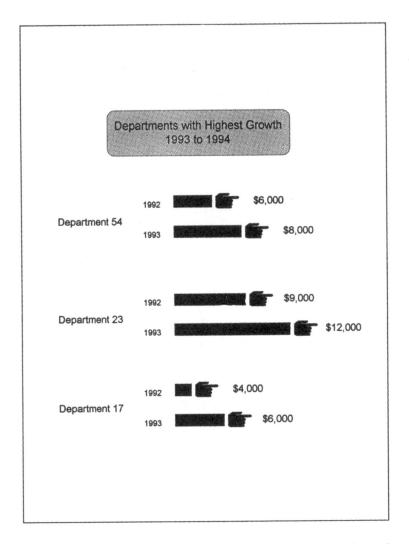

The fourth special shape, the Divided bar shape, enables you to show three categories of data as a portion of a 100% bar. You might use this shape when you want to show percentages as a bar instead of as a pie. To alter the percentages, you drag control handles to the right or left. The first control handle determines the percentage of the first category in the bar; the second control handle controls the second percentage in the bar. Drag the control handle to the left to make the percentage smaller; drag to the right to make the percentage larger. When you alter one or both of these percentages, the percentages for all three categories automatically change accordingly.

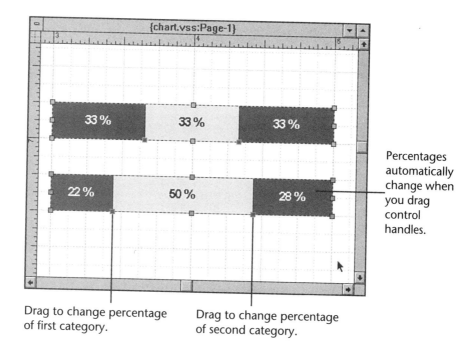

Percentages automatically change when you drag control handles.

Drag to change percentage of first category.

Drag to change percentage of second category.

Idea List

Try using some of the other shapes in the Visio Chart stencil to create these types of charts:

- X-Y graph
- X-Y-Z graph
- Exponential curve graph
- Normal curve graph

Computer Network Charts

In the high-tech world of computers, networks are key to communication. Through computer networks, you can share data with a colleague in the office next door or with a client halfway around the world. As the popularity and usefulness of personal computers have grown in the past decade, new types of computer networks have evolved.

To ensure that equipment is not overlooked and that the network runs correctly, diagramming a computer network is an important step in the planning process. Visio's Network stencil is designed to help you do that diagramming. The stencil contains 43 shapes that represent different types of networks, computers, and computer-related equipment (printers, disks, modems, FAX machines, and so on).

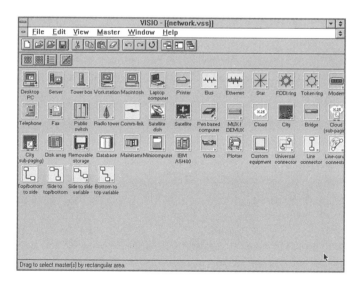

Before you actually start creating network drawings, you need to know some things about how the shapes in the Network stencil work. The five shapes that represent an actual network itself (Bus, Ethernet, Star, FDDI ring, and Token ring) contain several shaded green control handles. When you drag one of these control handles to a connection point on a computer or equipment shape, a connecting line appears, automatically glued to that shape. Once glued, you can move the computer or equipment shape to a new location and maintain its connecting line to the network.

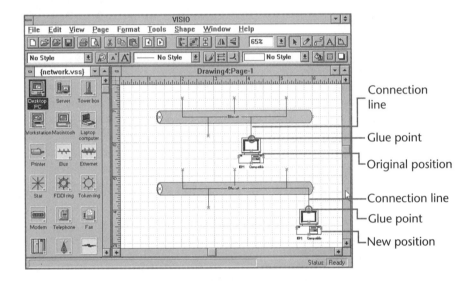

To connect a network control handle to a computer or equipment shape, select the network shape, then point to the control handle you want to use. The mouse pointer changes to a four-headed arrow. Drag the mouse to a connection point on the computer shape and release the mouse button. The control handle is displayed in red, indicating it is glued to the computer shape.

TIP: When you are working with the Network stencil, you need to display connection points and use Visio's Glue feature. To display connection points, click the Connection Points option on Visio's View menu. (A check mark appears next to the option on the menu when it's selected.) To turn on Glue, click the Glue toolbar button or choose the Tools Snap & Glue Setup command, then check the Glue check box and the Connection Points check box when the dialog box appears.

You don't have to use all of the control handles on a network shape. To remove a connector, drag the control handle back to its network line, as shown in the following figure.

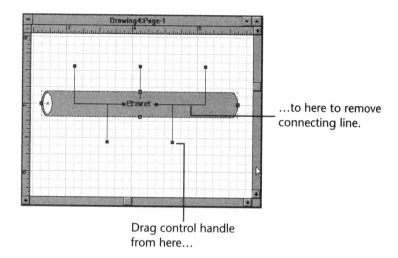

...to here to remove
connecting line.

Drag control handle
from here...

NOTE: Although some control handles on the Bus and Ethernet shapes appear above the "network line" and some appear below the line, you can drag any control handle to either side of the line.

Computer and equipment shapes in the Network stencil have text labels that appear just below the shape. Like network shapes, these shapes also have control handles, but they are used to reposition the text label, not to connect the shape to other shapes. To move a text label to the side of the shape, for example, simply drag the shape's control handle to the side.

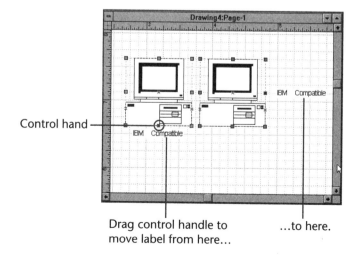

Control hand

Drag control handle to
move label from here...

...to here.

Creating a Simple Network Diagram

The simplest network diagram contains a network shape and the computer components that are connected to it. In the following drawing, the Bus shape is used to
illustrate a PC local area network, or PC LAN. Connected to the network are a DOS-
Based File/Print Server, an IBM PC, a Mac II, a Laptop computer, an IBM Compatible,
and a Laser printer.

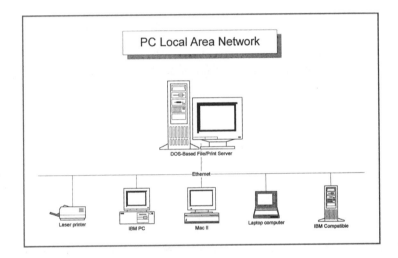

You might use a drawing like this to represent the exact components attached to a
LAN—that is, one of each component shown. Or, you might use it to represent the
exact number of components of a specific type attached to the LAN. In the latter case,
you might modify the existing labels to read, for example, *25* IBM PCs, *14* Mac IIs, *19*
Laptop computers, and so on.

To create this PC LAN drawing, follow these steps:

1. Open Visio using the Network template. The drawing page appears in Landscape orientation.

2. Choose File Print Setup, choose the Landscape option, and click OK.

3. Drag the Bus shape onto the drawing page. • Size the Bus shape to 8" or 9".
   • Type **Ethernet** to label the shape.

4. Drag a Server shape onto the drawing and position it above the Bus shape.
   Drag a corner handle to make the shape slightly larger. • Type the label
   DOS-Based File/Print Server. • Select the Bus shape and drag the center
   control handle on the upper side of the Ethernet to a connection point on
   the DOS-Based File/Print Server. The control handle turns red when you
   release the mouse button. • Drag the DOS-Based File/Print Server so it is
   roughly centered above the Ethernet.

NOTE: Make sure you select the Bus shape first, then point the mouse to the control handle until the four-headed arrow appears. If you try to drag one of the Bus shape's connection points before you select the shape, you'll accidentally move the whole Bus shape.

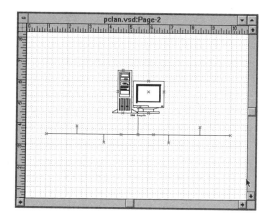

5. Drag the following shapes onto the drawing page and place them in order along the lower side of the Bus shape. (Don't worry about the spacing and horizontal alignment of the shapes right now.)

> Printer
>
> Desktop PC
>
> Macintosh
>
> Laptop computer
>
> Tower box (Type **IBM Compatible** for this shape.)

6. Select the Bus shape, and one by one drag a control handle to a connection point on each of the shapes listed in step 5.

7. Hold the Shift key as you click on all five shapes connected below the network line. • Click the Align Shapes toolbar button, then choose the last button from the drop-down menu.

8. Move the first and last shapes (the Printer and the IBM Compatible) an equal distance from their respective page borders (for example, 1½" or 2" from the left and right edges of the page). • Select all five shapes connected below the network line. • Click the Distribute Shapes toolbar button, then choose the third button from the drop-down menu.

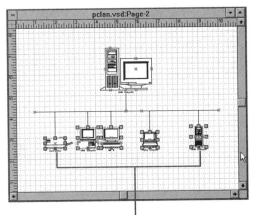

After you click the Distribute Shapes
button, these shapes are equally spaced..

9. Click the Text tool and type a title for the drawing.

Other Ideas

Earlier in this chapter, you learned that the Visio Network stencil contains shapes for five basic network types: Bus, Ethernet, Star, FDDI Ring, and Token Ring. Regardless of the type of network diagram you draw, you use the same basic techniques for working with these and other shapes in the stencil: drag a network shape onto the drawing, then drag a control handle from the network shape to a connection point on computer or equipment shapes. Once the shape is glued, you can move it to a new position around the network and the connecting line will automatically adjust to the proper angle and length.

The examples that follow illustrate how to draw various types of networks using these basic principles.

Token Ring Network Diagram

A *token ring network* has a hub, or ring, in the center, to which all network components are connected. To create the diagram shown on the following page, first drag the Token ring shape onto the drawing, size it, and place it where you want it to appear in the drawing. Drag other computer and equipment shapes onto the drawing, placing them around the ring. Glue control handles from the Token ring to connection points on each of the computer and equipment shapes, then adjust the position of the computer and equipment shapes as needed.

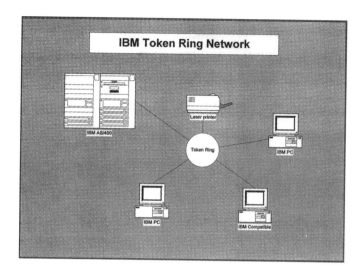

x.25 Network Diagram

An *x.25* network is a public packet switching network. Generally, an x.25 network connects computers or subnetworks at remote locations. In the following figure, the x.25 network connects different types of networks at four remote locations (Seattle, Boston, Los Angeles, and Dallas).

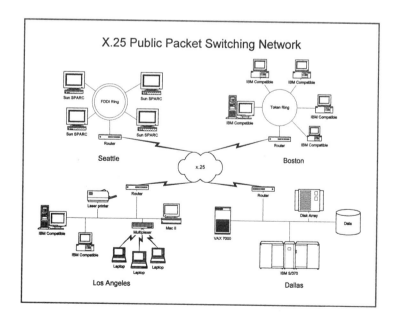

Although the Cloud shape represents a type of network (x.25) in this drawing, it differs from other network shapes (Bus, Ethernet, Token ring, and so on) in that it does not contain control handles. This is because computers are connected to an x.25 network by a communications link via a network device called a *Bridge*. To connect a Bridge to the Cloud shape, use the Comm-link shape, which has two endpoints. Glue one endpoint to a connection point on the Cloud; glue the other end to a connection point on a Bridge shape.

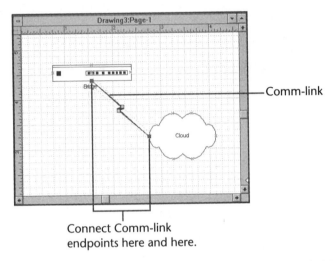

Connect Comm-link
endpoints here and here.

Although the x.25 drawing looks more complex than the PC LAN and IBM Token Ring network drawings, it is just as easy to create using the same basic principles. Begin by dragging the Cloud shape to the center of the drawing, then place four Bridge shapes around the Cloud shape. (For this example, change the Cloud label to **x.25** and the Bridge labels to **Router**.) Drag four Comm-link shapes onto the drawing to connect the routers to the x.25 shape, then build each of the four remote networks individually. Finally, use the Text tool to add labels for each city.

TIP: When a drawing contains multiple copies of the same shape (such as the IBM Compatible), drag one shape onto the drawing, size it appropriately, then copy it to other locations on the drawing. This saves time and ensures that the shapes are a consistent size throughout the drawing. To align and distribute shapes evenly, use the Align Shapes and Distribute Shapes toolbar buttons.

Wide Area Network Diagram

A *wide area network* is one in which computers at remote locations are connected via telephone lines, an FDDI network, or satellite link. The following figure depicts a satellite connection between Seattle, Boston, and Dallas. This is a conceptual type of network drawing as opposed to an actual network diagram. The drawing is enhanced by a map shape borrowed from another Visio stencil.

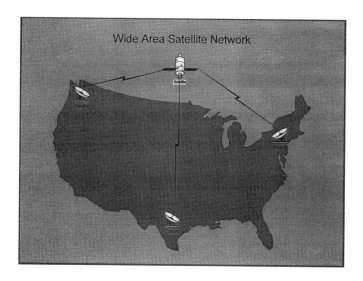

The shape of the United States is taken from the North America shape in the World Map stencil. To open this stencil, click the Open Stencil toolbar button, then double-click on World Map Stencil in the list. Drag the North America shape onto the drawing page, then click the Ungroup toolbar button or press Ctrl+U. Ungrouping the shape takes a few minutes (Visio ungroups more than 1300 separate shapes from this image). When the shape is ungrouped, delete all unwanted shapes until all you have left is the United States. Size the United States shape, then add the network shapes to the drawing.

From the Network stencil, drag the Satellite shape onto the drawing and center it above the United States. Use the Satellite dish shape in the location of each city. (Alternatively, you could use a combination of the Satellite dish shape and the City shape to represent each city.) Use the Comm-link shape to connect each satellite dish to the Satellite shape, then glue each endpoint of the Comm-link to connection points on the Satellite and Satellite dish shapes.

Creating an Equipment Inventory

Aside from creating network diagrams and conceptual drawings, you can use the shapes in the Network stencil to create a simple graphical inventory of computer equipment. To create a drawing like the one shown here, use a different shape to represent each piece of equipment, then add a count of the number of units. Just as you did for other network drawings, use the Align Shapes toolbar button to horizontally align shapes and text labels. Finally, you might want to include a revision date in the title for reference.

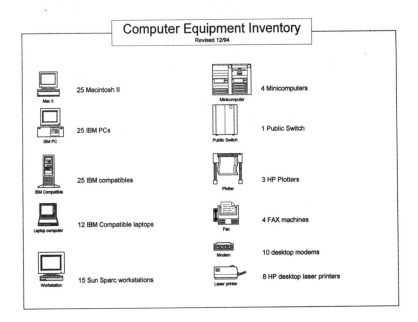

Idea List

Here are some other types of network drawings you can create using the methods described in this chapter:

- Star network diagram
- FDDI network diagram
- Stand-alone mainframe computer and disk farm

Business Forms

Every day, each of us encounters more forms than we realize—many, in fact, that we don't even notice. Every time you make a deposit or withdrawal at your bank, weed through your junk mail, fill out a warranty card for something you bought, pay a bill, or sign your name on the mailing list at your favorite store, you encounter forms of various kinds. The business world revolves around forms: you can't get a job without filling out an application, you can't collect a paycheck until you fill out a W4 form, and a company can't sell and get paid for products or services without receiving purchase orders and issuing invoices.

For *every* business (from the modest home business to the multi-million dollar corporation), forms are an inevitable reality. Many businesses use preprinted standardized forms that you can buy at your local office supply. But the majority of business forms require unique information and, therefore, a custom design. If you've ever been asked to design and create a custom business form, you know just how difficult and time consuming that task can be.

The purpose of Visio's Forms template is to simplify the task of creating business forms. At a minimum, most forms comprise lines, boxes, text labels, grids, and borders, all precisely positioned and aligned. Visio's Forms stencil contains shapes for all of these elements. You can mix and match these shapes in many different ways and, as usual, you can stretch, shrink, size, and modify them like all other kinds of shapes.

Visio makes it especially easy for you to create two of the most common business forms: a business card and a Fax cover sheet. The Forms stencil contains shapes for each of these two forms. (The full set of shapes in the Forms template is shown in the following figure.) Take a minute to read the shape names and think about how you might use each shape.

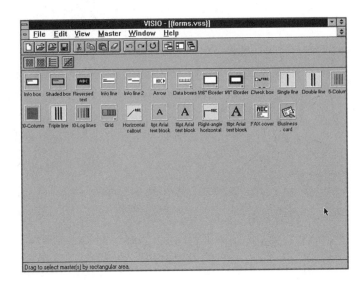

TIP: When creating any type of form, you can simplify the job of positioning and aligning shapes by using the grid lines on the drawing page, or by using horizontal and vertical guides. For a review of how to use the grid and guides, refer to Chapter 2. Visio's Snap and Glue features (discussed in Chapter 2) also come in handy when you want to align shapes precisely.

Creating a Business Card

For the first business forms example, let's start with a simple item that everyone is familiar with: a business card. You might not think of a business card as a form, but it has all the elements of a business form. In fact, you might never think of creating your own business cards, but you can easily do so with Visio.

The Business card shape in the Forms stencil contains text blocks for a company name, company address, and an individual's name and title. To create a business card like the one in the following example, you can slightly alter the Business card shape so that you can add a shape (such as the bicycle) from the Symbols stencil as a company logo. Once you have completed a single business card, you can copy it so that ten business cards fill a sheet of paper. You can then print the cards on heavy stock paper, or take a master copy to a professional printer and have the cards printed and cut to size.

When you drag the Business Card shape onto the drawing page, it is a grouped shape. To make changes to it, you must first open the group. Then edit the individual shapes as outlined in the following steps.

1. Open Visio using the Forms template.

2. Drag the Business card shape onto the drawing page.

3. Choose Edit Open Business card. A group window opens.

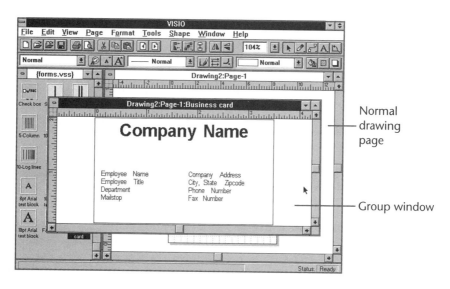

4. In the group window, click on the Company Name text block and type **Steve's Cycle Shop** or your own company name. • Click on the Font toolbar button and choose Coronet or a similar font. • Click on the down arrow next to the Font Size toolbar button and choose 30 pt. • Click the Left-Align Text toolbar button. • Size the text block so that the company name just fits within the text block. • Place the Company Name text block approximately ⅛" from the left edge and the top edge of the business card.

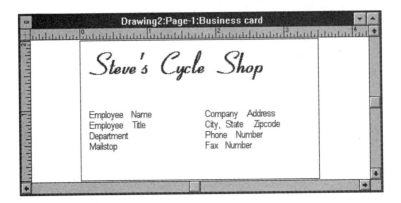

5. Click on the Open Stencil toolbar button and choose the Symbols Stencil.

6. Drag the bicycle shape onto the drawing page.

 TIP: If you have your company logo stored on your computer, you can insert it into the business card form in place of the bicycle shape by choosing the Page Insert Object command.

7. Choose Shape Ungroup or press Ctrl+U to ungroup the bicycle shape. • Click OK in response to the warning message. • Select the white background surrounding the bicycle and the text block below the bicycle, then press the Delete key.

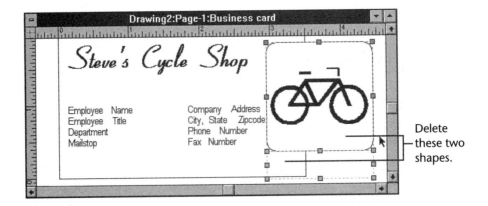

Delete these two shapes.

8. Select the bicycle shape, then drag a corner selection handle to size the bicycle to approximately ½" wide. • Move the bicycle into place to the right of the company name. • Click the Shadow toolbar button once.

9. Click on the Employee Name text block, then type the name and (optional) title, department, and mail stop, or other information such as CompuServe or Internet addresses.

10. Click on the Company Address text block, then type the address, city, state, ZIP code, phone number, and fax number.

11. Click on the business card outline or border. • Choose Format Line. • Choose Weight #1 and Color #15, then choose OK.

12. Double-click on the group window's Control-menu box to return to the regular drawing window.

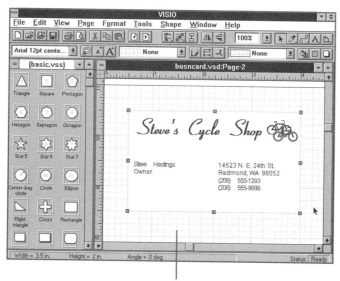

Regular drawing window

13. Click on the business card and align it at 10½"/1".

14. Hold the Ctrl key and drag a copy of the business card directly below the current one.

15. Repeat step 14 three more times so that you have five cards down one side of the page. • Select all five business cards at once (hold the Shift key as you click on each card, or use the Pointer tool to draw a selection box around all five cards). • Hold the Ctrl key and drag a copy of all five business cards to the right of the existing cards, aligning the inside edges.

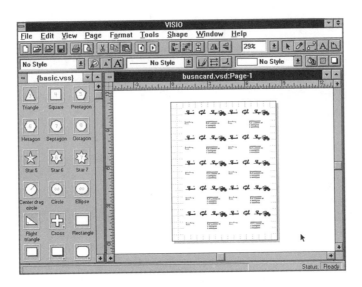

To achieve a different look or style for a business card, you can rearrange the text blocks on the Business card shape to suit your particular needs. In the business card below, the title text block was moved to the bottom of the card.

Fax Cover Sheet

Similar to the Business card shape, the FAX cover shape is a complete Fax cover page that includes the date, sender's and recipient's names, phone number, subject, and so on. At the bottom, it includes a text block in which you can enter a message to the recipient. You can use the FAX cover shape as is, or you can modify it. For a Fax cover sheet like the one in the following figure, move the Company Name/Address text block down and resize it to accommodate a globe shape from the Clipart stencil.

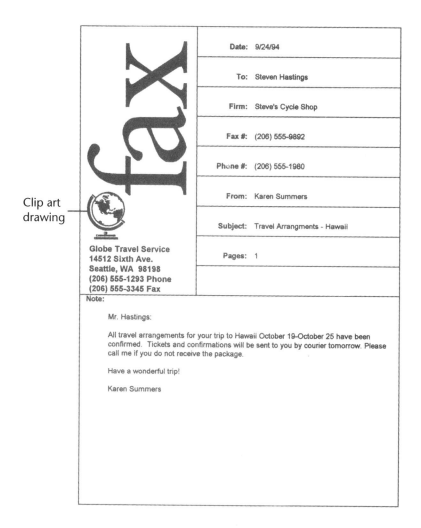

Clip art drawing

To create this Fax cover sheet, you use the same general steps you used to create the business card:

1. Drag the FAX cover shape from the Forms stencil onto the drawing page.

2. Choose Edit Open Fax cover to open a group window.

3. Type the correct name and address in the Company Name/Address text block.

4. (Optional) To add the globe shape shown in the example, click on the Open Stencil toolbar button, open the Clipart stencil, and drag the Globe shape onto the drawing page. You then size the globe, as well as the Company Name/Address text block, to fit within the given area.

5. To fill in the actual date, name, firm, phone numbers, and so on for the cover sheet, click twice on the Date *placeholder* (until the gray selection handles appear), then begin typing. Press Enter to move from one line to the next.

Other Ideas

The Business card and FAX Cover sheet shapes make creating these types of business forms easy because much of the work is already done for you. You can also create other types of business forms by using the various elements that go into most of them: that is, lines, boxes, labels, borders, and so on. Just drag the shapes onto the drawing page, arrange them how you want them, then move, size, alter, or enhance them as necessary.

The following is a list of some of the forms you can create using Visio.

- Time Sheet
- Address Label
- Vacation Request Form
- Permission Slip
- Sales Slip
- Request Form
- Grade Book
- Enrollment Form
- Questionaire
- Order Form
- Packing List

You can take the form you create to a professional printer and have duplicate and triplicate forms made. You can also have forms made into tear-off pads.

Copy Request Form

The copy request form shown on the following page is created using only four shapes from the Forms stencil: the Info line 2 shape, the Single line shape, the 18 pt. Arial text block shape, and the 1/16" Border shape.

The Info line 2 shape contains a label to the left of a blank line. This shape is very handy because it eliminates the need to painstakingly align text labels with blank lines. You can vary the length of each info line by stretching the width of the shape. You create other blank lines by rotating the Single line shape 90 degrees and sizing the lines to the proper length. Create the borders surrounding the form using the 1/16" Border shape and varying the line color. Create the form's title with the 18 pt. Arial text block shape. For a final touch, add a fill color, shadow, and curved corner to the title text block.

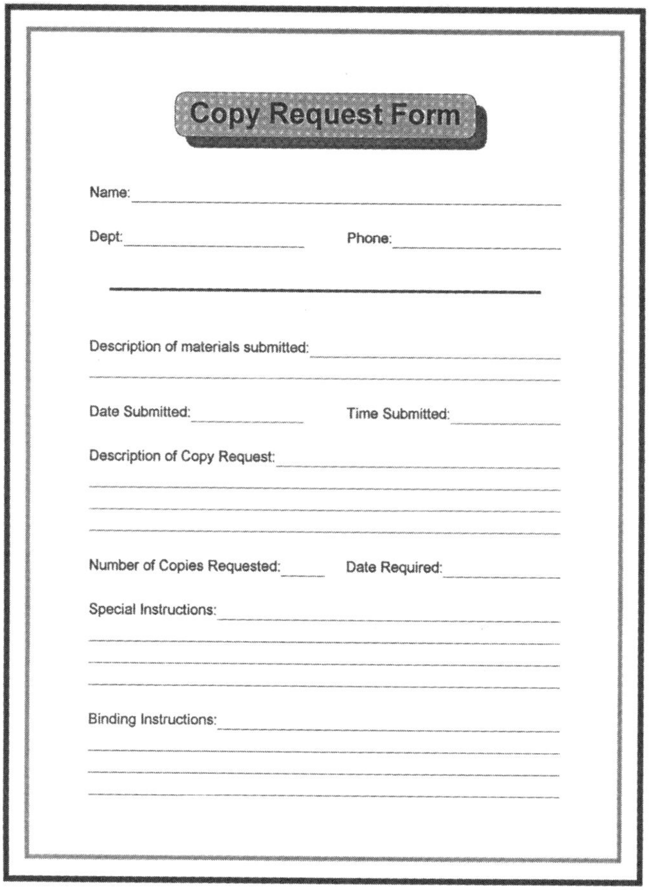
Copy Request Form

Name:

Dept: Phone:

Description of materials submitted:

Date Submitted: Time Submitted:

Description of Copy Request:

Number of Copies Requested: Date Required:

Special Instructions:

Binding Instructions:

Registration/Warranty Card

A common element in forms is the row of boxes—Visio calls them *data boxes*—in which you write or type individual characters (such as in a name or address). Data boxes help separate characters so that they can be identified easily. Check boxes are also commonly used on forms.

The Registration/Warranty Card shown here uses the Data boxes shape, the Check box shape, the Info line 2 shape, and the Reversed text shapes, all found in the Forms stencil. The 1/16" Border and 1/8" Border frame the form.

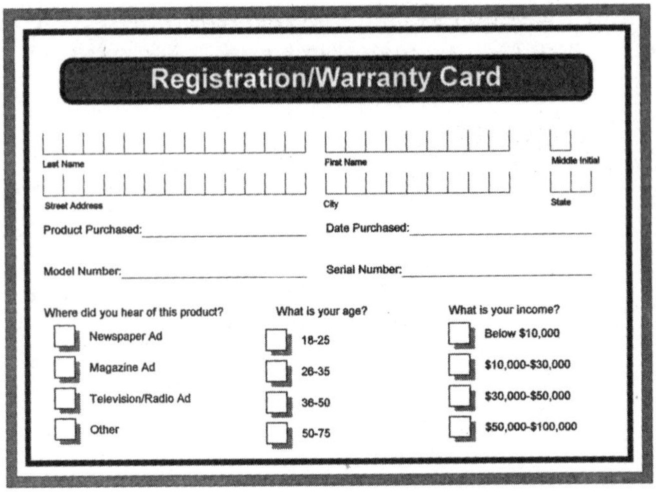

Initially, the Data boxes shape provides 8 boxes in which to enter characters. To provide more or fewer boxes, you vary the width of the entire shape by dragging a side selection handle. You can also vary the uniform width of the data boxes by dragging the shape's control handle right or left. To make the individual boxes narrower, drag the control handle to the left. To increase the width of the individual boxes, drag the control handle to the right.

Phone Message Pad

The phone message pad shown in the following figure consists of shapes from two stencils: the Forms stencil and the Border stencil. The Message for, From, Phone, and other lines should be familiar to you by now. They were created using the Info line 2 shape from the Forms stencil. The border, however, is created using the Art deco frame shape from the Border stencil.

When you drag the Art deco frame shape onto the drawing, the frame is wider than it is high. For this project, rotate the frame 90 degrees to make it higher than it is wide. Then add the title and information lines and size them appropriately. Creating this form is as simple as that!

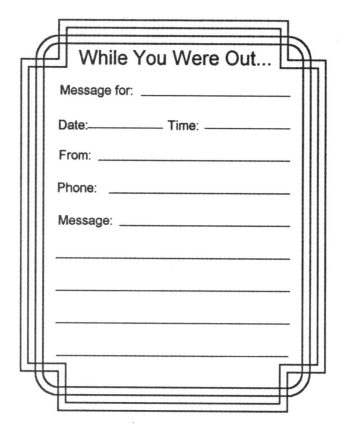

As with the example of the business cards, once the initial message pad is complete, you can group the shapes and copy them to fill the drawing page. Four message pads fit nicely on a page. You can then print copies and cut them to size. You can even take your message pad to a printer and have it printed on bright paper and cut and bound into message pads.

Idea List

Here are a few more business form ideas for you to try using the same basic steps and procedures you learned in this chapter.

- Job Application
- Marketing Questionnaire
- Inventory Forms
- Purchase Order Form

- Invoice Form
- Product Special Order Form
- Credit/loan Application Form
- Medical Questionnaire
- Expense Report
- Tracking Form
- Insurance Forms
- Membership Application
- Report Cards
- Transmittals
- Receipts
- Sales Proposals
- Coupons
- Mileage Report

Drawing House Plans

You probably wouldn't use Visio to create detailed architectural drawings or blue-prints, but you can use Visio's Space Planning stencil quite successfully to create accurate, scaled house plan drawings. You could use this type of drawing for a number of purposes, for example:

- as a starting point when designing a new home
- to illustrate house plans for real estate advertising
- as illustrations in home and decorating magazines
- as a sales tool for a residential building or construction company
- as diagrams for insurance documents
- as a diagram for potential remodeling

If you've ever tried to draw a house plan to scale, you know how time-consuming and challenging it can be—especially for those of us who are not architects. Even when you have all the proper drawing tools and scaled graph paper, you must calculate the dimensions of every wall, door, and window to scale, and it's easy to forget to include important dimensions, like the width of outside and inside walls.

In this chapter, you use Visio's Space Planning stencil (shown in the following figure) to draw several different house plan styles. The stencil includes a wide variety of shapes, some for the structure of the house itself and some for furniture inside of the house. Not only does the stencil contain many detailed shapes for indoor spaces (such as tables, chairs, and desks), it also contains the basic shapes you need to create a whole-house plan. The shapes you'll use most are the Wall square, Wall corner, Wall section, Door, and Window shapes. You'll use the other shapes in the Space Planning stencil in subsequent chapters.

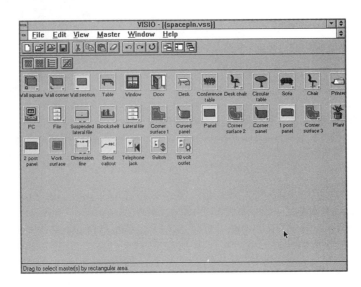

The three wall shapes (Wall square, Wall corner, and Wall section) each create walls that are 6" thick. To determine dimensions, Visio measures from the *inside* of the walls. For example, the Wall square shown below is 8' by 8', measured from the inside of the walls. The selection box that appears when you select the shape indicates the point from which the walls are measured. You can vary the thickness of the walls by dragging a wall shape's control handle.

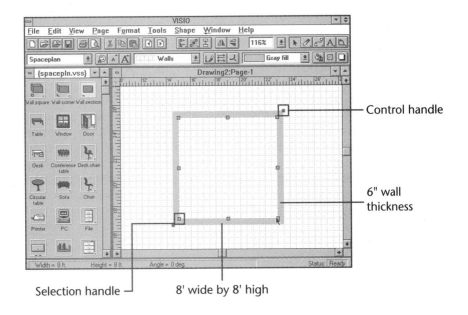

When you open Visio using the Space Planning template, the Space Planning stencil automatically opens, and the drawing page appears in landscape orientation. The drawing scale is ¼" = 1', making the drawing page 44' wide by 34' high. This is not quite large enough for most houses, so you'll probably want to change the drawing scale to at least ⅛" = 1', which creates a drawing page of 88' wide by 68' high. To change the drawing scale, choose the Page Page Setup command and click the Size/Scale button. In the Page Setup Size/Scale dialog box, choose the ⅛" = 1' scale from the Architectural drop-down box and click OK. Click OK again to close the Page Setup dialog box.

Drawing a One-Story Rectangular House

The one-story rectangular house shown in the figure below is the simplest type of house to draw; you use Visio's basic Wall square shape to create the outer walls, and use the Wall section shape to define the interior walls.

Use the following steps to create this house plan:

1. Open Visio using the Space Planning template.

2. Choose Page Page Setup. In the dialog box, click the Size/Scale button. • Click on the Standard option button and choose Letter Tall from the drop-down list. • Click on the Architectural option button, then choose ⅛" = 1'0" from the drop-down list. • Click OK twice. The drawing page is now 68' wide by 88' high.

3. Drag a Wall square shape onto the drawing and size it to 45' wide by 65' high. • Align the Wall square at 75'/15'.

4. To create the left bedroom, drag a Wall corner shape onto the drawing. • Size the Wall corner to 19½' wide by 20' high. • Click the right mouse button and choose Rotate Left from the shortcut menu. • Align the Wall corner at 55'/15'. • Drag a Door shape from the stencil onto the drawing. • Click the right mouse button and choose Rotate Left from the shortcut menu. • Click on the Flip Vertical toolbar button.• Align the door near the lower right corner of the bedroom at 39'/35'. • Drag a Window shape onto the drawing and size it to 8'. • Click the right mouse button and choose Rotate Left. • Align the Window shape at 46'/15'.

5. To create the laundry/storage room, drag a Wall section shape onto the drawing and size it to 20'. • Align the wall section at 49'/15'. • Hold the Ctrl key and drag a copy of the Door shape from the left bedroom, aligning it along the right laundry room wall at 52½'/35'.

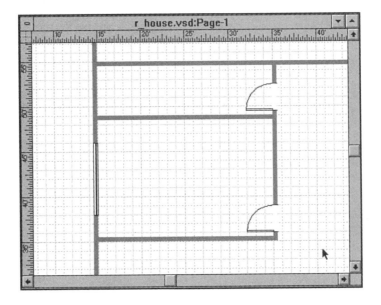

6. To create the inside walls on the right side of the house, drag a Wall corner shape onto the drawing. • Size the Wall corner to 20' wide by 42' high. • Align the Wall corner at 75'/40'.

7. To create the master bedroom, drag a Wall section shape onto the drawing. • Size the Wall section to 45'. • Align the wall section at 55'/15'. • Drag a Door shape onto the drawing and align it on top of the lower master bedroom wall at 55'/36'. • To create the door from the master bedroom to the bathroom, drag another Door shape onto the drawing. • Click the right mouse button and choose Rotate Right from the shortcut menu. • Align the door at 69½'/39½'. • Drag a Window shape onto the drawing and size it to 10'. • Click the right mouse button and choose Rotate Left from the shortcut menu. • Align the window along the left master bedroom wall at 75'/15'. • Drag another Window shape onto the drawing and size it to 10'. • Align the window along the upper master bedroom wall at 75'/15'. • Hold the Ctrl key and drag a copy of this window, aligning it at 75'/34' along the upper bedroom wall.

8. To add a fireplace to the master bedroom, drag a Corner surface 1 shape onto the drawing. • Click the right mouse button and choose Rotate Left from the shortcut menu. • Align the fireplace in the lower left corner of the master bedroom at 60'/15'.

9. To create the walk-in closet wall in the master bathroom, drag a Wall section shape onto the drawing and size it to 20'. • Align the Wall section at 60'/40'. • Drag a Door shape onto the drawing. • Click the Flip Vertical toolbar button. • Align the door at 60'/49'6". • Hold the Ctrl key and drag a copy of the door to the left of the first door. • Click the Flip Horizontal toolbar button. • Align the second door alongside the first door at 60'/46'6".

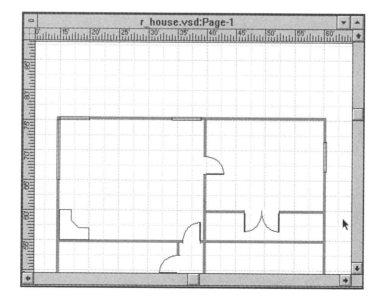

10. To create the toilet room in the master bathroom, drag a Wall square shape onto the drawing and size it to 5' wide by 7' high. • Click the right mouse button and choose Rotate Right from the shortcut menu. • Align the Wall square at 65'/53'. • Choose the Ellipse tool and draw an oval 3' wide by 2' high. • Align the oval at 63½'/56½'. • Drag a Door shape onto the drawing. • Click the Flip Vertical toolbar button. • Click the Flip Horizontal toolbar button. • Align the door at 65½'/53'.

11. To create the bathtub area, choose the Rectangle tool and draw a rectangle 4' wide by 7' high. • Align the rectangle at 72½'/56'. • Choose the Ellipse tool and draw an oval 2½' wide by 6' high. • Using the Pointer tool, click on the bathtub rectangle shape, hold the Shift key down, then click on the bathtub oval shape. • Click on the Align Shapes toolbar button and choose the second button from the drop-down menu to align the shapes vertically. • With both shapes still selected, press Ctrl+G to group the shapes. • Drag a Window shape onto the drawing. • Click the right mouse button and choose Rotate Right from the shortcut menu. • Align the window on the right bathroom wall at 71'6"/60'.

12. To create the master bathroom counter and sinks, choose the Rectangle tool and draw a rectangle 20' wide by 2'6" high. • Align the rectangle at 75'/40'. • Choose the Ellipse tool and draw an oval 1'9" wide by 1'6" high. • Align the oval at 74½'/45'. • Hold down the Ctrl key and drag a copy of the oval, aligning it at 74½'/52'.

13. To create the shower, click the Rectangle tool and draw a rectangle 4½' wide by 4½' high. Align the rectangle in the lower left corner of the master bathroom. • Drag a Door shape onto the drawing. • Size the door to 2' wide. • Click the right mouse button and choose Rotate Right from the shortcut menu. • Align the shower door at 63'3"/44'. • Choose the Shape Send to Back command.

TIP: When drawings call for precise measurements, use the information provided on the status bar to help you size shapes correctly. The height, width, and angle of a shape are always displayed on the status bar and are updated continuously as you change a shape's size.

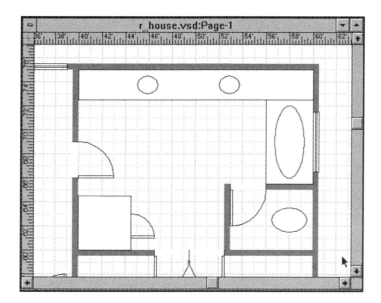

14. To create the guest bathroom, drag a Wall section shape onto the drawing
    and size it to 20'. • Align the wall at 45½'/40'. • Drag a Door shape onto the
    drawing. • Click the right mouse button and choose Rotate Right from the
    shortcut menu. • Align the door along the left bathroom wall at 49'/39½'.

15. To create the bathtub, click on the Rectangle tool and draw a rectangle 4'
    wide by 9' high. • Align the rectangle at 54½'/56'. • Choose the Ellipse tool,
    draw an oval 2½' wide by 6' high, and place it inside the rectangle. • Using
    the Pointer tool, click on the bathtub rectangle shape, hold the Shift key
    down, then click on the bathtub oval shape. • Click on the Align Shapes
    toolbar button and choose the second button from the drop-down menu to
    align the shapes vertically. • Click on the Align Shapes toolbar button again
    and choose the fifth button from the drop-down menu to align the shapes
    horizontally. • With both shapes still selected, press Ctrl+G to group the
    shapes.

16. To create the toilet, choose the Ellipse tool and draw an oval 2' wide by 3'
    high. • Align the oval at 54'/53'3".

17. To create the counter and sink, choose the Rectangle tool and draw a rect-
    angle 12' wide by 2½' high. • Align the rectangle at 54½'/40½'. • Using the
    Pointer tool, hold the Ctrl key and drag a copy of one of the sinks from the
    master bathroom to the guest bathroom counter. • Click on the counter
    rectangle first, hold the Shift key down, then click on the guest bathroom
    sink. • Click on the Align Shapes toolbar button and choose the second
    button from the drop-down menu to align the shapes vertically. • Click on
    the Align Shapes toolbar button again and choose the fifth button from the
    drop-down menu to align the shapes horizontally.

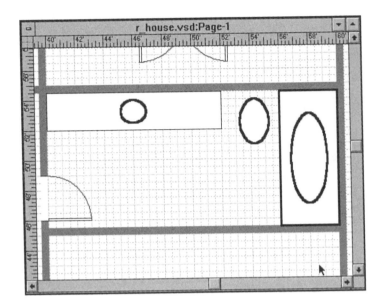

18. To complete the right bedroom, drag a Door shape onto the drawing. • Click the right mouse button and choose Rotate Right from the shortcut menu. • Click the Flip Vertical toolbar button. • Align the door at 44'6"/39'6". • Drag a Window shape onto the drawing and size it to 6'. • Click the right mouse button and choose Rotate Right from the shortcut menu. • Align the window at 42'/60'.

19. To create the kitchen and dining room walls, drag a Wall square shape onto the drawing and size it to 25' wide by 10' high. • Align the Wall square at 20'/35'. • Drag a Wall section onto the drawing and size it to 15'. • Place the Wall section directly on top of the upper kitchen wall, aligning it at 40' on the horizontal ruler. • With the Wall section still selected, click the Fill Style toolbar button and choose No Style from the drop-down menu. This makes the Wall section white to create an opening from the kitchen to the dining room.

20. Drag a Window shape onto the drawing and size it to 6'. • Click the right mouse button and choose the Rotate Right command from the shortcut menu. • Align the window along the right dining room wall at 29'/60'. • Drag another Window shape onto the drawing and size it to 4'. • Click the right mouse button and choose the Rotate Right command from the shortcut menu. • Align the window along the right kitchen wall at 17'/60'. • To make this a garden window, choose the Rectangle tool and draw a rectangle 1' wide by 4' high. Align this shape at 17'/60½'. • Drag another Window shape onto the drawing. • Click the Flip Vertical toolbar button. • Align the window along the lower kitchen wall at 10'/52'.

21. Complete the living room by dragging a Door shape onto the drawing and aligning it along the lower (outer) wall at 10'/29'. • Drag a Window shape onto the drawing and size it to 9'. • Click the Flip Vertical toolbar button. • Align the window along the lower living room wall at 10'/17½'. • Drag another Window shape onto the drawing and size it to 10'. • Click the right mouse button and choose Rotate Left from the shortcut menu. • Align the window along the left living room wall at 25'/15'. • To create the patio, choose the Rectangle tool and draw a rectangle 6' wide by 15' high. • Align the rectangle at 27½'/14½'. • Type **Patio** to label the rectangle.

22. To add a fireplace to the living room, drag a Corner surface 1 shape onto the drawing. • Click the right mouse button and choose Rotate Right from the shortcut menu. • Align the fireplace in the upper left corner of the living room at 35'/15'.

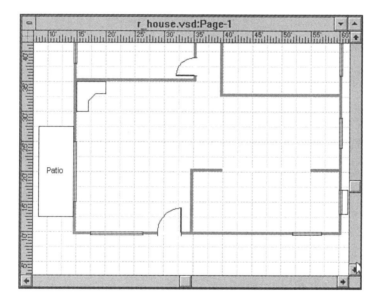

23. Label each room of the house as shown in the finished picture of this project at the beginning of these steps. To create labels, choose the Text Block tool, draw a text block large enough for the text label, and type the appropriate label. • To position each text block, choose the Pointer tool and drag the text block as necessary to position it in each room.

24. To add a title to the drawing, choose the Text tool, click near the top center of the drawing, and type the title. While the title is selected, you can change the font, font size, fill color, or line color. Or you can add a shadow to the title by clicking the Font, Font Size, Fill Style, Line Style, or Shadow tools on the toolbar.

Another Idea: Drawing an L-Shaped House

The next figure shows a standard L-shaped house with bedrooms and bathrooms along the hallway on the long side of the L. Except for the L-shape, the drawing is created using the same principles used in the one-story rectangular house. You create the L-shape by using the Wall section creatively to hide wall sections.

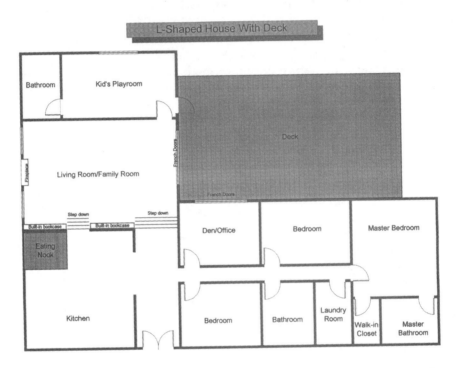

To create the L-shape, begin by drawing a rectangle using the Wall square shape. In the figure below, the Wall square shape is 78' wide by 54' high. Create the L-shape by dragging a Wall Corner shape onto the drawing, sizing it to 49' wide by 28' high, and aligning it as shown in the figure.

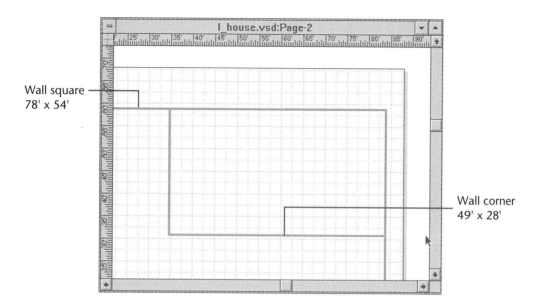

Wall square
78' x 54'

Wall corner
49' x 28'

Now you need to somehow delete the upper right portion of the original Wall square shape. You can't delete part of a shape, but you can obscure it by placing another shape on top of it. To hide this section of the Wall square, drag another Wall corner shape onto the drawing and size it to 48½' wide by 27½' high, then click the Flip Horizontal and Flip Vertical toolbar buttons and align the shape exactly over the wall sections you want to hide. When the shape is positioned properly, click the Fill Style toolbar button and choose Normal or White fill from the drop-down menu. A white Wall corner shape now hides the upper right section of the Wall square.

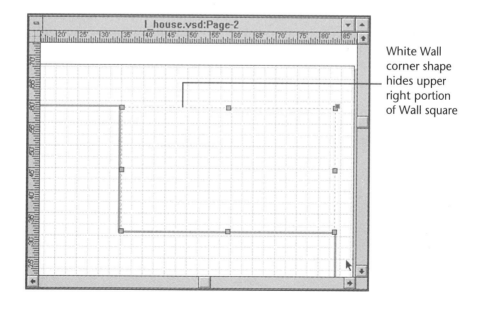

White Wall
corner shape
hides upper
right portion
of Wall square

You can complete the drawing using the same basic methods you would use for any house plan drawing. As a finishing touch, add the deck by drawing a rectangle using the Rectangle tool.

Idea List

Once you've had some practice, try creating house plans for these types of drawings:

- U-shaped house
- Two-story or three-story house using multiple drawing pages
- Tri-level or split-level house
- House additions like garages, extra rooms, and so on
- Layout for finishing a basement or attic
- Office or retail space or building

Planning Spaces for Businesses, Schools, and Organizations

In all types of groups—businesses, schools, and other organizations—space planning is a crucial factor. When offices, classrooms, and meeting rooms are dark, cramped, or inaccessible, workers are not as efficient or productive as they might otherwise be. When public and customer spaces are uncomfortable, poorly planned, and uninviting, business suffers.

Unfortunately, spaces are often poorly planned because space planning is a challenging task. Without the proper tools, space plan drawings are difficult to create, difficult to change, and often subject to error. But with Visio, space planning is a snap. The Space Planning template in Visio enables you to plan any type of space that has walls, doors, windows, and furniture. Whether you're designing a reception area/ waiting room or drawing a floor plan of a banquet ballroom, you'll find just about every shape you need. The Space Planning template includes shapes for walls, doors, windows, and even panel walls for creating modular spaces like office cubicles. Once you have created your space, you can furnish it with furniture shapes that include tables, desks, chairs, file cabinets, bookshelves, computers, printers, and even plants. This figure shows the complete set of shapes in the Space Planning stencil.

Space Planning shapes

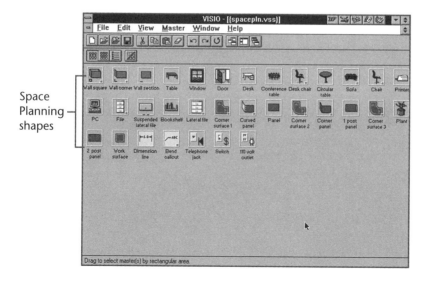

When you open Visio using the Space Planning template, the drawing page is shown in landscape orientation, and the vertical and horizontal rulers display feet rather than inches. Using a scale of ¼" = 1', the drawing area shown is approximately 44' wide by 34' high. You can change the scale by choosing the Page Page Setup command, clicking the Size/Scale button in the Page Setup dialog box, then choosing an option from the Architectural Drawing Scale box. For instance, if you choose a scale of ⅛" = 1', the drawing area is approximately 88' wide by 68' high. You can also change the page orientation from landscape to portrait by choosing the Page Page Setup command, clicking the Size/Scale button in the Page Setup dialog box, then choosing the Letter Tall option in the Standard Printed Page Size box.

TIP: Space planning often involves exact measurements and careful alignment of shapes. For whatever type of space planning you do, you'll find horizontal and vertical guides helpful for placing shapes precisely. Visio's Snap and Glue features also help you to align shapes. For a review of these features, refer to Chapter 2.

Creating a Conference/Banquet Seating Chart

The first example in this chapter is a simple one: a seating chart that can be used for a luncheon, company party, reunion, fund-raising dinner, fashion show, or banquet. Guests at these type of functions are often assigned to specific tables. This type of chart could be included with each guest's information. The chart could also be used by the table service staff to indicate assigned sections.

In this project you are introduced to some of the most basic shapes in the Space Planning stencil: walls and doors. You also use the table, circular table, and chair shapes to add the furniture in the room. Horizontal guides help you position the tables in the ballroom.

TIP: When your drawing calls for precise measurements, use the information provided on the status bar to help you size shapes correctly. The height, width, and angle of a shape are always displayed on the status bar and are updated continuously as you change a shape's size.

Rainier Ballroom Seating Chart

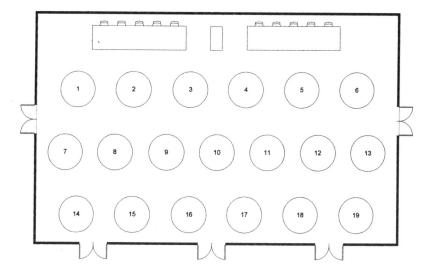

1. Open Visio using the Space Planning template.
2. Choose File Print Setup. • Choose Landscape and choose OK.
3. Choose Page Page Setup. • Choose the Size/Scale button. • Choose the Architectural ¹/₈" = 1'0" option, then choose OK. • Choose OK again.
4. Drag the Wall square shape to align with 55'/5'. • Stretch the Wall square to 7¹/₂'/82¹/₂'.

 TIP: Recall from the introduction of this book that "7¹/₂'/82¹/₂'" means to align the upper left corner of a selected shape at 7¹/₂' on the vertical ruler and 82¹/₂' on the horizontal ruler. The vertical ruler point is always given first.

5. Create three horizontal guides at 43', 30', and 17'.
6. Drag a Circular table shape onto the drawing page. • Size the circular table to 7¹/₂' by 7¹/₂'. • Align the top edge of the Circular table shape to the first horizontal guide (at 43') and align the left edge at 10'. When you release the mouse button, the shape is glued to the horizontal guide, indicated by the red selection handles.

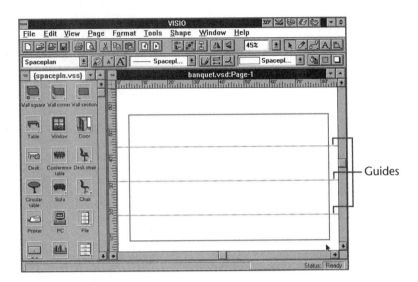

7. Glue a copy of the Circular table shape to the first horizontal guide (at 43')
   and align the left edge at 70'. • Press and hold the Ctrl key and drag a copy of
   the Circular table shape along the first horizontal guide. • Use this same
   method to drag three more Circular table shapes between these two circle
   shapes along the first horizontal guide. • Select all six table shapes. • Click
   the Distribute Shapes toolbar button and choose the first button from the
   drop-down menu. Or choose the Tools Distribute Shapes command, choose
   the first Left/Right button, and choose OK.

8. Copy one Circular table shape and glue it to the second horizontal guide (at
   30' and 7¹/₂'). • Glue a copy of the Circular table shape along the second
   horizontal guide at (at 25') and align the left edge at 72¹/₂'. • Copy five more
   table shapes between these two along the second horizontal guide. • Select all
   seven shapes along the second horizontal guide. • Click the Distribute Shapes
   toolbar button and choose the first button from the drop-down menu. Or
   choose the Tools Distribute Shapes command, choose the first Left/Right
   button, and choose OK.

9. Select all tables in the first row and copy them to the third horizontal guide
   (at 25').

10. Beginning with the first row, number all tables consecutively from left to
    right by selecting each table and typing the correct number.

11. Drag the Table shape from the stencil to any location on the drawing page.

12. Size the table to 20' by 5'. • Align the table at 52¹/₂'/17'. • Copy the table
    shape and align at 52¹/₂'/50'. • Drag another Table shape onto the drawing
    page. • Rotate the Table shape 90 degrees. • Align the Table shape at
    52¹/₂'/42¹/₂'.

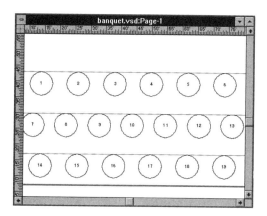

13. Drag a Chair shape onto the drawing page and rotate 90 degrees clockwise.
• Place the Chair shape close to the left end of the left-hand table. • Copy
four more Chair shapes along the left-hand table, placing the last chair near
the right end of the table. • Select all five chairs. • Click the Distribute Shapes
toolbar button and choose the first button from the drop-down list. Or
choose the Tools Distribute Shapes command, choose the first Left/Right
button, and choose OK. • With all five chairs still selected, choose Shape
Send to Back. • Copy all five chairs to the right-hand table. • Choose Shape
Send to Back.

14. Drag a Door shape along the lower ballroom wall ($7^1/_2'$) and align at $17^1/_2'$.
• Click the Flip Vertical toolbar button. • To create double doors, copy the
Door shape and drag it to the left of the first door. • Choose the Flip Horizontal toolbar button. • Align the doors side by side. • Select both doors and
press Ctrl+G to group the doors.

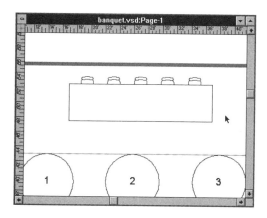

15. Select the double doors by clicking on them. Then press and hold the Ctrl key and drag a copy of the double doors to 15' along the lower ballroom wall. • Drag another copy of the double doors anywhere along the lower ballroom wall between the other two doors. • Select all three double doors by holding the Shift key as you click them. • Click the Distribute Shapes toolbar button and choose the first button from the drop-down menu. Or choose the Tools Distribute Shapes command, choose the first Left/Right button, and choose OK.

TIP: Use the Zoom toolbar button to zoom in on the drawing to at least 100% to correctly align the door.

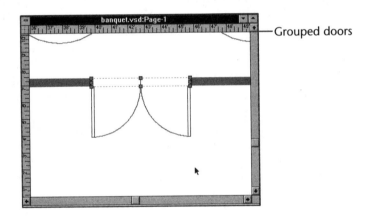

Grouped doors

16. Copy one group of double doors anywhere on the drawing page. • Choose Rotate Left from the shortcut menu, then align the bottom edge of the doors at the 30' guide on the left ballroom wall. • Copy the double doors to the right ballroom wall. • Click the Flip Horizontal toolbar button. • Align the bottom edge of the doors at the 30' guide on the right ballroom wall.

17. Near the top of the drawing, type a title for the drawing. • From the Font Size button, choose 24 points.

18. Click on the ballroom walls, then click on the title. • Click the Align Shapes toolbar button and choose the second button from the drop-down menu. Or choose the Tools Align Shapes command, choose the second Left/Right button, and choose OK.

TIP: You could easily add text labels indicating smoking and non-smoking sections/tables to a seating chart of this type.

Creating a Cubicle Design

Cubicles are a common alternative to private offices in large companies. A cubicle is a semi-private office built of wall panels that are 5 or 6 feet high. The modular design of cubicles makes them quick and easy to assemble. Cubicles are usually built in groups of four or more, as shown below.

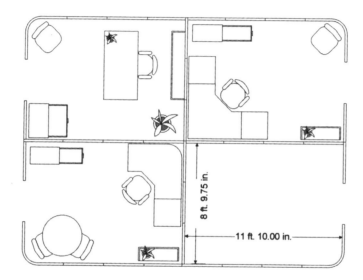

You use the Space Planning template to create this four-unit cubicle design. To give you the flexibility to vary the placement of furniture, the cubicle walls are created on a background page, and furniture placement is done on a foreground page. This enables you to create different arrangements in foreground pages without having to redraw the outer cubicle walls each time. (Chapter 3 discusses the use of foreground and background pages in Visio in more detail.) Because this project is very different from the banquet seating chart project, the specific steps for creating cubicles appear on the following page.

In this drawing, you use the Dimension line shape, which consists of a line and a text label showing a measurement. The measurement adjusts automatically depending on the length of the dimension line. You can use the dimension line as a guide for sizing an object to an exact dimension, or you can use it to indicate the exact length or width of an object.

Before you begin, make sure that Snap and Glue are on by clicking the Snap & Glue toolbar buttons. (Or, choose the Tools Snap & Glue Setup command. In the dialog box, make sure an X appears in the Snap and Glue check boxes and click OK.) Click the Connection Display button on the toolbar or choose the View Connection points command to turn off the display of connection points.

1. Open Visio using the Space Planning template.

2. Choose Page Page Setup. • Choose Background. • Enter "Cubicle Walls" in the Name box. • Choose OK.

3. Set the zero point for the top ruler at 2' from the top of the drawing page and the zero point for the side ruler at 2' from the left edge of the drawing page. (To move ruler zero points, hold the Ctrl key as you drag the square in the upper left corner where the rulers meet.)

4. Draw vertical and horizontal guide lines at both zero points. (To draw a guide, click on a ruler and drag the mouse onto the drawing page.)

5. Drag a Curved panel shape to 0'/0'. • Drag a corner selection handle to make the Curved panel shape 3' x 3'. • Click the right mouse button and choose Rotate Right.

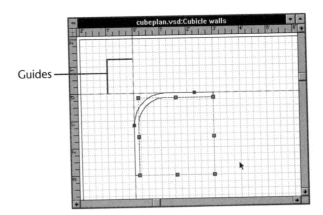

Guides

6. Drag a Panel shape onto the drawing page. If necessary, adjust to make it 3' wide. • Click the Flip Vertical toolbar button. • Glue the Panel shape to the right end of the Curved panel shape (at 0'/3'). • Hold the Ctrl key, drag a duplicate of the Panel shape to the right, and align it at 0'/6'. • Press F4 to duplicate the Panel shape one more time (at 0'/9'). • Drag another Panel

shape anywhere on the drawing and adjust it to 3'. • Click the right mouse button and choose Rotate Right from the shortcut menu. • Align the shape at 6'/0'. You now have the left and top walls of a single cubicle, with a doorway between 3' and 6'.

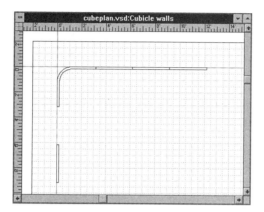

7. Select all shapes (left and top wall panels) and group them by selecting Shape Group or pressing Ctrl+G. This group will be called the Outer Walls.

8. Make a copy of the Outer Walls and place at 10'/0'. Click the Flip Vertical toolbar button. • Make a copy of the Outer Walls and place it at 0'/13'. Click the Flip Horizontal toolbar button. • Make another copy of the Outer Walls and place it at 10'/13'. Click the Flip Vertical button, then click the Flip Horizontal button.

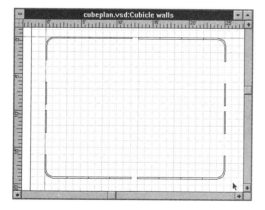

9. To draw the inside walls between cubicles, drag a Panel shape onto the drawing, adjust it to 3' wide, and glue it at 9'/0'.

10. Hold the Ctrl key as you drag a duplicate shape to 9'/3'. • Press F4 six times to add six duplicate panels.

11. Drag another Panel shape into the drawing area and adjust it to 3' wide. • Click the right mouse button and choose Rotate Left from the shortcut menu. • Align the shape at 0'/12'. • Hold the Ctrl key as you drag a duplicate copy of the panel to 3'/12'. • Press F4 four times to create four more duplicate panels.

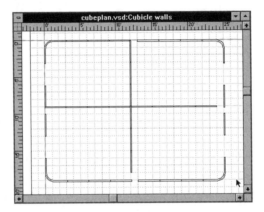

12. Move the lower left Outer Walls to 9'/0'. • Move the upper right Outer Walls to 0'/12'. • Move the lower right Outer Walls to 9'/12'. The four cubicle walls are now built.

13. To display length and width dimensions in the lower right cubicle, drag the Dimension line shape into the lower portion of the cubicle. Size the Dimension line shape to reach from the left to the right cubicle wall. • Press F2 to select the dimension line's text block, then choose 12-pt. from the Font Size toolbar button. • Drag another Dimension line shape onto the drawing page, click the right mouse button, and choose Rotate Left from the shortcut menu. • Press F2 to select the dimension line's text block, then choose 12-pt. from the Font Size toolbar button. • Move the Dimension shape near the left wall of the cubicle and size to fit between the upper and lower cubicle walls.

TIP: Zoom in very close on the cubicle walls to size the dimension lines correctly. To zoom in, click the Zoom toolbar button and choose a setting from the drop-down menu.

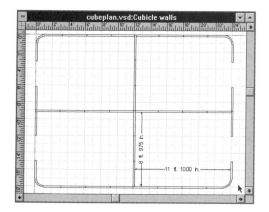

14. Choose Page New Page. • Choose Foreground. • In the Name box, type **Cubicle Furniture 1**. • From the Background drop-down list, choose Cubicle Walls. • Choose OK.

15. Turn Snap off by choosing the Tools Snap & Glue Setup command. In the dialog box, click the Snap check box to remove the X, then click OK.

16. To place furniture in the upper right cubicle, drag the Corner surface 1 shape into the lower left corner. • Attach a Work surface shape to the left and right sides of the Corner surface 1 shape. • Drag a Desk chair shape in front of the Corner surface 1 shape. • Drag the Desk chair's control handle to point to the lower left corner of the shape. This rotates the chair to face the desk. • Drag the File shape into the upper left corner of the cubicle. • Click the right mouse button and choose Rotate Left from the shortcut menu. • Drag the File shape's control handle to the right to show the file drawer fully open. • Drag a Chair shape into the upper right corner of the cubicle. • Drag the Chair shape's control handle to point to the lower left corner of the shape. This rotates the chair to face towards the desk. • Drag a Bookshelf shape into the lower right corner of the cubicle. • Drag a Plant shape onto the bookcase and size it to fit.

TIP: Create custom furniture shapes and save them in the Space Plan stencil or a separate stencil.

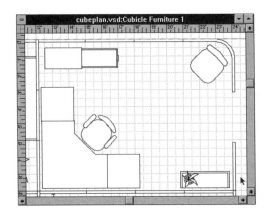

17. To place furniture in the upper left cubicle, drag a Desk shape into the drawing area. • Click the right mouse button and choose Rotate Left from the shortcut menu; then align the desk at 1'/6'. • Drag a Plant shape into the upper left corner of the desk and size it appropriately. • Drag a Desk chair shape into the drawing area. • Drag the shape's control handle to point to the left side of the chair. This rotates the chair 180° (to face the desk). • Align the chair at 2½'/8'. • Click the Shape Send to Back button to put the chair under the desk. • Drag a Bookshelf shape into the drawing area. • Click the right mouse button and choose Rotate Left from the shortcut menu. • Align the Bookshelf shape at 1'/11', then size the Bookshelf to the same length as the desk. • Drag the Plant shape into the lower right corner of the cubicle.
• Drag a Lateral file shape into the lower left corner of the cubicle. • Click the right mouse button and choose Rotate Left from the shortcut menu. • Drag the Lateral file's control handle to the right to show the file drawer fully open. • Drag a Chair shape into the upper left corner of the cubicle. Drag the Chair's control handle to point to the lower right selection handle. This turns the chair to face diagonally into the cubicle.

TIP: To distinguish file cabinets from bookshelves, lateral files, and suspended files, add labels to furniture by selecting the shapes and typing names.

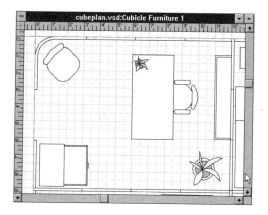

18. To place furniture in the lower left cubicle, drag the Corner surface 3 shape into the upper right corner of the cubicle. • Click the right mouse button and choose the Rotate Right command from the shortcut menu twice. • Attach a Work surface shape to the right side of the Corner surface 3 shape. • Select both shapes and press Ctrl+G. • Align the shapes near the upper right corner of the cubicle. • Drag the Desk chair shape onto the drawing area and place it near the diagonal of the Corner surface 3 shape. • Drag the shape's control handle to point to the upper right corner of the shape. This rotates the shape to face the desk. • Drag the File shape into the upper left corner of the cubicle. • Click the right mouse button and choose Rotate Left from the shortcut menu. • Drag the control handle to the right to show the file drawer fully open. • Drag the Bookshelf shape into the lower right corner of the cubicle. • Drag and size a Plant shape on top of the Bookshelf. • Drag two chair shapes into the lower left corner of the cubicle. • Use the control handles on each chair to rotate the chairs as shown in the figure. • Drag a Circular table shape into the lower left corner of the cubicle and size to 3' square. • Arrange the table and chairs in the lower left corner of the cubicle.

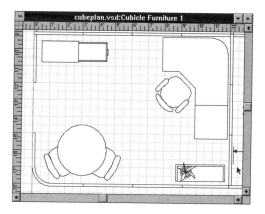

TIP: Create additional pages for different furniture variations. Be sure to assign Cubicle Walls as the background for new pages.

Other Ideas

Once you use Visio to plan spaces, you'll find out just how easy it is. In the two previous projects, you learned the basic steps for building a space by using wall, panel, and furniture shapes. You also learned how to use a very important shape, the dimension line, to help you indicate precise measurements.

An important thing to remember when planning spaces is to draw the space the same way you would if you were building it. In other words, you wouldn't start arranging furniture before you built the walls of a room; so draw the walls first when you begin drawing. If you follow this simple rule, you minimize potential problems in sizing and arranging shapes.

The following sections outline additional projects you can create using Visio. You're not limited to these projects, so use your imagination and adapt them to your needs. You can create any of the following projects using the techniques you have already learned—no unusual methods are used. The projects include the same basic shapes introduced earlier in this chapter.

Cubicle Floor Plan

Earlier in this chapter you saw an example of a four-unit cubicle. You can carry this design one step further by drawing an entire floor plan of 24 cubicles; 12 interconnected cubicles on the left and 12 on the right.

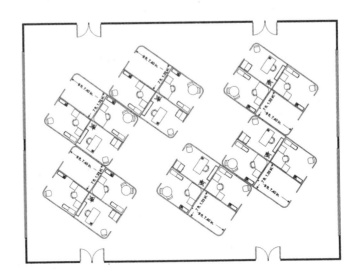

For this drawing, create the room's outer walls, doors, and windows first. Arrange three four-unit cubicles in a staggered pattern, then group and rotate them to the right 35 degrees. Then copy this grouped arrangement of 12 cubicles to the right side of the drawing, and flip them vertically and horizontally. By copying and flipping the original group of cubicles, you save yourself the trouble of independently arranging, grouping, and angling the 12 cubicles on the right side of the room.

Fire Evacuation Map

Fire evacuation maps are an essential item for most large buildings (such as hotels, office buildings, convention centers, and so on). In the following fire evacuation drawing, create the outer walls using the Wall corner and Wall section shapes from the Space Planning stencil. Create the individual rooms using the Line tool. For the stairs, use the 5-Column shape in the Forms stencil (although you could just as easily create the stairs using the Line tool).

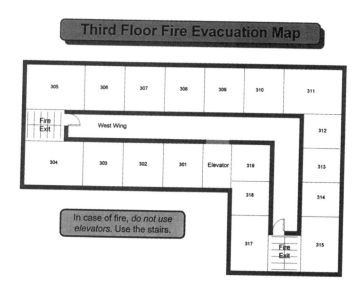

Management Office

The following management office drawing contains many of the same shapes from the Space Planning stencil used in the cubicle design drawing. The only additional shapes used in this drawing are the Window, PC, and Printer shapes.

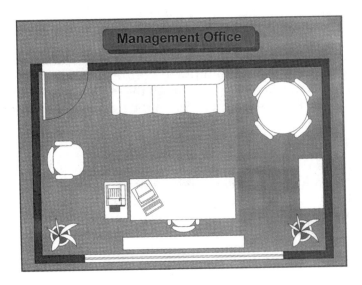

The gray background for this drawing was created using the Rectangle tool after the drawing was complete. You need to create it last because the most recent shape you draw always appears on top of other shapes that it overlaps; therefore, the rectangle momentarily obscures the entire drawing when you draw it. To place the rectangle beneath all other objects, click Shape Send to Back, then shade the rectangle using the Format Fill command or the Fill Pattern toolbar button.

TIP: If the shapes in this management office are drawn to scale, you can move and reposition them until you find the best arrangement. If you want to experiment with drawings for a variety of furniture arrangements, you can create the office outer walls on a background page and create different furniture arrangements on foreground pages. This technique is described in the cubicle design drawing earlier in this chapter. Using foreground and background pages is also discussed in Chapter 3.

Reception Area/Waiting Room

You can draw the reception area/waiting room drawing using many of the same shapes you used for the management office. You use the same method to draw the reception area that you used to draw the management office, with one exception. Because the reception area contains a lot of furniture that is aligned along the side and lower walls, you should glue furniture shapes to horizontal and vertical guides. Using guides (instead of simply using the Align Shapes toolbar button) can really be to your advantage if you need to move all of the furniture, because you can move furniture glued to a guide as a single unit simply by moving the guide. This makes it easy to vary the distance of the furniture from the outer walls, for example. See Chapter 2 for more information on guides.

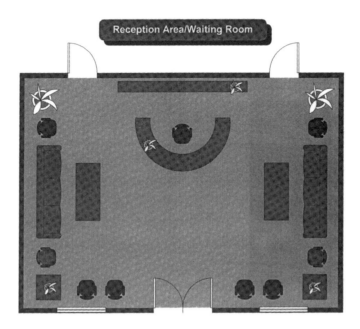

Computer Training Room

For this layout of a computer training room, create the outer walls, doors, and windows first. Then create and group one complete table with two computers and two chairs. Once you have grouped the tables, chairs, and computers, copy them around the room. Use the Align Shapes and Distribute Shapes toolbar buttons to correctly align and space the tables.

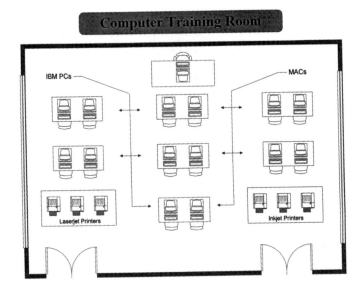

Create the printer tables using the Table shapes from the Forms stencil and the Printer shapes from the Clipart stencil. You can draw the callout lines indicating which computers are IBM PCs and which are MACs in one of two ways. You can draw the lines using the Line tool and then click the Line Ends toolbar button to add the arrows. Or you can open the Callout stencil and use an arrowhead callout.

Cafeteria/Lunch Room

You can easily create this cafeteria/lunch room floor plan using some of the same techniques you used to create the conference/banquet seating chart earlier in this chapter. The cafeteria tables are positioned horizontally using guides and are equally spaced apart from one another using the Distribute Shapes toolbar button.

A unique shape in this drawing is the L-shaped cafeteria food line counter. Create this shape by overlapping two rectangles at right angles, selecting both shapes, then choosing the Shape Union command. This command combines the two shapes into one. For a discussion of the Shape Union command, refer to Chapter 3.

The booths are bordered by Panel shapes placed end-to-end: eight on the left side and fourteen on the top side. To create the booths, use the Rectangle tool to draw booths 5' wide by 5' high. Place one booth in the corner, three booths on the left side, and six booths along the top. To create the booth tables, use the Rectangle tool to draw a rectangle approximately 4' wide by 2' high, then click the Shadow toolbar button once. Place three copies of this table in the booths along the left side. Then make another copy of this table and rotate it to the left using the Rotate Left command on the shortcut menu (click the right mouse button to display the shortcut menu). Place six copies of the rotated table in the booths along the top. The table in the corner booth is created the same way, but its size is approximately 3' by 2'.

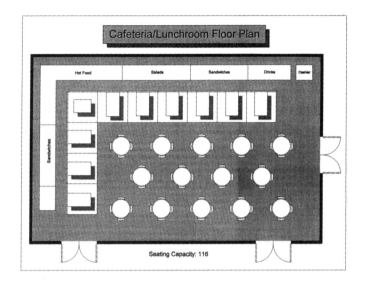

Idea List

Here are a few more space planning projects that you can create using Visio:

- Computer room floor layout
- Conference/presentation room
- Convention/trade show floor plan
- Employee gym/workout room
- Classroom layout
- Classroom seating chart
- Library floor plan
- Trade show booth

Planning Retail Spaces

Chapter 9 introduced you to the Space Planning template and space plan drawings for businesses, schools, and organizations. In this chapter, you use the same template to design floor plans for retail spaces.

No matter what kind of retail business you work for or own, designing your floor plan in Visio can save you hours of time and help you avoid costly errors. By creating drawings of your floor plan online, you can try many different arrangements before you decide which one will help you sell the most product. Visio is an especially useful tool for these types of drawings because it enables you to draw the space plans to scale.

Although the Space Planning stencil contains many office-oriented shapes such as desks, chairs, and computer equipment, it also contains shapes that you can use to represent rounders (round clothing racks), shelving, tables, dressing rooms, cashier desks, and so on. For custom furnishings, you can draw your own custom shapes using the drawing tools.

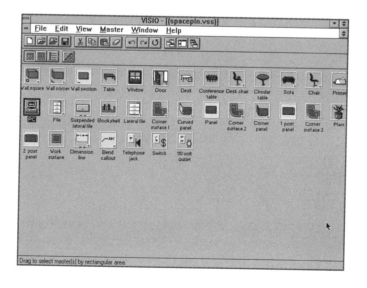

When you open Visio using the Space Planning template, the drawing page appears in landscape orientation, and the rulers show feet as the unit of measurement. Using the ¼" = 1' Architectural scale, the drawing page measures 44' wide by 34' high. To change the scale or page orientation, choose Page Page Setup and click the Size/Scale button. In the Page Setup Size/Scale dialog box, choose the Letter Tall option in the Standard Printed Page Size box to change the page orientation to portrait. To change the scale, choose an option in the Architectural Drawing Scale box.

TIP: When your drawing requires precise measurements, use the information provided on the status bar as you draw. The status bar displays the height, width, and angle of a shape and continuously updates these fields as you change the size or angle of a shape.

Creating a Clothing Boutique Floor Layout

The boutique floor layout shown below is a perfect example of how Visio can help you plan spaces. The boutique is relatively small (35' wide by 23' deep), so the floor space must be carefully planned. There are dressing rooms on both side walls; there are hanging racks on the back wall and right wall; and rounders, small rectangular tables, and shelving occupy the remainder of the floor space. After drawing the layout shown below, you might try to arrange the store's fixtures differently on a new drawing page.

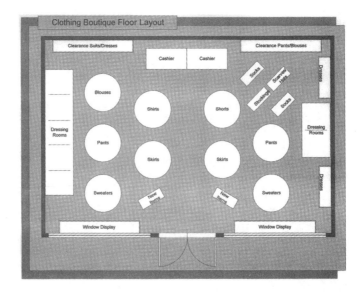

To draw the boutique floor space layout, follow these steps.

1. Open Visio using the Space Planning template.

2. Drag a Wall square shape onto the drawing. • Size the shape to 35' wide by 23' high and align it at 30'/5'.

3. Drag a Window shape onto the drawing and size it to 12'6" wide. • Align the Window shape along the lower edge of the Wall square at 9'/7½'. • Hold the Ctrl key and drag a copy of the Window shape, aligning it along the lower wall at 9'/27'.

4. To create the window displays, drag a Bookshelf shape onto the drawing and size it to 10' wide by 1'6" high. • Type **Window Display** to label the shape. • Align the shape in front of the left front window. • Hold the Ctrl key and drag a copy of the window display, aligning it in front of the right front window.

5. Drag a Door shape onto the drawing and size it to 3'6" wide. • Click the Flip Vertical toolbar button. • Align the Door shape along the lower wall at 9'/22½'. • Hold the Ctrl key and drag a copy of the door, aligning it at 9'/19'. • Click the Flip Horizontal toolbar button.

6. To create the clearance hanging racks, drag a Bookshelf shape onto the drawing and size it to 10' wide by 1'6" high. • Click the Flip Vertical toolbar button. • Align the Bookshelf shape along the upper wall at 30'/6'. • Hold the Ctrl key and drag a copy of the Bookshelf shape to 30'/29'. • Select the first Bookshelf shape and type **Clearance Suits/Dresses**. • Select the second Bookshelf shape and type **Clearance Pants/Blouses**.

7. Drag another Bookshelf shape onto the drawing and size it to 5' wide by 1'6" high. • Click the right mouse button and choose Rotate Right from the shortcut menu. • Align the shape along the right wall at 28'. • Type **Dresses** to label the shape. • To rotate the text label, select the Text Block tool to display text rotation handles. • Place the mouse pointer over a corner rotation handle, and drag the mouse in either direction 180 degrees. (Refer to Chapter 2 for detailed instructions on rotating text labels.) • Hold the Ctrl key and drag a copy of the Dresses shape, aligning it at 15' along the right wall.

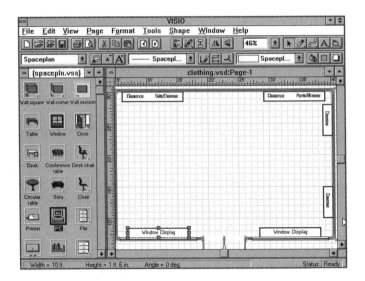

8. To create the cashier tables, drag a Table shape onto the drawing and align it at 29'/17½'. Label the shape **Cashier**. • Hold the Ctrl key and drag a copy of the Table shape, aligning it along the right side of the previous Table shape.

9. To create a rounder, drag a Circular table shape onto the drawing and size it to 4'6" wide and 4'6" high. • Align the Circular table shape at 26'/10'. • Make two copies of the Circular table, aligning them below the first shape at 20' and 14' on the vertical ruler. • Hold the Shift key and click on all three Circular table shapes in the order in which you created them; then click the Align Shapes toolbar button. • Choose the second button from the Align Shapes drop-down menu.

10. Use the same method outlined in step 9 to create the remaining rounders, spacing each approximately 1½' apart.

11. When you have created all of the rounders, select each one and label it with the appropriate name.

12. To create the display tables, drag a Table shape onto the drawing and size it to 3' wide by 1'3" high. • Type the label **New Items**. • Hold the Ctrl key and drag a copy of the shape anywhere on the drawing. • Select the first shape, click the Rotation tool, then rotate the shape 30 degrees. • Align it at 12½'/16½'. • With the Rotation Tool still active, select the second shape and rotate it –30 degrees. • Align the shape at 12½'/25½'.

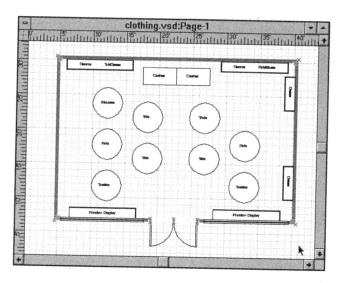

13. Drag a Table shape onto a blank area of the drawing and size it to 3' wide by 1'3" high. • Make three copies of the Table shape and align them approximately 1½' apart in a cross fashion. • Label the four shapes as shown in the following figure.

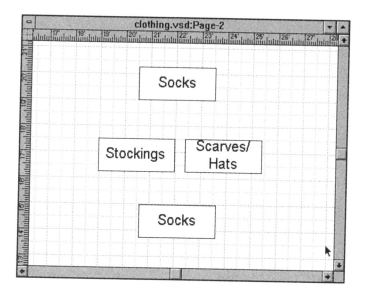

14. Select all four Table shapes, then press Ctrl+G to group the shapes. • Click the Rotation Tool and rotate the shapes 45 degrees. • Click the Pointer tool and align the grouped shapes at 27½'/29'.

15. To create the left wall dressing rooms, click the Rectangle tool and draw a rectangle 3'6" wide by 15" high. • Type **Dressing Rooms** to label the shape. • Click the Line tool and draw a horizontal line to mark the wall between rooms. • Copy the line three times, then select all four lines. • Click the Align Shapes toolbar button and choose the second button on the drop-down menu to vertically align the shapes.

16. With all four lines still selected, click the Distribute Shapes toolbar button and choose the last button on the Distribute Shapes drop-down menu. • Select all four lines and the box, then press Ctrl+G to group the shapes. • Align the dressing rooms along the left wall at 26½'.

17. To create the right wall dressing rooms, click the Rectangle tool and draw a rectangle 3'6" wide by 6½' high. • Type **Dressing Rooms** to label the shape. • Click the Line tool and draw a horizontal line at the middle of the shape to mark the wall between rooms. • Align the dressing rooms along the right wall at 22½'.

Other Ideas

Using the Space Planning template, you can create a drawing for just about any type of retail business. The shapes you use might vary from drawing to drawing, and in some cases you might need to create custom shapes. But the method for creating a space planning drawing is fairly consistent from drawing to drawing. Just follow these general steps:

- Choose a page orientation.

- Set the architectural scale you want to use.

- Draw the outer walls, then add windows and doors.

- Add inner walls, if necessary.

- Add furniture and fixtures.

Bookstore

The bookstore shown below is 38' wide by 28' high. The store contains both wall shelves and freestanding shelves labeled by subject. The front wall contains two 12-foot windows and window displays.

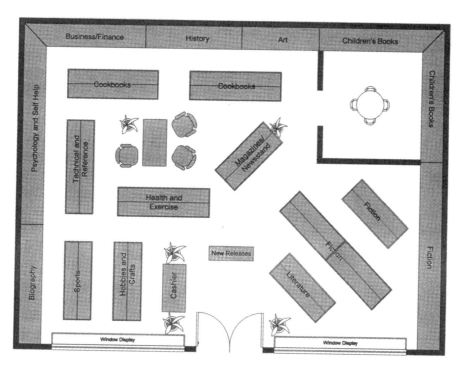

To create the bookstore layout shown above, use Visio's Shape Union command to create the wall bookshelves. Place three Bookshelf shapes on the left, back, and side walls of the bookstore and overlap them at the corners. To combine the shapes into one, select all three shapes and choose Shape Union. Create the mitered upper left and upper right corners using the Line tool. Then use the Text Block tool to create the labels on the wall shelves. To rotate text left or right, keep the Text Block tool active and rotate the label by dragging the rotation handle left or right.

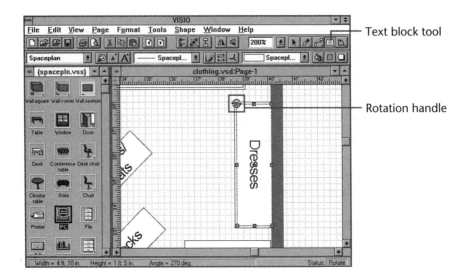

Create the freestanding bookshelves by placing two Bookshelf shapes back to back and grouping the shapes. Rotate some 45 degrees, and rotate some 90 degrees. The bookstore also contains two seating areas; create both of them using the Desk chair, Table, and Circular table shapes.

Nutrition Store

The nutrition store layout shown in this figure primarily contains rectangular shelving, tables, refrigerators, and freezers. The juice bar, the cashier stand, and the back and right wall shelving are custom shapes created using the Shape Union and Shape Fragment commands. (Refer to Chapter 3 for a complete discussion of these features.) As in the bookstore drawing, create the freestanding shelves by placing two Bookshelf shapes back to back and grouping the shapes. Along the juice bar, use the Chair shape for bar stools. You can illustrate shopping carts by overlapping several Chair shapes on one another.

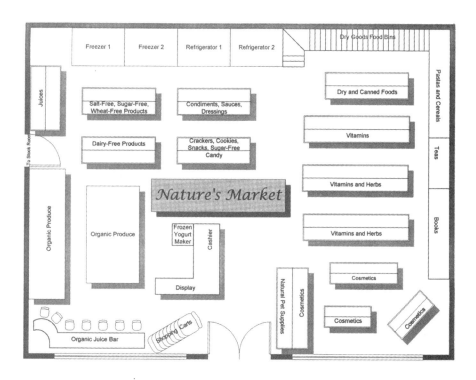

Idea List

Use the principles you learned in this chapter to create floor layouts for these types of stores:

- Video store
- Gift/card shop
- Restaurant
- Delicatessen
- Sporting goods store
- Toy store
- Hair salon
- Liquor store
- Laundromat
- Shoe store

Designing Home Spaces

There is no doubt that planning a room arrangement or moving furniture can be a challenging task. Some of us just begin moving things and see what happens: we drag a desk from one wall only to find that it's too long to fit on another wall. Or we unload the entire bookcase intending to move it under the window before realizing the bookcase is too tall to fit under the window sill.

Others of us actually take measurements and draw pictures. We might even cut out bits of paper to represent each piece of furniture and arrange them on a scaled floor plan drawing. Although this method is better than none, it's time consuming and often inaccurate (a crucial measurement might be incorrect, an important item of furniture might be overlooked, or the drawing scale might not be exact).

With Visio, you can create a drawing in a fraction of the time it would take to draw a room arrangement by hand, and you can rely on Visio's drawing scale to be accurate. The added bonus is that you can print a copy of your arrangement, study it, and think about how "livable" the arrangement is before you actually start moving furniture. You also can easily create alternate arrangements using the same shapes from your original drawing.

In this chapter you use the Space Planning template (shown in this figure) to plan home spaces. When you open Visio using this template, the drawing scale is ¼" = 1', creating a drawing page that is 44' wide by 34' high. To draw smaller rooms, such as 12' by 14', it's best to change the drawing scale to ⅜" = 1' or ½" = 1'. A larger scale is easier to work with because all the shapes on the drawing page appear larger. When you choose the ⅜" = 1' scale, the drawing page is approximately 29' by 23'. When you choose the ½" = 1' scale, the drawing page is 22' by 17'.

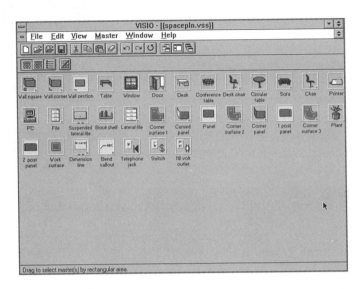

To change the drawing scale, choose Page Page Setup, then click the Size/Scale button. In the Page Setup Size/Scale dialog box, choose a new scale from the Architectural drop-down box and click OK.

Designing a Child's Bedroom

The child's bedroom shown in the following figure is 12' wide by 10' deep (using the ½" = 1' architectural scale). The corner window in the upper right corner of the room has built-in bookshelves below the windows; create this shape using Visio's Union feature. The Space Planning stencil doesn't include a shape for closet doors, so the Window shape is used to represent closet doors. The doors are shaded in gray to distinguish them from other windows. The drawing also contains one custom shape, the lamp. Create the top-down view of the lamp by layering circles on top of one another and adding the "spokes" for the lamp shade holder.

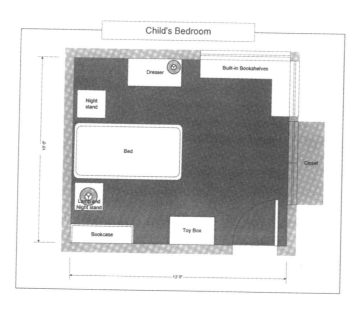

To create this drawing, follow these steps:

1. Open Visio using the Space Planning template.

2. Choose Page Page Setup, then click the Size/Scale button. • In the Page Setup Size/Scale dialog box, choose the ½" = 1' setting in the Architectural drop-down box, then click OK.

3. Drag a Wall square shape onto the drawing and size it to 12' wide by 10' high. • Align the Wall square at 14'/5'.

4. Drag a Window shape onto the drawing. • Align the Window along the upper bedroom wall at 12'. • Drag another Window shape onto the drawing and size it to 3'. • Click the right mouse button and choose Rotate Right from the shortcut menu. • Align the Window shape along the right bedroom wall at 14'.

5. To create the closet doors, drag another Window shape onto the drawing and size it to 2'3". • Click the right mouse button and choose Rotate Right from the shortcut menu. • Click the Fill Style toolbar button and choose 10% Gray. • Align the Window shape along the right bedroom wall at 10¾". • Hold the Ctrl key and drag a copy of the Window shape directly below the first one (aligned at 8½') along the right bedroom wall.

6. Select the Rectangle tool and then draw a rectangle 1'6" wide by 4'6" high. • Click the Fill Style toolbar button and choose 10% Gray. • Type **Closet** to label the shape. • Align the shape to the right of the closet doors at 10¾'/17½'.

7. Drag a Door shape onto the drawing and size it to 2'6". • Align the Door shape along the lower bedroom wall at 14'.

8. Drag a Dimension line onto the drawing and size it to 12'. • Align the Dimension line at 3¼'/5'.

9. Drag another Dimension line onto the drawing and size it to 10'. • Click the right mouse button and choose Rotate Left from the shortcut menu. • Align the Dimension line at 14'/4½'.

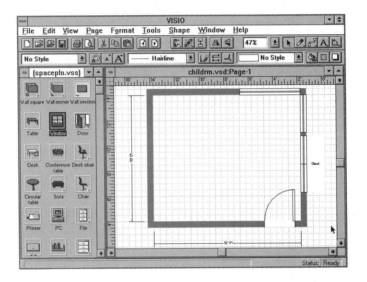

10. To create the bed, drag the Table shape onto the drawing and size it to 6' wide by 3' high. • Click the Corner Rounding toolbar button once. • Drag another Table shape onto the drawing and size it to 5'9" wide by 2'8". • Click the Corner Rounding toolbar button once. • Align the smaller rectangle inside of the larger rectangle. • Label the smaller shape **Bed**. • Select both rectangles and press Ctrl+G to group them. • Align the bed shape at 10½'/5¼'.

11. To create a night stand, drag a Table shape onto the drawing and size it to 1'7" square. • Align the shape at 7⅛'/5⅛'. • Hold the Ctrl key and drag a copy of the night stand to 12⅛'/5⅛'. • Type the label **Night stand** on the second night stand shape only. (You will add the label for the first night stand in step 15.)

12. Drag a Table shape onto the drawing and size it to 3' wide by 1'6" high. • Label the shape **Dresser**. • Align the dresser along the upper bedroom wall at 8'.

13. To create the custom lamp shape, click on the Ellipse tool. • Hold down the Shift key and create a circle 9" wide by 9" high. • Inside of the first circle,

hold the Shift key and draw another circle 3½" wide by 3½" high. (Don't worry about centering the circles.) • Inside of the second circle, hold the Shift key and draw another circle ½" wide by ½" high. Click the Fill Color toolbar button three times until the ½" circle is black. • Select all three circles. • Click the Align Shapes toolbar button and select the second button from the drop-down menu to align the shapes vertically. • Click the Align Shapes toolbar button and select the fifth button from the drop-down menu to align the shapes horizontally. • Select the Line tool and draw three "spokes" from the center circle to the middle circle. • Select all three spokes and all three circles, then press Ctrl+G to group the shapes.

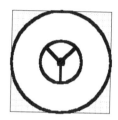

14. Align the lamp shape in the upper right corner of the dresser. • Hold the Ctrl key and drag a copy of the lamp shape onto the lower night stand. • Select the Text Block tool and type **Lamp and Night stand** in a freestanding text block. Align the text block on top of the lamp and lower night stand.

15. Drag a Table shape onto the drawing and size it to 2'6" wide by 1'6" high. • Label the shape **Toy Box**. • Align the shape along the lower wall at 10¼'.

16. Drag a Bookshelf shape onto the drawing and size it to 3'6" wide by 1' high. • Label the shape **Bookcase**. • Align the bookcase in the lower left corner of the bedroom at 4'/5'.

17. To create the custom built-in window bookshelves, drag a Bookshelf shape onto the drawing and size it to 5' wide by 1' high. • Align the Bookshelf shape along the upper bedroom wall at 12'. • Drag another Bookshelf shape onto the drawing. • Click the right mouse button and choose Rotate Left from the shortcut menu. • Align the second Bookshelf shape along the right bedroom wall at 14'. • Select both bookshelf shapes, then choose the Shape Union command to create the custom shape. • Label the shape **Built-in Bookshelves**. • To center the label in the upper part of the shape, select the Text Block tool. • Drag the Bottom center selection handle of the text block up until the label is centered over the bookshelf.

18. While the Text Block tool is still active, click near the top center of the page and type a title to your drawing.

Other Ideas

You can create an endless variety of drawings for your home, including living rooms, bathrooms, kitchens, workshops, and so on, that you can use for remodeling, rearranging furniture, or adding on to your home. Remember to use shapes creatively—in the Space Planning stencil and other stencils as well. For instance, the Bookshelf shape doesn't have to represent a bookshelf; it could represent a built-in cabinet in a kitchen. To open other stencils, just click the Open Stencil toolbar button. (Refer to Appendix B for an illustration of the shapes in each Visio stencil.)

When creating drawings for your home, remember to adjust the drawing scale, if necessary, using the Page Page Setup command. The ½" = 1'0" scale gives you a drawing page that's 22' by 17'. The ⅜" = 1'0" scale gives you a drawing page that's 29'4" by 22'8". The following sections include designs for a home office and a kitchen.

Designing a Home Office

The home office shown below is 15' by 17', which means the ⅜" = 1' scale is used to draw this layout. The office contains the essential equipment for working at home: a desk, chair, telephone, computer and printer, and FAX machine. The size of the office allows for additional items such as a full wall of bookshelves; a file cabinet; a second desk and chair; a reading corner with chair, ottoman, and reading table; and two house plants. The telephone and notepad shapes are borrowed from the Clipart Stencil. The FAX machine is a custom shape you can create by modifying the Printer shape. (The Clipart Stencil contains a shape for a FAX machine, but the shape is a front view instead of a top view.)

The methods for creating this home office drawing are the same as those used to create the child's bedroom. To add the clip art shapes, click the Open Stencil toolbar button, select the Clipart Stencil, and click OK. Then drag the Business Telephone and Notes shapes onto the drawing and size them to fit on the desk.

To customize the Printer shape and turn it into a FAX machine, follow these steps:

1. Drag the Printer shape from the Space Planning stencil onto the drawing and then choose the Edit Open Printer command. Visio opens a group window.

2. Select the gray paper tray and control panel shapes, and press Delete.

3. Choose the Rectangle tool and draw a small square to represent a keypad button. • Click the Line Style toolbar button and choose the Hairline setting from the drop-down menu. • To complete the keypad, make eight copies of the button and arrange all of them in three rows and three columns. • Select all nine keypad buttons and use the Align Shapes toolbar button to align the buttons vertically and horizontally. • Press Ctrl+G to group the keypad button shapes.

4. To create the telephone handset, use the Rectangle tool to draw a long narrow rectangle in the upper right box of the printer. • Click the Line Style toolbar button and choose the Hairline setting from the drop-down menu. • Click the Corner Rounding toolbar button once. • Select the Pencil tool. • Click on the side control points and drag them slightly to the center, creating the curves in the handset. • Double-click the group window's Control-menu box to return to the regular drawing window.

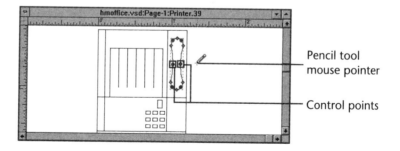

Pencil tool
mouse pointer

Control points

Designing a Kitchen

You can create the kitchen design shown on the following page using shapes exclusively from the Space Planning stencil. As you work on this drawing, note the fact that with Visio, you can create quality drawings without having specialized shapes. (The same kitchen design is drawn again in Chapter 16 using shapes from Visio's Home Planning add-on shapes package.)

For this kitchen plan, use the ½" = 1'0" Architectural scale. In the drawing, use white shapes to represent floor cabinets, and shade the wall cabinets with gray. You draw the corner floor cabinets using the Corner surface 1 shape, and draw the wall cabinets using the Bookshelf shape. The Bookshelf shape is also used to represent a garden window above the kitchen sink.

To create the outer walls, use the Wall square shape. You create the doorway openings by placing a Wall section shape directly on top of a portion of the Wall square and changing the fill color to white.

The kitchen drawing contains several custom shapes: the sink, the stove, the island, and the stools, all of which are so easy to create they can scarcely be called "custom." The sink is simply a rounded rectangle drawn using the Rectangle tool and one click on the Corner Rounding toolbar button. (You could also use the Rounded Rectangle shape from the Basic stencil to create the sink.)

Create the stove using rectangles: two large and two small circles represent the burners (the small burners aren't visible), and four tiny circles represent the stove knobs. Use the Shape Send Backward command to group these shapes, then place the stove under the wall cabinets but on top of the floor cabinets.

You create the kitchen island using a rectangle and a circle. Place the rectangle on top of the circle to make the circle appear like a half-circle countertop extension. Create the stools by placing a circle on top of a square and aligning the shapes vertically and horizontally. The square gives the appearance of four legs at the corner of each stool.

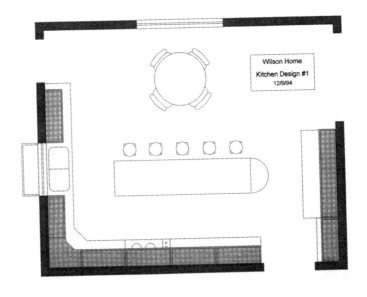

Wilson Home
Kitchen Design #1
12/9/94

Idea List

Here are a few more project ideas for home spaces:

- Workshop
- Exercise room
- Living or family room
- Project/bonus room
- Basement (finishing or organizing storage space)

Outdoor Spaces

Without Visio, you might never think to plan your outdoor spaces using a computer program. You would be missing out on a lot of fun, though. The wide variety of stencils available in Visio makes it possible, even easy, to plan many types of outdoor spaces, from parks to swimming pools to gardens. If you've been wanting to add a deck to your house, but you're concerned that it will be too expensive, save yourself tons of money by drawing up the plans yourself instead of hiring an architect to do it for you. Or perhaps you've always wanted a beautiful, landscaped garden of your very own, but the sheer enormity of the planning involved has overwhelmed you. Put it off no longer! Visio makes an easy process of deciding which plants should go where, which colors next to which, etc.—the whole trial and error process without ever even getting your hands dirty. In this chapter, you learn to use a number of Visio stencils to draw plans for these and other common outdoor spaces.

Planning a Neighborhood Park

During the planning stages of a new residential development, builders often include a neighborhood park. The park shown in the following figure has a combination baseball/soccer field, basketball court, tennis court, picnic area, playground area, and swimming pool area. Trails surround the park and lead through the middle of the park to provide access to the major areas.

The park drawing is drawn to scale: 1" on the drawing page equals approximately 18'. The drawing purposely shows only the major areas of the park and very little detail (such as the specific layout for the swimming pool and playground areas).

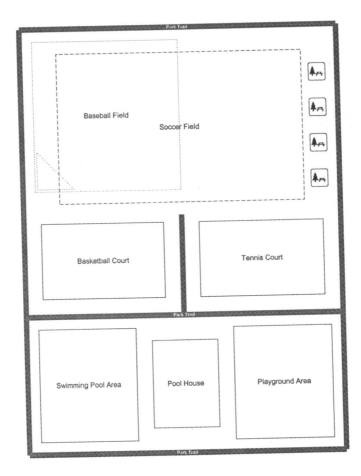

You'll use several stencils to create this drawing. To begin, open Visio using the Basic stencil. Draw the park trails using a road shape from the Map stencil, then add the symbol depicting the picnic areas, which comes from the Symbols stencil.

To draw the park plan, follow these steps:

1. Open Visio using the Basic template.

2. Choose Page Page Setup.• Click the Size/Scale Button. • In the Page Setup Size/Scale dialog box, choose the Letter Tall option in the Printed Page Size box.• Click the Custom option button in the Drawing Scale box, then type **0ft.0.0048in.** in the first Custom box. This sets the dimensions of the drawing page to approximately 150' by 190'. • Click OK. • Change Measurements to Feet and click OK.

3. If Snap and Glue are not on, turn them on by clicking the Snap and Glue toolbar buttons. If these buttons aren't available, choose the Page Snap &

Glue Setup command. When the dialog box appears, check the Snap and Glue check boxes, then click OK.

4. Click the mouse on the vertical ruler, and drag a vertical guide to 75' on the horizontal ruler.

5. To create the park trails, use the Road square shape from the Map stencil. • Click the Open Stencil toolbar button. • Choose the Map stencil, then click OK.

6. Drag a Road square shape onto the page. • Size the road to 130', then align the road at 180'/10'. • Hold down the Ctrl key, drag a copy of the road, and align it at 10'/10'. • Press and hold the Ctrl key and drag another copy of the road onto the drawing, then click the right mouse button and choose Rotate Right. • Size the road to 170', then align at 180'/140'. (The road glues itself to the right endpoints of the horizontal road shapes.) • Copy the side road and align it at 180'/10'. (The road glues itself to the left endpoints of the horizontal road shapes.)

7. Select the top Road square shape, then hold the Ctrl key as you drag a copy of the road to 65'/10'.

8. Drag another Road square shape from the stencil onto the drawing. • Click the right mouse button and choose Rotate Right from the shortcut menu. • Size the road to 40'. • Align the road at 105'/75'. (The road glues itself to the vertical guide and the middle horizontal road.) • Select each horizontal road separately and label each road **Park Trail**.

9. Choose Edit Select All, then press Ctrl+G to group the road shapes. Your drawing now looks like this:

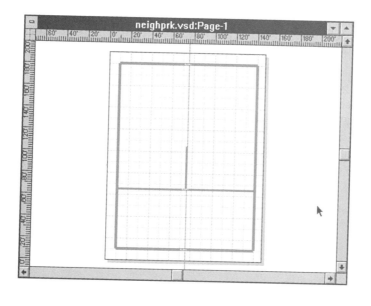

10. Double-click the Control-menu box in the Map stencil window to close the stencil.

11. Click on the Rectangle tool on the toolbar.

12. Hold the Shift key as you draw a square 60' by 60'. • Align the square at 175'/15'. • Click the Line toolbar button, then choose the Short Dash option from the Style drop-down list. • With the square still selected, type **Baseball Field.** • From the Basic stencil, drag a Right triangle shape onto the drawing page and size it to approximately 15' by 15'. • Click the Line Style toolbar button and choose the Short dash option. • Align the Right triangle in the lower left corner of the baseball field shape to illustrate the backstop. • Select the Right triangle and the baseball field shape, and press Ctrl+G to group the two shapes.

13. Using the Rectangle tool, draw a rectangle 100' wide by 60' high. • Click the Line style toolbar button, then choose the Long dash option from the drop-down list. • Align the rectangle at 170'/25'. • With the square still selected, type **Soccer Field.** • Click the Fill Style toolbar button and choose the None option from the drop-down box.

14. Using the Rectangle tool, draw a rectangle 50' wide by 30' high. • Align the shape at 102'/116'. • With the shape still selected, type **Basketball Court.**

15. Use the Ctrl key to copy the basketball court shape and align it at 102'/82'. • With the shape still selected, type **Tennis Court.**

16. Click the Open Stencil toolbar button. • Choose the Symbols Stencil and click OK.

17. Drag a Park shape onto the drawing. • Size the Park shape to 7' by 7'. • Align the Park shape at approximately 164'/128'. • Hold the Ctrl key as you copy three more Park shapes directly below the first, aligning the last Park shape at approximately 122'/128'. • Select all four Park shapes. • Choose the second button from the Align Shapes drop-down menu. • With all four shapes still selected, choose the fifth button from the Distribute Shapes drop-down menu. • Your drawing now looks like the figure on the following page.

18. Use the Rectangle tool to draw a rectangle 40' wide by 45' high. • Align the rectangle at 60'/15'. • With the rectangle still selected, type **Swimming Pool Area.**

19. Use the Rectangle tool to draw a rectangle 27' wide by 35' high. • Align the rectangle at 55'/62'. (The center of the rectangle glues itself to the vertical guide.) • With rectangle still selected, type **Pool House.**

20. Copy the swimming pool rectangle and align it at 62'/95'. • With the rectangle still selected, type **Playground Area.**

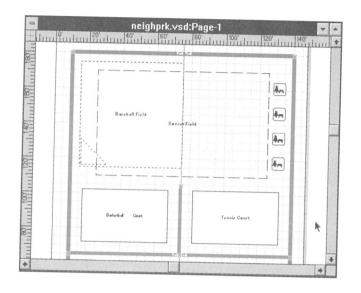

Other Ideas

You can use the same basic principles and techniques that you used to create the neighborhood park to create other outdoor area drawings. As you work, open whatever stencils are helpful to you. (Appendix A of this book shows all of the shapes included in each Visio stencil.) Get creative with stencil shapes! You can often use a shape for something entirely different from what it was designed to represent.

Here are some additional tips to keep in mind as you're drawing:

- Remember to use guides and guide points to help you align and move related shapes.

- Use the Align Shapes and Distribute Shapes buttons frequently to help you position shapes on your drawing.

- Group shapes that belong together, such as a table and chairs. If you group them, you can't inadvertently move one without the others.

Swimming Pool Area

The previous drawing of the neighborhood park included a swimming pool area. Create the drawing below to show the detail of this swimming pool area. Because the drawing contains several furniture shapes, use the Space Planning template when you create the new drawing.

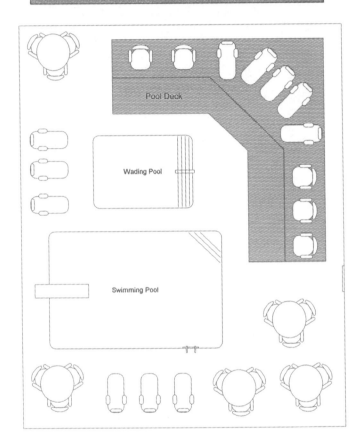

To draw the drawing to scale, use the ⅛" = 1' 0" Architectural scale. This scale makes the drawing area about 88' by 68'. If you require a larger drawing area, choose the 3/32" = 1' 0". You select an architectural scale by choosing the Page Page Setup command and then clicking the Size/Scale button in the Page Setup dialog box. Draw the easiest shapes—the swimming pool and wading pool—first using the Rectangle shape. Round the corners using the Corners Rounding tool; draw the straight lines that represent steps using the Line tool; and add a separate rectangle to the large pool to represent the diving board. Once all these shapes are in place, group the shapes that make up each pool using the Shape Group command.

Use the Chair and Circular table shapes from the Space Planning stencil to create the seating areas. Group three chairs with one table, then copy the group to various locations in the pool area. Draw the pool deck area using the Corner surface 1 shape from the Space Planning stencil. You can control the depth of the diagonal cut across this shape by dragging the shape's control handle. Apply a lined pattern to the pool deck area, and place the Chair shape in several places along the pool deck.

The lounge chair is the only custom shape in the drawing. You create it by overlapping rounded rectangles, as shown in the following figure. Again, once each shape is in place, select and group all of them.

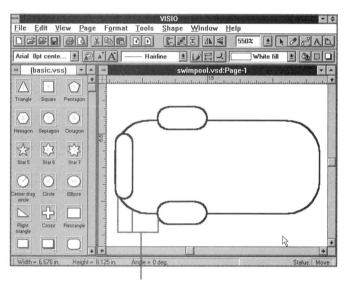

Rounded rectangles

Deck

If you're thinking of adding a deck to your house, you could have an architect draw up the plans, or you could plan it yourself using Visio. Whether you're creating a very simple deck or a more complex one, Visio's Space Planning template gives you the tools you need. The figure on the following page shows a fairly basic bilevel deck.

By default, the Space Planning template uses a drawing page of approximately 35' by 44'. If you choose the ⅛" = 1' 0" architectural scale, the drawing page is approximately 68' by 88'. To specify the scale, choose the Page Page Setup command, click the Size/Scale button in the Page Setup dialog box, and make your choice from the Architectural drop-down box.

Although the deck shown in the following figure is more complex than a simple rectangular deck, it isn't difficult to create. However, it does take patience and a little creativity—and creativity begins with using shapes creatively. The primary shape used in the following drawing is the Corner surface 1 shape. Although the Corner surface 1 shape is designed to represent a desktop or working surface in an office, it works quite well for the basic shape of this deck. Use the Corner surface 1 shape to draw the main deck area, and use another Corner surface 1 shape to draw the steps down to the lower level of the deck. (Use the Line tool to draw the lines that represent the individual steps.)

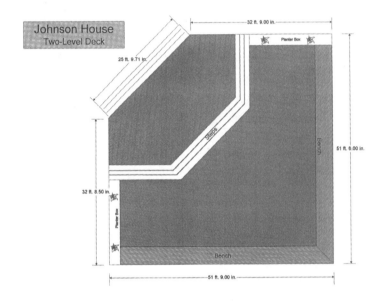

Although there are probably many possible ways to draw this deck, the overlapping of shapes is the key to this drawing. The steps overlay the lower level of the deck, and the upper level of the deck overlays the steps. The benches along the edge of the deck overlay the upper level of the deck, and the planter boxes overlay both the upper-level deck and the benches. Create the mitered corner of the benches by overlapping two rectangular shapes and using the Pencil tool to reshape the bottom edge of the vertical bench to a diagonal line. (Refer to Chapter 2 for instructions on using the Pencil tool.) Finally, place the Dimension line shape on all outside edges of the deck to note the outer dimensions.

Playground

The playground area shown in the next figure requires no special stencils; you can create the entire drawing using Visio's Basic template. As in previous drawings, if you want to draw the playground to scale, choose the Page Page Setup command, then click the Size/Scale button. In the Size/Scale dialog box, choose an appropriate scale from the Architectural drop-down box.

The three custom shapes in this drawing are the climber, the swing set, and the L-shaped platform at the left end of the climber. Create the notched corner of the climber using Visio's Fragment feature. First, draw the large rectangle, then draw a small square that overlaps the upper left corner of the rectangle. Choose Shape Fragment, and Visio breaks the two overlapping shapes into separate shapes, then simply select the square shape and delete it.

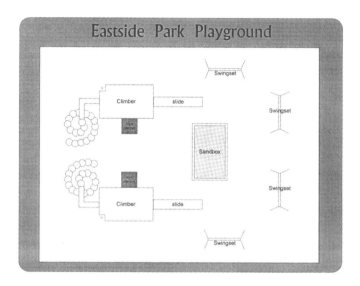

The swing set shape is a combination of a narrow rectangle and diagonal lines. Draw the rectangle first, then draw one diagonal line at a corner of the rectangle to represent a swing set leg. To ensure that all legs are the same length and angle, copy the leg three times and use the Flip Horizontal and Flip Vertical buttons to orient each leg. Move each leg into position at the four corners of the rectangle, then group all the shapes.

Create the L-shaped platform that leads from the climber to the spiral by drawing two small rectangles, overlapping their ends perpendicular to one another and then choosing the Shape Union command. Visio instantly transforms the two rectangles into a single shape—just like that.

The spiral log steps that lead to the climber are not really a custom shape. Simply draw overlapping circles in a spiral configuration, then group all the shapes.

Flower Garden

Any gardener knows that there is a real art to planning a flower garden. Once you choose an area for your garden, you must decide the location of each plant based on its tolerance for sun, as well as its height, size, color, and blooming season. It's always best to plan a garden on paper before you actually plant one—but that usually requires a lot of erasing and redrawing. Using Visio, all that erasing and redrawing becomes much simpler. You can draw your garden plan on-screen and change it as needed.

Here's your chance to test your freehand drawing ability! The garden plan shown below is drawn entirely using Visio's Pencil tool. Actually, it's not as difficult as it looks. Recall from Chapter 2 that when you drag the Pencil tool in a circular motion, you can draw elliptical arcs. This drawing is nothing more than a series of elliptical arcs. Practice getting used to the Pencil tool a bit before you begin your drawing.

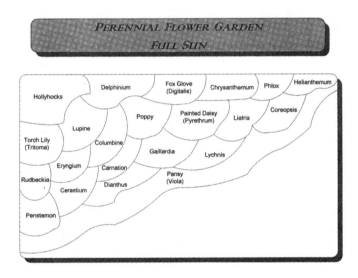

To draw a single arc, click the Pencil tool and drag the mouse in a circular direction. Release the mouse button when the arc is the size and shape you want. To draw a line that curves in several directions, drag the mouse in a circular direction. When you want to change the direction of your curve, click the Pencil tool and—without changing its position—begin dragging the mouse in a circular direction again. (If you change the position of the mouse after you click, you draw two separate arcs as opposed to one continuous curving line.)

Remember, you can change the shape of a curve by dragging a control point (a circle-shaped handle). You can move a vertex (a diamond-shaped handle) by dragging it to a new position. For both control points and vertices, be sure to click twice on the handle until it turns magenta, then drag. Refer to Chapter 2 if you need more detailed instructions.

TIP: Before you begin drawing, drag a vertical and a horizontal guide onto the drawing page to use as the top and left "anchor" positions or borders of your garden area.

When you finish drawing the arcs, label each area using the Text tool. When you have finished labeling the areas and the garden drawing is complete, add the rectangular frame, then click the Send to Back toolbar button or choose the Shape Send to Back command.

Idea List

Here are a few more ideas for outdoor spaces. Use Visio's Basic, Space Planning, or other stencils appropriate for your project. And remember to use Visio's drawing tools (Pencil, Line, Arc, and so on) to create custom shapes.

- Picnic/barbecue area
- Campground/recreational areas
- Fairgrounds
- Flower border
- Vegetable garden
- Home or business landscaping
- In-ground sprinkler system

Creating Maps

If you've ever tried to draw a map using a computer drawing program, you know how difficult and time-consuming it can be. Whether you're drawing a map to your home or drawing a visitor's map for out-of-town clients, Visio makes the process easy by providing typical map shapes in the Map template. The template not only includes shapes for roads, railroads, and metro lines, it also includes shapes for traffic and highway signs, as well as common landmarks such as gas stations, churches, airports, and schools. To depict congested areas and neighborhood areas, the Map stencil includes shapes for buildings, cities, and houses.

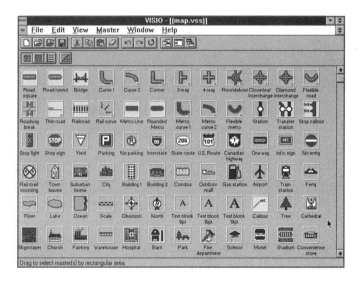

To create a map, you combine straight and curved sections of roads, railroads, and metro lines, then stretch or shrink them as necessary. The most difficult road sections—intersections, 3- and 4-way stops, cloverleafs, diamond interchanges, and roundabouts—are easy to create because Visio provides distinct shapes for each one. You can also indicate the scale and orientation of a map using the Scale and Direction shapes.

When you open the Map template, Visio displays a portrait-style drawing page, and the vertical and horizontal rulers display inches. To change either of these settings, choose the Page Setup command from the Page menu.

TIP: When you are creating maps, remember to use Visio's Zoom feature to your advantage by clicking the Zoom button on the toolbar. Zooming in close to connect road sections makes it easier to align the roads correctly (especially if you're not using Snap or Glue). As you continue to create the map, you might need to zoom in and out frequently, alternating between an overall perspective of the drawing and a detailed area.

Creating a Neighborhood/Real Estate Map

To introduce you to Visio's Map template, let's create a simple map: a neighborhood map. Real estate or construction companies might use this type of map to advertise and promote a new neighborhood, or a neighborhood homeowner's association might use it for a community directory. Drawn to scale, a map of this type might also be useful for electric or utility companies who are planning the location and placement of wires, cables, and pipes in a new neighborhood development.

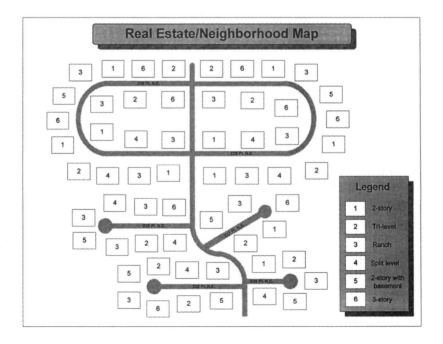

In this project, you build neighborhood roads using the round and square road shapes, and you learn how to create a cul-de-sac by altering a square road shape using the Pencil tool. Each road shape contains a built-in text label, which makes it easy to mark road names and numbers. The map also includes a legend identifying different home styles.

1. Open Visio using the Map template.

2. Choose File Print Setup. • Choose Landscape and choose OK.

3. Drag a vertical guide to 5½".

4. Using the Text tool, click near the top center of the drawing, then type the title **Real Estate/Neighborhood Map**. • Click the Increase Font Size toolbar button until the font is 30 points. • Size the text block so that the title appears all on one line. • Glue the text block to the center vertical guide ½" from the top of the page.

5. Drag a vertical guide to 4¾".

6. Drag a Road round shape onto the drawing page. • Click the right mouse button and choose Rotate Left from the shortcut menu. • Align the Road round shape at 7" and at the 4¾" vertical guide. • Drag the bottom endpoint of the Round road shape to 2⅞". • Drag a Curve 2 shape onto the drawing page. • Click the right mouse button and choose Rotate Left from the shortcut menu twice. • Align the shape at the bottom of the Road round shape (approximately 2⅞"/4¾").

7. Drag another Curve 2 shape onto the drawing and connect it to the previous curve (aligned at approximately 2⅛"/5⅜").

8. Drag a Road round shape onto the drawing and connect it to the second curve (aligned at 1½"/5⅛"). • Drag the lower endpoint of the Road round shape so that the road ends at ⅝" on the vertical ruler.

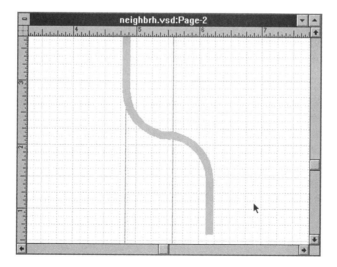

TIP: Zoom in close on the drawing (100% or more) to align roads correctly.

9. To create the first cul-de-sac side road, drag a Road square shape onto a blank area of the drawing. • Size the shape to a length of 1". • Select the Pencil Tool. • Drag the right endpoint slightly to the left to expose the circular control point. • Click on the circular control point; the handle turns magenta. • Drag the circular control point ½" to the right to create a "bulb" at the end of the road. • Align the road at approximately 1½"/6". • Click on the control point (the circular handle with an X inside) at the right end of the Road round shape. (The control point turns magenta.) • Drag the control point ¾" to the right.

 NOTE: A circular control point appears at both ends of the Road square shape. You must drag the endpoint out of the way before you can select the circular control point.

10. To create the lower-left-side cul-de-sac road, use the same method described in step 9, but with the following changes: Before making the bulb, size the road to 2⅛". • Place the cul-de-sac at the left end of the road. • Align the road at 1⅜"/4".

11. To create the upper-left-side cul-de-sac road, copy the road you created in step 10 and align it at 2⅞"/2¾".

12. To make the upper-right-side cul-de-sac road, use the method described in step 10, with the following changes: Size the road to 1¼". • Select the road, then drag the left endpoint downward to angle the road at approximately 25 degrees (refer to the status bar).

13. Position the left end of the road near the midpoint of the first Curve 2 shape (approximately 2¼"/5⅛").

14. Click the Zoom button and select the Width option.

15. To create the circular street at the top of the drawing, drag four Road round shapes onto the drawing, gluing two to the right side of the main road and two to the left side of the main road. Align the top two at 6⅜" and the lower two at 4⅝" on the vertical ruler. • Drag a Curve 2 shape onto the drawing and align it next to the upper right road. • Make a copy of the curve, choose the Flip Vertical toolbar button, then align it with the lower right road. • If necessary, drag the endpoints of each of the curves to meet one another. • Select both curves and copy them to the left side of the drawing. • Click the Flip Horizontal toolbar button, then align both curves with the left-facing roads to complete the circle.

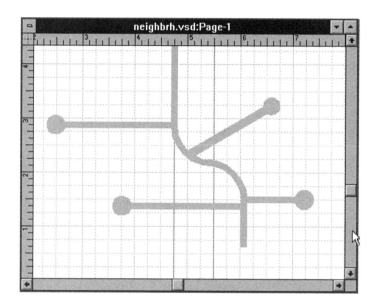

16. Draw a selection box around all roads. • From the Fill Style toolbar button, choose 20% Gray. • Select Format Font. • Choose Black #0 in the Color box and click OK. • Label the roads as they appear on the final drawing (shown at the beginning of this section).

17. Using the Rectangle tool, draw a rectangle approximately ½" wide by ⅓" high to represent a house.

18. Copy the house shape around the drawing, labeling each with a style number after you copy it.

19. To create the drawing legend, make six copies of the house shape near the lower right corner of the drawing. • Select all six shapes, click the Align Shapes toolbar button, then choose the second button (Align Vertical Centers) from the drop-down list. • Select each house shape individually and label it with a number from 1 to 6. • Next to each house shape, type the description of the house type using the default font (Arial 12-point). • Using the Text tool, type **Legend** above the legend key. From the Font toolbar button, choose Arial. From the Font Size toolbar button, choose 18 pts. • Draw a rectangle surrounding the legend key and its title. • Click the Send to Back toolbar button or choose the Shape Send to Back command. • From the Fill Pattern toolbar button, choose the 10% Gray fill option. • Click the Shadow button once. • Draw a selection box around the legend rectangle. • Press Ctrl+G or choose Shape Group.

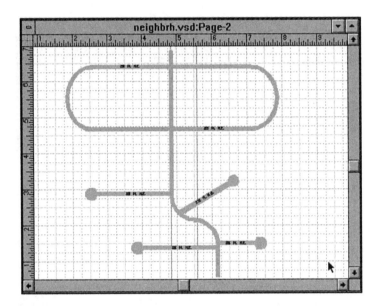

20. Use the Rectangle tool on the toolbar to draw a rectangle around all of the elements in the drawing. Leave a ¼"–½" border on the drawing page. • Click the Send to Back toolbar button or choose the Shape Send to Back command.

Other Ideas

The real estate/neighborhood map is a relatively simple map because it contains only roads and rectangular shapes (houses). But the wide variety of shapes included in Visio's Map template provides many possibilities for other types of maps—some with more complex shapes and greater detail than the real estate/neighborhood map. However, regardless of the complexity of the map you create, the techniques you use to create the map are simple: drag shapes onto the drawing page, then size and position them appropriately. There's nothing complex about that.

You can create all of the maps shown in this section using these basic techniques.

TIP: To position shapes easily and more accurately, use horizontal and vertical guides, as well as the Align Shapes and Distribute Shapes toolbar buttons. (See Chapter 2 for information on guides.)

Subway Map

As you saw earlier in this chapter, Visio's Map template contains shapes for metro lines as well as for roads and railroads. You can create the subway map shown here using primarily the Metro Line, Metro curve 1, Metro curve 2, Station, and Transfer Station shapes.

You draw each subway line by combining straight and curved sections of metro shapes. To distinguish subway lines, add a color or pattern to each line using the Format Fill command or the Fill Style and Fill Pattern buttons on the toolbar.

Once you have completed the subway lines, add subway stops to each line using the Station shape. Each station is labeled using the Stop callout shape, which has two endpoints and consists of a triangular-shaped arrow and a text label. By dragging either endpoint of the Stop callout shape, you can change the direction in which the arrow points and align the blunt end of the arrow correctly next to a Station shape. To label a station, simply select the Stop callout shape and begin typing.

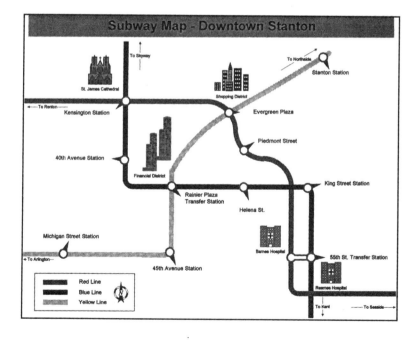

When you have completed the subway lines and stations, add major landmarks to the map and size them appropriately. Create the legend by copying small sections of each colored or patterned metro line to the lower left corner of the drawing. Label each subway line using the Text block 10pt shape, and add the North shape to indicate the orientation of the map.

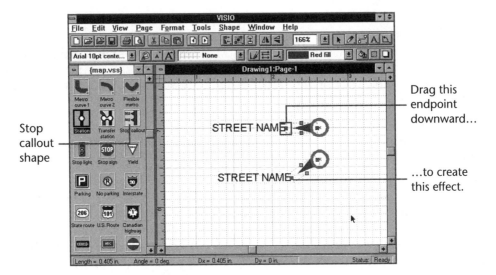

To create the directional arrows that read "To Arlington," "To Seaside," and so on, you need the Practice stencil. To open this stencil, click the Open Stencil button on the toolbar, then choose the Practice Stencil item in the list. From the stencil, you can use either the YES result or NO result arrow. Size the arrow to the proper length, then type a text label to replace the Yes or No label.

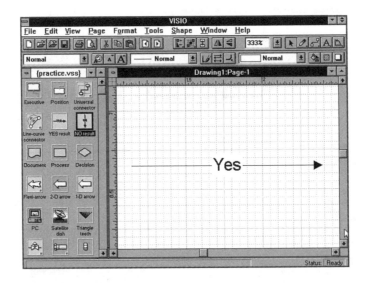

Corporate Campus

A corporate campus map can be very useful in a large corporation, especially one that has a large site with many buildings. For example, new employees and visitors might find this type of map helpful as they try to make their way to the proper buildings or location.

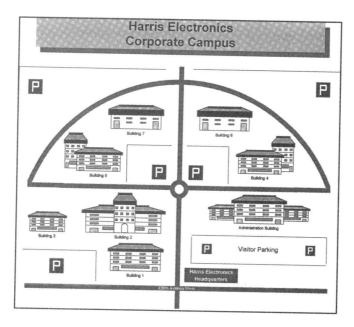

To create the example map, use the Building 2 shape from the Map template for buildings 1 and 3. Then, to create the remainder of the buildings, vary the Building 2 shape either by combining several shapes in different sizes and grouping them, or by altering the detail of the original shape. For instance, you can create the administration building using three Building 2 shapes of different sizes. Offset the shapes to depict the depth of the building, then group all three shapes.

Create the roadways by first dragging the Roundabout shape onto the drawing page and then adding the perpendicular roadways. To create the curved roadway at the top of the map, use the Flexible road shape, and size it to the appropriate width.

City Center Map

A city center map can be useful for many different organizations, from a local tourist bureau to an advertising agency. And, depending on who will be using the map, you can customize it to show as little or as much detail as you want to include.

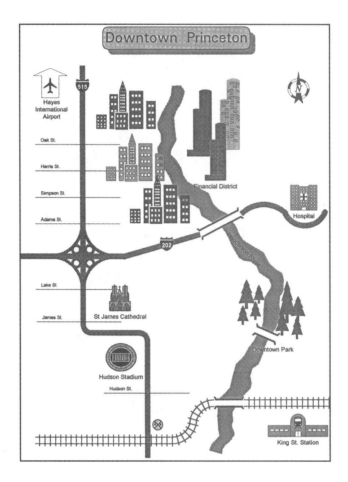

This downtown map shows a great deal of detail—buildings, skyscrapers, bridges, a railroad, a hospital, a cathedral, a stadium, and a train station. To create a map like this, simply drag the appropriate shapes from the Map template onto the drawing page, then size and position them as necessary.

The river is the unique shape in this drawing. You can create it in one of two ways: by dragging one River shape onto the drawing and stretching it or by connecting several River shapes. In either case, you use the Pencil tool to change the path of the river, as the following figure illustrates.

When you select the River shape with the Pencil tool, you see circular and diamond-shaped handles. The circular handles are control points that enable you to change a line to an arc. The diamond-shaped handles are vertices that enable you to reshape the angle between the two lines that form the vertex. To create the bends in the river, drag the control points and vertices.

If necessary, you can add a vertex to the River shape by pointing to the location where you want to add the vertex, then holding the Ctrl key as you click on that location. To delete a vertex, select the vertex (it turns magenta), then press the Delete key on the keyboard. For more information about using the Pencil tool, refer to Chapter 2.

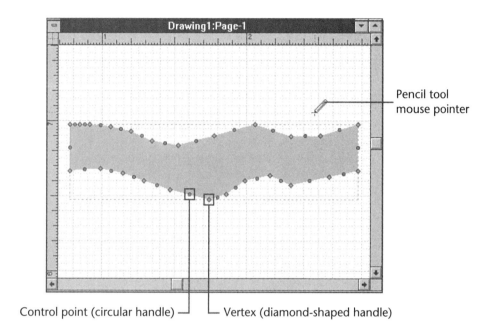

Pencil tool
mouse pointer

Control point (circular handle) ⎤   ⎣ Vertex (diamond-shaped handle)

Attractions Map

An attractions map shows a city's tourist attractions. It can be used in visitor's information centers or by tourist bureaus, travel agencies, rental car companies, hotels, and motels. The map below shows Seattle's downtown and waterfront area.

You should already be familiar with some of the shapes in this map—the roads, railroad, interstate signs, skyscrapers, trees, and buildings—from other drawings. You can create the Road and Railroad shapes' angled effect using the Rotation tool. Remember that it's helpful to zoom in close on the drawing when connecting sections of road and railroad. Use the Callout shape to label specific sites around the city.

The Ocean is the most difficult part of this drawing to create. If the waterfront followed a straight line, you could create the entire waterfront using just one Ocean shape and stretching it to the proper length. To create the curved waterfront line shown in this drawing, place several Ocean shapes side by side and rotate them to follow the waterfront line, as shown in the next figure. (It helps if you draw the waterfront street and waterfront trolley first to establish the proper waterfront line.) You must use the Pencil tool to display the vertices (diamond-shaped handles) and control points (circular handles of each Ocean shape).

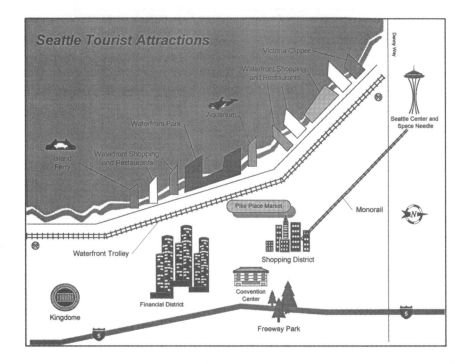

TIP: Dragging a vertex changes the angle between two lines; dragging a control point changes a line to an arc or changes the shape of an existing arc.

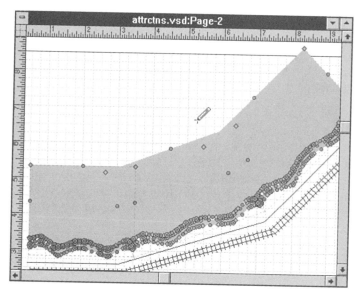

To fill in the ocean shape, you must drag the upper vertices of the left and middle Ocean shapes upward to fill in the area to the top of the map. Then drag the upper right vertex of the right Ocean shape downward to meet the line across the top of the map. Once the borders of the Ocean shapes are correct, select all three shapes and group them by pressing Ctrl+G.

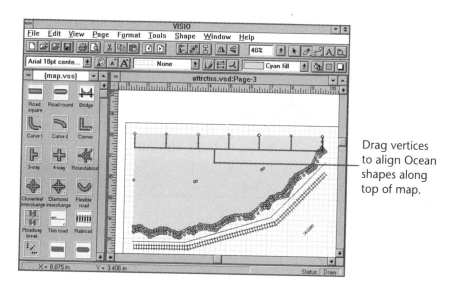

Drag vertices to align Ocean shapes along top of map.

The custom shapes in this drawing are the Space Needle and the buildings along the waterfront. You can create the Space Needle using the Pencil, Line, Arc, and Ellipse tools. You can draw the waterfront buildings in one of two ways. You can draw them freehand using the Line tool, or you can draw rectangles with the Rectangle tool and then alter their shape using the Pencil tool to drag vertices.

Home Map

One of the most useful maps you can create is a map to your home. We've all had the experience of trying to give someone directions to our home and wishing we had a map to check the name of a certain street. And most of us have also had the experience of getting lost when trying to follow someone else's handwritten (often hurriedly written) directions to his home. A map like the one shown here is easy to follow and has printed directions.

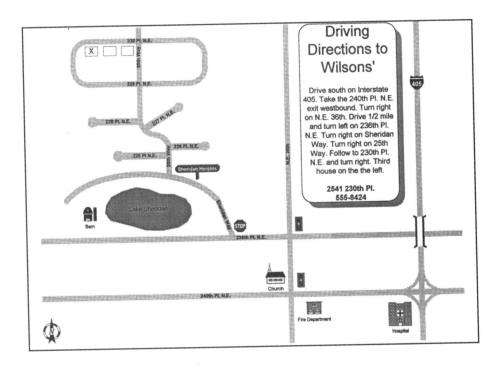

This map is easy to draw because it is made up of the most basic shapes from the Map stencil. Earlier in this chapter, you learned how to create neighborhood streets and cul-de-sacs; the rest is simple. Create major streets using the Road square shape, label them, then add lakes, rivers, landmarks, and traffic signs where appropriate. A helpful feature on this map is the driving directions. If you include driving directions on your map, use a large font that's easy to read.

Idea List

Here are a few more ideas for you to try using the same basic steps and procedures you learned in this chapter.

- Scavenger hunt
- School map
- School campus
- Hotel rooms
- City attractions
- Historic or architectural tours
- Nature or walking trails
- Campground map

Special Projects

As you've seen in Chapters 4 through 14, some of Visio's stencils are designed for creating specific types of drawings or diagrams. For instance, you use the shapes in Visio's Space Planning stencil to draw an office or home floor plan; and you use the shapes in the Map stencils to draw maps and directions. In addition to these "obvious" stencils, however, Visio includes several other stencils that you can use for many different types of projects—some that might never occur to you because, technically, they aren't *drawings* (such as a thank-you card and a Flags-of-the-World game). In this chapter, you discover some creative ways to use the wide selection of shapes available in Visio.

Bordered Thank-You Card

The following thank-you card is created using a Greek border design from Visio's Border stencil. The card is printed in the lower right corner of an 8½ x 11 inch sheet of paper. The paper is folded in half crosswise and then lengthwise to create a card that opens up like a card from the greeting card store.

Creating this thank-you card is easy if you make sure Visio's Snap and Glue features are turned on before you begin drawing. Place horizontal and vertical guides on all four sides of the border so that the border shapes snap right into place when you drag them onto the drawing.

To create the card, use these steps:

1. Open Visio using the Basic template.

2. Click the Open Stencil toolbar button and choose the Border stencil.

3. Choose the File Print Setup command. • Choose Landscape. • Click on OK. The drawing page is 11" wide by 8½" high.

4. Choose the Tools Snap & Glue Setup command. • In the dialog box, check both the Snap and Glue check boxes. In both the Snap to and Glue to boxes, check the Guides and Connection points boxes. • Click on OK.

5. From the left ruler, drag two vertical guides onto the drawing, one at 5¾" and the other at 10⅝". (These will be referred to as the left and right guides.) • From the top ruler, drag two horizontal guides onto the drawing, one at 4" and the other at ¼". (These will be referred to as the upper and lower guides.)

6. Use the Zoom toolbar button to zoom in on the rectangular area enclosed by the guides.

7. Drag a Greek corner shape to the upper left corner where the left and upper guides intersect. Let the shape snap into place and glue itself to both guides.

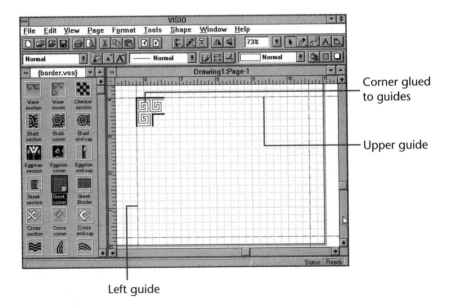

Corner glued to guides

Upper guide

Left guide

8. Drag a Greek Border shape onto the drawing and let it snap into place next to the right arm of the Greek corner. The shape glues itself to the upper guide. • Size the Greek Border shape so that 9 motifs appear in the shape. (Drag the right edge of the shape to 10".) One *motif* is equivalent to a single "square" of the Greek design.

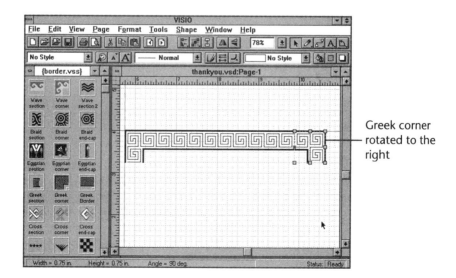

One motif in the Greek Border shape

9. Press and hold the Ctrl key and drag a copy of the Greek corner shape to the corner where the upper and right guides intersect. • Click the right mouse button and choose Rotate Right from the shortcut menu.

Greek corner rotated to the right

10. Drag another Greek Border shape onto the drawing.

11. Click the right mouse button and choose Rotate Right from the shortcut menu. • Align the Greek Border shape under the upper right corner along the right guide. • Size the Greek Border shape so that 6 motifs appear in the shape. (Drag the lower edge to 1".)

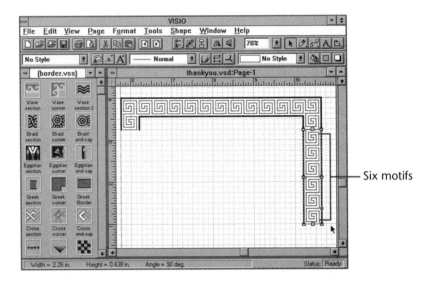

— Six motifs

12. Copy the Greek corner shape (from step 9) to the corner where the lower and right guides intersect. • Click the right mouse button and choose Rotate Right from the shortcut menu.

13. Copy the Greek Border shape from the upper guide and drag it into place along the lower guide.

14. Press and hold the Ctrl key as you click on the Greek corner shape (from step 12). Then drag a copy of the shape to the corner where the left and lower guides intersect. • Click the right mouse button and choose Rotate Right from the shortcut menu.

15. Press and hold the Ctrl key to copy the Greek Border shape from the right guide to the left guide and align it between the two left corners.

16. Hold down the Shift key and click on each shape to select all of the shapes. Press Ctrl+G to group the shapes.

17. Choose Format Line. • Choose Line Color #14 and choose OK.

18. Select the Text tool. • Near the center of the card, draw a text box and type **Thank You.** • Choose Format Font. • In the Font dialog box, choose Footlight MT Light font, 48 points, Color #20; then click OK.

19. Align the Thank You in the center of the border. (The center point is 2¼"/8⅛".)

TIP: For a different flair, change the squared corners of the motif to rounded corners. Select the entire border, choose Format Line, then choose a style in the Round Corners box. Choose Apply to preview the style. Choose OK to use the style.

Picture Wall

You might never think to use Visio (or *any* computer program, for that matter) to help you arrange pictures on the wall, but Visio is actually a good tool for this task. The fact that Visio lets you draw to scale and draw shapes to exact sizes makes Visio perfect for this project. In addition, the frame shapes in Visio's Border stencil (shown here) enable you to represent picture frames realistically, instead of simply drawing rectangles to represent pictures. Using Visio, you can decorate every wall in your house, without making a bunch of holes seeing what looks best where.

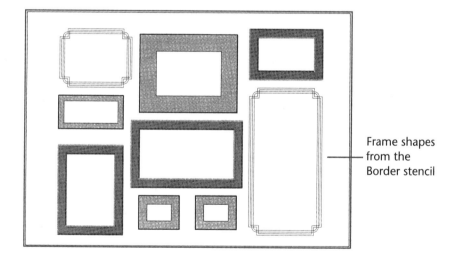

Frame shapes from the Border stencil

To create a drawing like the one in the previous figure, open Visio using the Basic template. Visio displays a drawing page in landscape orientation with an architectural scale of 1" = 1' 0", which makes the drawing page 11' wide by 8½' high. (You could use a smaller scale for a larger drawing area.) Draw each shape to size using frame shapes from the Border stencil. Then arrange the shapes on top of a rectangular shape that represents the available wall space (10' wide by 7' high).

Using Visio for this type of project enables you to experiment with many different arrangements until you find the one you like best. Or, you could create several pages in a single drawing to save a variety of arrangement options.

Personal Stationery

The personal stationery shown in this figure is so easy to create that it almost requires no explanation. The only shape used is the Rectangle, so open Visio using the Basic template.

Just drag a Rectangle shape onto the drawing, size it to about 7½" wide by 10" high, and position it in the upper left corner of the page. Then, while the rectangle is still selected, click the Fill Style toolbar button and choose None to make the rectangle transparent. Press and hold the Ctrl key to drag a copy of the rectangle and position it slightly below and to the right of the first rectangle. Then add your initials to the stationery using the Text tool. You can choose a font for your initials by clicking the Font toolbar button while the text is still selected. To add a shadow to the text, click the Shadow toolbar button.

Certificate

Visio's Border stencil and wide selection of fonts make it easy to create a professional-looking certificate. To create a certificate like the one shown, use the Wave section shape on the Border stencil for the upper and lower borders. For a more formal look, you could use one of the Frame shapes from the Border stencil or simply draw lines or rectangles in different weights and colors using the Line and Rectangle tools. To create this type of text, use the Lucida Calligraphy font in a variety of sizes.

TIP: Visio's Clipart Stencil contains such shapes as the Award Circle, Diamond label, and 1st place ribbon that could be used in certificates.

Flags-of-the-World Game

If you have children, you can easily create this fun and educational Flags-of-the-World game for them using Visio's Flags stencil. The stencil includes 34 national flags from around the world.

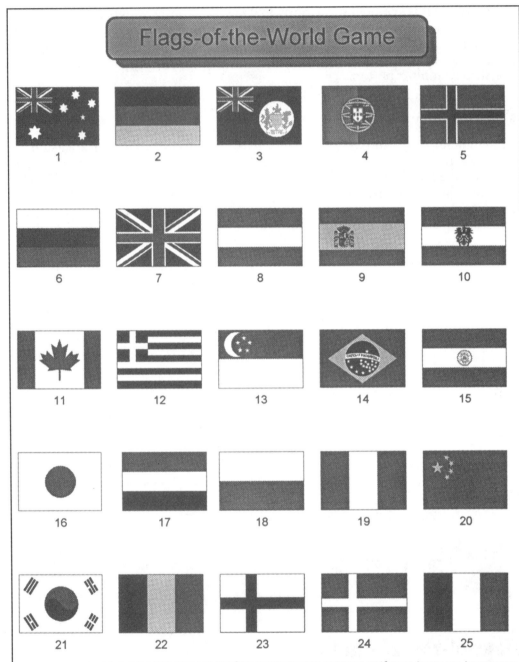

Flags-of-the-World Game

To create this drawing, drag the flag shapes you want to use onto the drawing page and size them using a corner selection handle. (The flags in the example are 1¼" wide.) Use horizontal guides to position the flags in rows, then use the Distribute Shapes toolbar button to space the flags evenly across each row. Once the flags are positioned on the page, go back to each one and label it in consecutive order.

You can add a title like the one shown by choosing the Text tool and drawing a text block approximately 3½" wide by ½" high. In the text block, type **Flags-of-the-World Game**, then click the Font Size toolbar and choose 18 pt. from the drop-down menu. With the text block still selected, choose the Pointer tool, then click the Shadow toolbar button once. To add a fill color to the title text block, click the Fill Color toolbar button repeatedly until you find a color you like. Or, choose the Format Fill command, select a Foreground color from the drop-down list, and click OK. Finally, drag the title text block so that its center selection handle glues itself to the guide at the vertical center of the page (4¼").

Leave some room at the bottom of the page for the answer key. Use the Text tool to type the answers in a text block. Then click the right mouse button and choose Rotate Right or (Rotate Left) from the shortcut menu twice to turn the answers upside down.

Idea List

Use your creativity to make some of the projects listed below:

- Notepad
- Personalized greeting cards
- Place cards
- Party invitation
- Sale flyers
- Continents game (World Map stencil)
- United States game (States of the U.S.A. stencil)

Projects Using Visio's Add-On Shapes

The introduction to this book discusses the various Visio products that Shapeware Corporation produces. Visio and Visio Home both include the Visio program itself along with a wide variety of templates, stencils, and shapes. For specialized projects, you can purchase any of 15 Visio Shape packages (prices range from $39 to $79). These are *add-on* packages that contain only templates, stencils, and shapes. Each package contains hundreds of shapes. You use the add-on packages to create anything from mechanical engineering drawings to accident scene diagrams. Refer to the Introduction for a complete list of these products.

As an added bonus, this book includes a disk that contains 12 stencils from Visio's Home Planning, Landscape Planning, Insurance, and Kids add-on packages. On the disk you get over 200 additional master shapes free of charge—a bonus to you worth well over $100.00. With the shapes in these stencils, you can complete all of the drawings shown in this chapter. (For a preview of these stencils, refer to Appendix A.)

Master Bathroom/Closet

To create the bathroom diagram shown on the following page, open Visio using the Bathroom Plan template, which in turn opens three stencils: hm_walls.vss, hm_bath.vss, and hm_elec.vss. (All three stencils are visible on the screen at once, as you'll see in later figures.) These three stencils give you structural shapes, bathroom fixtures, and electrical fixtures. The drawing page is 22' high by 17' wide. The following steps walk you through this project from creating the rectangular room using the Premade wall shape to opening up the lower right wall of the bathroom and adding the walk-in closet walls.

Master Bathroom/Walk-In Closet

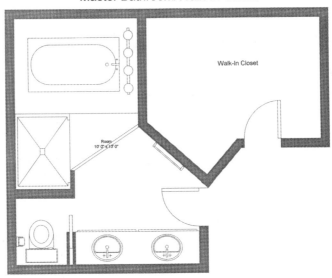

NOTE: The following instructions include approximate alignment positions. To accurately align and position shapes, remember to use Visio's Zoom feature and the Align Shapes and Distribute Shapes buttons, and to turn Glue and Snap on and off as necessary.

1. Open Visio using the Bathroom Plan template.

2. To change the orientation of the drawing page, choose Page Page Setup and click the Size/Scale button to display the Size/Scale Page Setup dialog box. • Click on the Standard option button, then choose Letter Wide from the drop-down list. The drawing page is now 22' wide by 17' high.

3. From the hm_walls.vss stencil, drag a Premade wall shape onto the drawing. • Size the walls to 10' wide by 13' high. (The lower right wall of this rectangular room will be changed later.) • Align the shape at 14½'/2½'.

4. From the hm_bath.vss stencil, drag a 36" shower shape onto the drawing. • Size the shower to 4' wide by 3' high. • Click the right mouse button and choose Rotate Left from the shortcut menu. • Align the Shower at 9½' along the left bathroom wall.

5. From the hm_walls.vss stencil, drag a Wall shape onto the drawing. • Size the Wall to approximately 3½'. • Align the wall along the left bathroom wall and at the bottom edge of the Shower (at approximately 5').

6. From the hm_walls.vss stencil, drag a Wall shape onto the drawing. • Size the Wall shape to approximately 1' wide by 3" high (a half-width wall). • Click the right mouse button and choose Rotate Left from the shortcut menu. • Place the wall along the right side of the lower right corner of the shower, forming a right angle with the previous shower wall.

 TIP: To accurately align shapes, turn Snap and Glue off as necessary by clicking the Snap and Glue toolbar buttons.

7. From the hm_walls.vss stencil, drag a Pocket door shape onto the drawing. • Size the Pocket Door to 3'6" wide. • Click the right mouse button and choose Rotate Left from the shortcut menu. • Align the Pocket Door along the lower bathroom wall at approximately 5¼'.

8. From the hm_bath.vss stencil, drag a Toilet 1 shape onto the drawing. • Click the right mouse button and choose Rotate Left from the shortcut menu. • Align the shape along the lower bathroom wall at 3'.

9. From the hm_bath.vss stencil, drag a TP dispenser shape onto the drawing. • Click the right mouse button and choose Rotate Left from the shortcut menu. • Align the shape along the left bathroom wall at 3'.

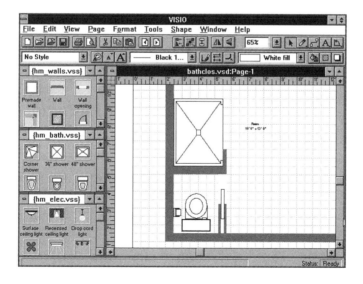

10. From the hm_bath.vss stencil, drag a 34" bathtub onto the drawing. • Click the right mouse button and choose Rotate Right from the shortcut menu. • Align the bathtub at 13½'/3¼'.

11. From the hm_elec.vss stencil, drag a Track light shape onto the drawing.
• Size the Track light to 3'6" wide. • Click the right mouse button and choose
Rotate Left from the shortcut menu. • Align the Track light shape at 14'/8½'.

12. From the hm_walls stencil, drag a Wall shape onto the drawing. • Size the
wall to 5'10". • Click the right mouse button and choose Rotate Right from
the shortcut menu. • Align the wall along the upper bathroom wall at 9¾'.

13. Click the Line tool, then draw a line at 9½' from the left bathroom wall to the
wall at the right end of the bathtub.

14. To draw the step up to the shower and tub, use the Line tool to draw two
diagonal lines from the new right bathroom wall to the lower right corner
of the shower.

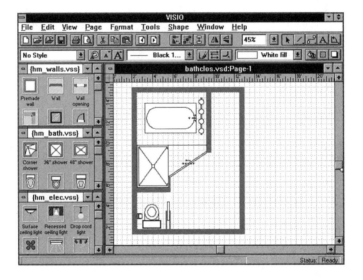

15. From the hm_bath.vss stencil, drag a 24" cabinet shape onto the drawing.
• Size the cabinet to 6'9" wide. • Click the right mouse button and choose
Rotate Left twice. • Align the 24" cabinet along the lower bathroom wall
between the right outer wall and the pocket door.

16. From the hm_bath.vss stencil, drag two Countertop sink 2 shapes onto the
drawing and space evenly on the 24" cabinet.

17. From the hm_walls.vss stencil, drag a Door shape onto the drawing. • Click
the right mouse button and choose Rotate Left. • Align the Door at 5½' along
the lower right bathroom wall.

18. To create the bathroom's diagonal wall, drag a Wall shape onto the drawing from the hm_walls.vss stencil. • Connect one end of the Wall to the existing right bathroom wall where it meets the upper right corner of the door. • Connect the other end of the wall to the 5'10" wall that borders the bathtub, sizing the wall as necessary. (The approximate angle of the wall is –41°.) • From the hm_bath.vss stencil, drag a Towel rack shape onto the drawing, size it to 2', rotate it to approximately –41°, and align it against the diagonal wall.

19. To hide the right wall of the original Premade Wall shape, drag the Wall opening shape onto the drawing from the hm_walls.vss stencil. • Click the right mouse button and choose Rotate Right. • Align the Wall Opening at 15'/12½', directly on top of the original right wall of the bathroom. • Size the Wall Opening to 9'6" to open the entire right wall down to the door.

20. Click on the 45° diagonal wall you drew in step 18, then click the Bring to Front toolbar button.

21. Now complete the closet walls using the Wall shape from the hm_walls.vss stencil. Adjust the alignment as necessary so that the walls are square. • Draw one Wall shape approximately 3' long, rotate it approximately 50°, and align it perpendicular to the diagonal wall drawn in step 18. • Draw a wall approximately 4'7" to create the lower wall of the closet. • For the right closet wall, draw a Wall shape approximately 7' long and rotate it to the right. • For the upper closet wall, draw a Wall shape 7'.

22. From the hm_walls.vss stencil, drag a Door shape onto the drawing. • Align the Door shape along the lower edge of the closet wall at approximately 15'.

23. Click the Text tool, then type **Walk-In Closet** near the center of the closet shape.

24. Use the Text tool to add a title to the drawing.

Kitchen

You can create a kitchen like the diagram shown in the following figure using Visio's Kitchen Plan template. The Kitchen Plan template automatically opens five stencils: hm_furn.vss, hm_appl.vss, hm_walls.vss, hm_kit.vss, and hm_elec.vss. These stencils provide appliance shapes, structural shapes, special kitchen shapes (such as base and wall cabinets), and electrical shapes. The drawing page is 17' wide by 22' high.

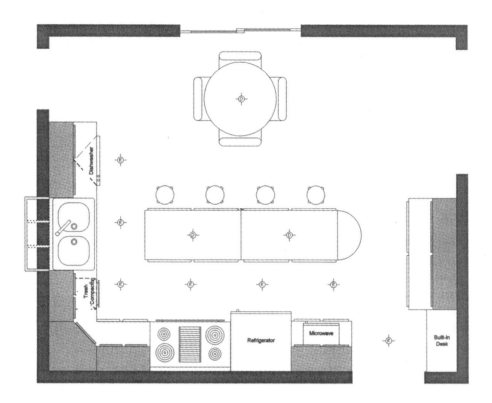

The wall cabinet shapes in the hm_kit.vss stencil are shallower than the base cabinet shapes so that base cabinets are visible below wall cabinets in the drawings. In the drawing, base cabinets appear in white, whereas wall cabinets are shaded in gray. It's best to add wall cabinets to the drawing after the base cabinets.

NOTE: The following instructions include approximate alignment positions. To accurately align and position shapes, remember to use Visio's Zoom feature and the Align Shapes and Distribute Shapes toolbar buttons, and to turn Glue and Snap on and off as necessary.

1. Open Visio using the Home-Kitchen Plan template.
2. To change the orientation of the drawing page, choose Page Page Setup and click the Size/Scale button to display the Size/Scale Page Setup dialog box.
   • Click on the Standard option button, then choose Letter Wide from the drop-down list. The drawing page is now 22' wide by 17' high.

3. From the hm_walls.vss stencil, drag a Premade wall shape onto the drawing. • Size the walls to 17' wide by 11' high. • Align the walls at 13'/2½'.

4. From the hm_kit.vss stencil, drag an L-shaped countertop shape onto the drawing. • Click the right mouse button and choose Rotate Left from the shortcut menu twice. • Align the L-shaped countertop in the lower left corner of the room. • Size the L-shaped countertop to 10' high by 4'3" wide.

5. From the hm_appl.vss stencil, drag the Range 3 shape onto the drawing. • Click the Flip Vertical toolbar button. • Align the range along the lower wall of the kitchen next to the L-shaped countertop (approximately 3½'/7¼').

6. From the hm_appl.vss stencil, drag a Refrg 1 shape onto the drawing. • Click the Flip Vertical toolbar button. • Align the refrigerator along the lower wall of the kitchen next to the Range shape (approximately 4'/10½').

7. From the hm_kit.vss stencil, drag a Utility cabinet 2 shape onto the drawing. • Click the Flip Vertical toolbar button. • Align the Utility Cabinet along the lower kitchen wall next to the refrigerator (approximately 3½'/13').

8. From the hm_appl.vss stencil, drag the Microwave shape onto the drawing. • Align the Microwave above the Utility Cabinet next to the refrigerator (approximately 3½'/13½').

9. From the hm_appl.vss stencil, drag the Dishwasher shape onto the drawing. • Click the right mouse button and choose Rotate Left from the shortcut menu. • Align the Dishwasher along the left kitchen wall (approximately 11'/3').

10. From the hm_kit.vss stencil, drag the Sink 2 shape onto the drawing. • Click the right mouse button and choose Rotate Left from the shortcut menu. • Align the sink along the left kitchen wall (approximately 8½'/3').

11. From the hm_walls.vss stencil, drag the Garden window shape onto the drawing. • Click the right mouse button and choose Rotate Left. • Align the Garden Window to the left of the sink (approximately 8½'/2').

12. From the hm_appl.vss stencil, drag the Trash Compactor shape onto the drawing. • Click the right mouse button and choose Rotate Left from the shortcut menu. • Align the trash compactor near the left kitchen wall at approximately 5¼'/3'.

13. From the hm_kit.vss stencil, drag a Base peninsula 2 shape onto the drawing. • Extend the width of the Base Peninsula 2 shape to 4'. • Align the Base peninsula 2 shape at 8'/7'. • Copy the shape and align it at 8'/11'. • From the hm_kit.vss stencil, drag a Peninsula end-shelf onto the drawing. • Click the Flip Horizontal toolbar button. • Align the end shelf at the right end of the rightmost Base peninsula (approximately 15'/8').

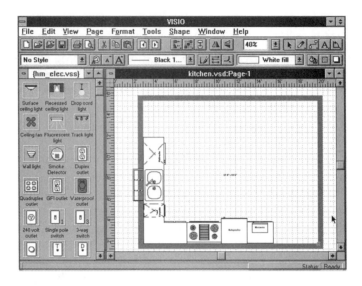

14. From the hm_furn.vss stencil, drag a Stool shape onto the drawing. • Align the stool along the upper edge of the Base peninsula (approximately 9'/7½'). • Make three copies of the stool and align them along the upper edge of the Base peninsula. (Hold the Ctrl key and drag a shape to make a copy.) • Use the Align Shapes and Distribute Shapes toolbar buttons to position the stools.

15. From the hm_furn.vss stencil, drag a Circular dining table onto the drawing. • Size the table to 3' by 3'. • Align the table at 14'/8¾'. The island and dining area of the kitchen should now look like this:

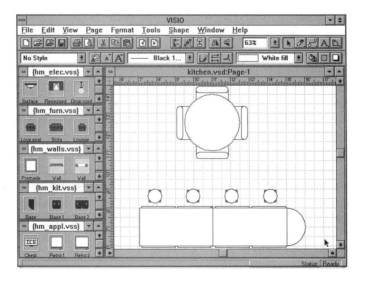

16. From the hm_kit.vss stencil, drag a Utility cabinet 2 onto the drawing. • Click the right mouse button and choose Rotate Right from the shortcut menu. • Size the cabinet to 4'6" by 2'. • Align the cabinet along the right kitchen wall (approximately 8½'/18').

17. Choose the Rectangle tool and draw a rectangular desk 1'3" wide by 2'6" high. • Align the desk in the lower right corner of the kitchen (approximately 4'/18¾").

18. From the hm_walls.vss stencil, drag a Wall opening shape onto the drawing. • Align the Wall opening along the lower kitchen wall at approximately 15¾'. • Drag another Wall opening shape onto the drawing. • Size the Wall opening to 5'. • Click the right mouse button and choose Rotate Right from the shortcut menu. • Align the Wall opening along the right kitchen wall at 14½'. • Drag another Wall opening shape onto the drawing. • Size the Wall opening to 2'6". Click the right mouse button and choose Rotate Left from the shortcut menu. • Align the Wall opening along the left kitchen wall at 14½'. • From the hm_walls.vss stencil, drag a Sliding door shape onto the drawing. • Align the Sliding door along the upper kitchen wall at 8½'.

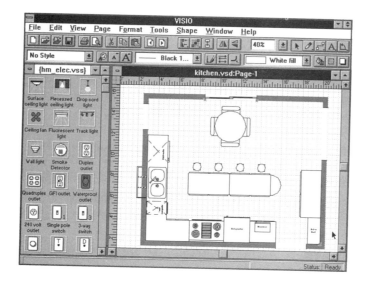

19. To add the upper wall cabinets, from the hm_kit.vss stencil, drag a Wall 2 shape onto the drawing. • Click the right mouse button and choose Rotate Left from the shortcut menu. • Align the Wall 2 shape above the Trash Compactor (approximately 5¾'/3').

20. Hold the Ctrl key and drag to copy the Wall 2 shape that's above the Trash Compactor to the wall above the Dishwasher. • Adjust the height of the Wall 2 cabinet to 3'. • Align the Wall 2 shape at 11½'/3'.

21. From the hm_kit.vss stencil, drag a Wall corner shape onto the drawing. • Click the right mouse button and choose Rotate Left from the shortcut menu. • Align the Wall corner in the lower left corner of the kitchen at approximately 3½'/3'.

22. Drag another Wall 2 shape onto the drawing. • Click the right mouse button and choose Rotate Left twice. • Align the Wall 2 shape along the lower kitchen wall at approximately 5'. • Size the Wall 2 shape to fit between the Wall corner and the Range (approximately 2'3" wide).

23. Hold the Ctrl key and drag to copy the Wall 2 shape you created in step 22 and align it along the lower kitchen wall to the right of the refrigerator (approximately 13'). • Size the Wall 2 shape to measure the same length as the cabinet below (approximately 2'6").

24. From the hm_kit.vss stencil, drag a Wall 2 shape onto the drawing. • Click the right mouse button and choose Rotate Left twice. • Align the Wall 2 shape along the right kitchen wall above the floor cabinet (approximately 8½'/19'). • Extend the height of the Wall 2 shape to 4'6".

25. Click on all upper wall cabinet shapes that you added to the drawing in steps 19 through 24. • From the Fill Style pull-down menu, choose Gray 10%.

26. From the hm_elec.vss stencil, drag a Drop cord light onto the drawing and center it over the dining table.

27. Make two copies of the Drop cord light and space them evenly above the island using the Align Shapes and Distribute Shapes toolbar buttons if necessary.

28. From the hm_elec.vss stencil, drag a Recessed ceiling light onto the drawing and center it in front of the dishwasher.

29. Make two more copies of the Recessed ceiling light and place them in front of the sink and trash compactor. Use the Align Shapes and Distribute Shapes toolbar buttons to position the lights.

30. Make three more copies of the Recessed ceiling light and place them in front of the range, refrigerator, and microwave. Use the Align Shapes and Distribute Shapes toolbar buttons to position the lights.

31. Copy one more Recessed ceiling light and center it above the doorway at the right end of the lower kitchen wall.

Accident Scene

Two of the stencils found in Visio's Insurance Shapes add-on package are included on the enclosed disk. When you open Visio using the Insurance Diagrams template, Visio opens the insauto1.vss and insauto2.vss stencils automatically. The drawing page is a standard 8½" by 11".

Using shapes in the insauto1.vss and insauto2.vss stencils, you can draw roadway shapes to designate streets, highways, or freeways, to which you can add vehicles, traffic signs, and pedestrians as needed. The location of impact in a vehicle accident diagram is marked by a Crash shape. To add comments or notes to a diagram, use a Text callout shape.

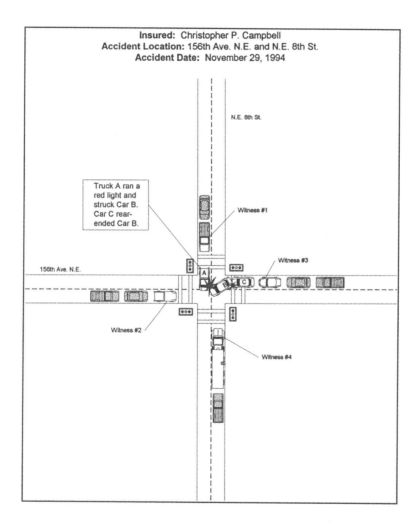

To create a drawing like the example accident scene above, use the Cross shape to illustrate the intersection. Add crosswalks and Stop lights at all four corners of the intersection. Then use both the insauto1.vss and insauto2.vss stencils to add cars and other vehicles to the streets. Rotate the vehicle shapes and their respective text blocks, and size them as necessary. Use the Callout shape to indicate witnesses to the accident, and use the Boxed callout to describe the accident.

Landscape Plan

Three of the stencils in Visio's Landscape Planning add-on package are included on the enclosed disk. The lssite.vss stencil contains structural and site shapes such as walls, doors, brick sidewalks, decks, fences, and gates. The lsplant.vss stencil contains a variety of shapes for trees, shrubs, grasses, cacti, and potted plants. And for designing recreational areas, the lssports.vss stencil contains pools, spas, sports courts (basketball, tennis, volleyball, and badminton), outdoor furniture, and play structures. Use the shapes from these three stencils to create the landscape plan shown here or a similar landscape plan.

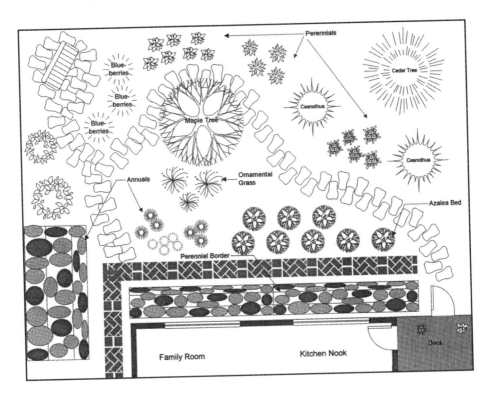

Dinosaurscape

Visio isn't just for adults, it's for kids, too! Visio's drag-and-drop technique makes it the easiest drawing program for kids to use. The final project in this chapter shows you some of the most popular shapes from Visio's Kids Shapes package: dinosaurs.

To create the dinosaurscape shown on the following page, open the Dinosaur template, and the mountainous terrain appears automatically. Drag dinosaur shapes, trees, and grass onto the drawing page, then size or flip them as necessary. You can change the color of a dinosaur's individual parts by selecting the shape, then choosing the Edit Open *Shape* command (such as Edit Open Tyrannosaurus). Visio opens a group window in which you can alter individual components of the shape. Double-click on the group window's Control-menu box to return to the drawing page.

Part 3

Visio Visual Guide

The appendices are a great place to browse and get good ideas for creating fun and interesting projects using Visio. Appendix A is a handy visual index of the stencils you will be using in Visio, and provides a great way to quickly find the stencil you are looking for without searching through the program. Appendix B is chock-full of finished Visio projects. Have fun browsing, but be warned: this appendix will undoubtedly get your creative juices flowing, and inspire more ideas than you'll have time to try. Appendix C walks you through the steps you need to install Visio on your machine.

Stencil Gallery

Visio 3.0 comes with the following stencils:

The Basic Stencil

1	2	3	4	5	6	7	8	9	10	11	12	13
14	15	16	17	18	19	20	21	22	23	24	25	26
27	28	29	30	31	32	33	34	35	36	37	38

1. Triangle
2. Square
3. Pentagon
4. Hexagon
5. Septagon
6. Octagon
7. Star 5
8. Star 6
9. Star 7
10. Center drag circle
11. Circle
12. Ellipse
13. Right triangle
14. Cross
15. Rectangle
16. Shadowed box
17. 3-D box
18. Rounded rectangle
19. Rounded square
20. 45 degree single
21. 60 degree single
22. Fancy arrow
23. 45 degree double
24. 60 degree double
25. Hints
26. 45 degree tail
27. 60 degree tail
28. Flexi-arrow 1
29. Flexi-arrow 2
30. Flexi-arrow 3
31. Double flexi-arrow
32. Universal Connector
33. Line connector
34. Line-curve connector
35. Side to top/bottom
36. Top/bottom to side
37. Bottom to top variable
38. Side to side variable

The Block Diagram Stencil

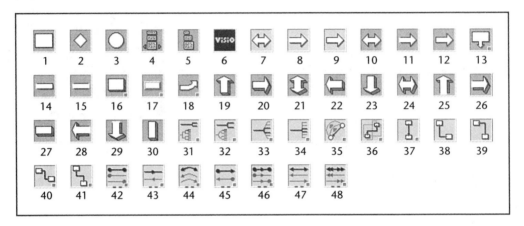

1. Box
2. Diamond
3. Circle
4. Auto-height box
5. Auto-size box
6. Arrow hints
7. 1-D double
8. 1-D open end
9. 1-D single
10. 2-D double
11. 2-D open end
12. 2-D single
13. Arrow bar
14. Open-closed end bar
15. Open end bar
16. 3-D box

17. Button
18. Curved arrow
19. 3-D Up arrow
20. 3-D right arrow
21. 3-D up/down
22. 3-D left arrow
23. 3-D Down arrow
24. 3-D left/right
25. 3-D up open end
26. 3-D right open end
27. 3-D horiz. bar
28. 3-D left open end
29. 3-D down open end
30. 3-D vertical bar
31. Double tree square
32. Double tree sloped

33. Multi-tree sloped
34. Multi-tree square
35. Line-curve connector
36. Universal Connector
37. Line connector
38. Top/bottom to side
39. Side to top/bottom
40. Side to side variable
41. Bottom to top variable
42. Dotted line
43. Mid-arrow
44. Arced arrow
45. Dot & arrow
46. Mid-arrow dotted
47. Single arrowhead
48. Double arrowhead

The Border Stencil

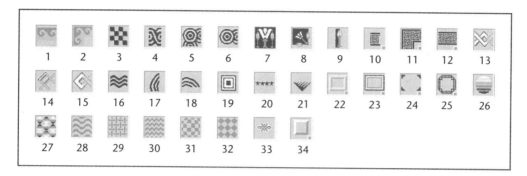

1. Wave section
2. Wave corner
3. Checker section
4. Braid section
5. Braid corner
6. Braid end-cap
7. Egyptian section
8. Egyptian corner
9. Egyptian end-cap
10. Greek section
11. Greek corner
12. Greek Border
13. Cross section
14. Cross corner
15. Cross end-cap
16. Wave section 2
17. Wave corner 2
18. Wave corner 3
19. Roman section
20. Star section
21. Triangle section
22. Chiselled frame
23. Square frame
24. Photo frame
25. Art deco frame
26. Art deco circle
27. Art deco tile
28. Wave tile
29. Weave tile
30. Zigzag tile
31. Op-art tile
32. Diamond tile
33. Celtic ornament
34. Button ornament

The Callout Stencil

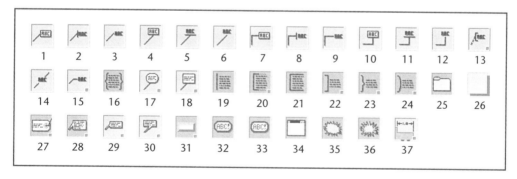

1. Side box callout
2. Side line callout
3. Side text callout
4. Mid box callout
5. Mid line callout
6. Mid text callout
7. Side elbow box
8. Side line elbow
9. Side elbow callout
10. Mid elbow box
11. Mid line elbow
12. Mid elbow callout
13. Annotatic
14. Center text callout
15. Bend callout
16. Braces with text
17. Oval callout
18. Box callout
19. Line with text
20. Partial bracket text
21. Full bracket text
22. Side bracket
23. Side brace
24. Side parentheses
25. File
26. Yellow note
27. Tag
28. 2-D word balloon
29. Balloon horizontal
30. Balloon vertical
31. Button
32. Angled stamp
33. Rounded stamp
34. Window
35. Blunt starburst
36. Sharp starburst
37. Automatic dimension

The Chart Stencil

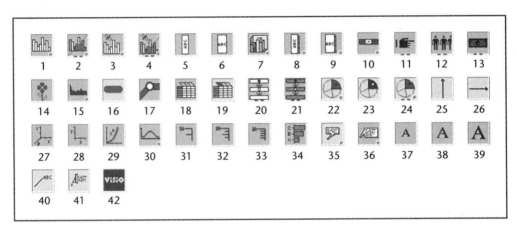

1. Bar graph 1
2. Bar graph 2
3. Bar graph 3
4. Bar graph 4
5. Vertical text bar
6. Horizontal text bar
7. 3-D axis
8. Vertical 3-D bar
9. Horizontal 3-D bar
10. Divided bar
11. Extend-o-hand

12. People
13. Stretchable dollars
14. Growing flower
15. Line graph
16. Graph line
17. Data point
18. Flow header
19. Column header
20. Yes/No box 1
21. Yes/No box 2
22. Pie chart slice 1

23. Pie chart slice 2
24. Super smart slice
25. Vertical axis
26. Horizontal axis
27. X-Y-Z axis
28. X-Y axis
29. Exponential curve
30. Normal curve
31. Graph-scale 2
32. Graph-scale 4
33. Graph-scale 5

34. Row/Column header
35. 1-D word balloon
36. 2-D word balloon
37. Text block 8pt
38. Text block 10pt
39. Text block 12pt
40. Horizontal callout
41. Annotation
42. Hints

The Clip Art Stencil

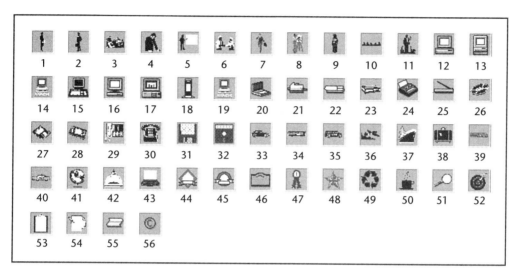

1. Business woman
2. Man walking
3. Meeting
4. Woman with telephone
5. Presentation
6. Handshake
7. Man running
8. Man with chart
9. Man with folder
10. Audience
11. Politician
12. Large Macintosh
13. Small Macintosh
14. IBM PS/2
15. Dumb terminal
16. Workstation
17. IBM-PC AT
18. Tower
19. Detailed IBM PS/2

20. Laptop computer
21. Laserjet printer
22. LaserWriter
23. Dot matrix printer
24. Facsimile machine
25. Flatbed scanner
26. CD
27. Disk
28. Video cassette
29. Business telephone
30. Telephone
31. 3.5" disk
32. 5.25" disk
33. Compact car
34. City bus
35. Car pool
36. Jet
37. Cruise ship
38. Luggage

39. Train symbol
40. Taxi symbol
41. Globe
42. Government
43. Open briefcase
44. Diamond label
45. Award circle
46. Aztec label
47. 1st place
48. Gold star
49. Recycle symbol
50. Coffee cup
51. Magnifying glass
52. Target
53. Clipboard
54. Notes
55. Scroll
56. Copyright

The Connector Stencil

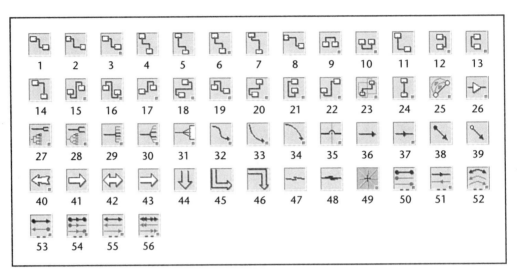

1. Side to side	20. Bottom to side 1	39. Flow director 2
2. Side to side fixed	21. Bottom to side 2	40. Flexi-arrow
3. Side to side variable	22. Bottom to side 3	41. 1-D single
4. Bottom to top	23. Universal Connector	42. 1-D double
5. Bottom to top fixed	24. Line connector	43. 1-D open end
6. Bottom to top variable	25. Line-curve connector	44. Hollow connect 1
7. Bottom to top fixed	26. Control transfer	45. Hollow connect 2
8. Side to side fixed	27. Double tree square	46. Hollow connect 3
9. Top to top	28. Double tree sloped	47. Comm-link 1
10. Bottom to bottom	29. Multi-tree square	48. Comm-link 2
11. Top/bottom to side	30. Multi-tree sloped	49. Star
12. Side to same side	31. One to many	50. Dotted line
13. Side to same side	32. Curve connect 1	51. Mid-arrow
14. Side to top/bottom	33. Curve connect 2	52. Arced arrow
15. Bottom to top 2	34. Curve connect 3	53. Dot & arrow
16. Bottom to top 2	35. Jumper	54. Mid-arrow dotted
17. Side to top/bottom	36. Directed line 1	55. Single arrowhead
18. Side to side 2	37. Directed line 2	56. Double arrowhead
19. Side to top	38. Flow director 1	

The Electrical Engineering Stencil

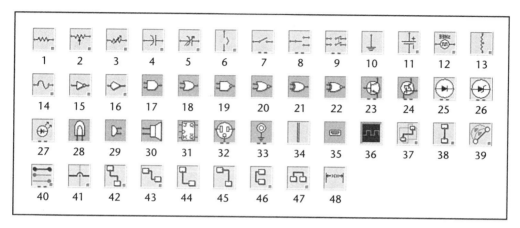

1. Resistor
2. Adjustable resistor
3. Variable resistor
4. Capacitor
5. Variable capacitor
6. Circuit breaker
7. SPST
8. SPDT
9. DPDT
10. Ground
11. Battery
12. Clock
13. Inductor
14. Fuse
15. Inverter
16. Operational amplifier

17. AND 2 input
18. OR 2 input
19. NAND 2 input
20. NOR 2 input
21. XOR 2 input
22. XNOR 2 input
23. Bipolar NPN
24. Latch
25. Diode
26. Zener Diode
27. LED/photo-diode
28. Lamp
29. Microphone
30. Speaker
31. J-K flip flop
32. F/M 3-conductor

33. Shielded jack/plug
34. Magnet core
35. Small D connector
36. Square
37. Universal Connector
38. Line connector
39. Line-curve connector
40. Dotted line
41. Jumper
42. Bottom to top variable
43. Side to side variable
44. Top/bottom to side
45. Side to top/bottom
46. Side to same side
47. Top to top
48. Dimension line

The European Map Stencil

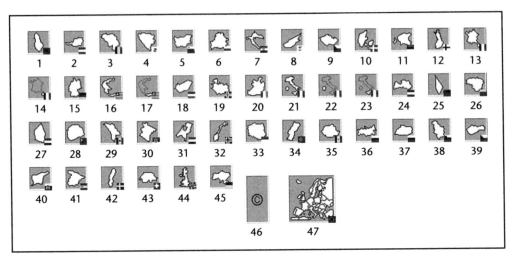

1. Albania	17. Crete	33. Poland
2. Austria	18. Hungary	34. Portugal
3. Belgium	19. Iceland	35. Romania
4. Bosnia	20. Ireland	36. Russia
5. Bulgaria	21. Italy	37. Kaliningrad
6. Byelarus	22. Sardinia	38. Serbia
7. Croatia	23. Sicily	39. Slovakia
8. Cyprus	24. Latvia	40. Slovenia
9. Czech Republic	25. Liechtenstein	41. Spain
10. Denmark	26. Lithuania	42. Sweden
11. Estonia	27. Luxembourg	43. Switzerland
12. Finland	28. Macedonia	44. United Kingdom
13. France	29. Moldavia	45. Ukraine
14. Corsica	30. Montenegro	46. Copyright
15. Germany	31. Netherlands	47. Europe
16. Greece	32. Norway	

The Flags Stencil

1. Australia
2. Austria
3. Belgium
4. Brazil
5. Canada
6. China
7. Denmark
8. European Council
9. Finland
10. France
11. Germany
12. Greece
13. Hong Kong
14. Hungary
15. Iceland
16. India
17. Ireland
18. Italy
19. Japan
20. Luxembourg
21. Netherlands
22. Norway
23. Poland
24. Portugal
25. Russia
26. Singapore
27. South Korea
28. Spain
29. Sweden
30. Switzerland
31. Taiwan
32. Ukraine
33. United Kingdom
34. United States

The Flowchart Stencil

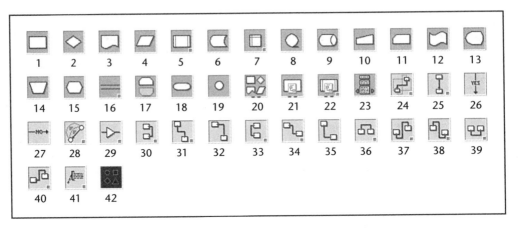

1. Process
2. Decision
3. Document
4. Data
5. Predefined process
6. Stored data
7. Internal storage
8. Sequential data
9. Direct data
10. Manual input
11. Card
12. Paper tape
13. Display
14. Manual operation
15. Preparation
16. Parallel mode
17. Loop limit
18. Terminator
19. Connector
20. Flowchart shapes
21. Process (sub-paging)

22. Predef proc (sub-paging)
23. Auto-height box
24. Universal Connector
25. Line connector
26. Result
27. No result
28. Line-curve connector
29. Control transfer
30. Side to same side
31. Bottom to top variable
32. Side to top/bottom
33. Side to same side
34. Side to side variable
35. Top/bottom to side
36. Top to top
37. Bottom to top 2
38. Bottom to top 2
39. Bottom to bottom
40. Side to top/bottom
41. Annotation
42. Hints

The Forms Stencil

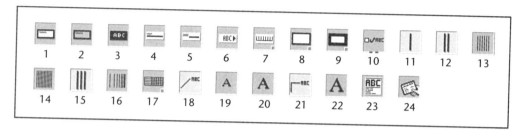

1. Info box
2. Shaded box
3. Reversed text
4. Info line
5. Info line 2
6. Arrow
7. Data boxes
8. 1/16" Border
9. 1/8" Border
10. Check box
11. Single line
12. Double line

13. 5-Column
14. 10-Column
15. Triple line
16. 10-Log lines
17. Grid
18. Horizontal callout
19. 8pt Arial text block
20. 10pt Arial text block
21. Right-angle horizontal
22. 18pt Arial text block
23. FAX cover
24. Business card

The Map Stencil

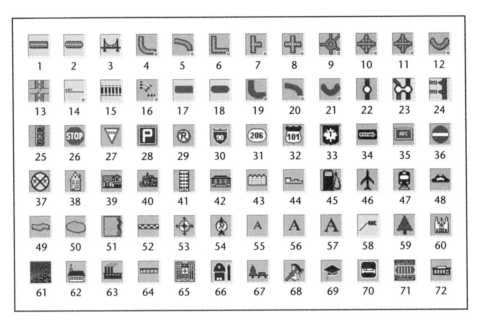

1. Road square
2. Road round
3. Bridge
4. Curve 1
5. Curve 2
6. Corner
7. 3-way
8. 4-way
9. Roundabout
10. Cloverleaf interchange
11. Diamond interchange
12. Flexible road
13. Roadway break
14. Thin road
15. Railroad
16. Rail curve
17. Metro Line
18. Rounded Metro

19. Metro curve 1
20. Metro curve 2
21. Flexible metro
22. Station
23. Transfer station
24. Stop callout
25. Stop light
26. Stop sign
27. Yield
28. Parking
29. No parking
30. Interstate
31. State route
32. U.S. Route
33. Canadian highway
34. One way
35. Info. sign
36. No entry

37. Railroad crossing
38. Town house
39. Suburban home
40. City
41. Building 1
42. Building 2
43. Condos
44. Outdoor mall
45. Gas station
46. Airport
47. Train station
48. Ferry
49. River
50. Lake
51. Ocean
52. Scale
53. Direction
54. North

55. Text block 8pt
56. Text block 10pt
57. Text block 18pt
58. Callout
59. Tree
60. Cathedral
61. Skyscraper
62. Church
63. Factory
64. Warehouse
65. Hospital
66. Barn
67. Park
68. Fire department
69. School
70. Motel
71. Stadium
72. Convenience store

The Network Stencil

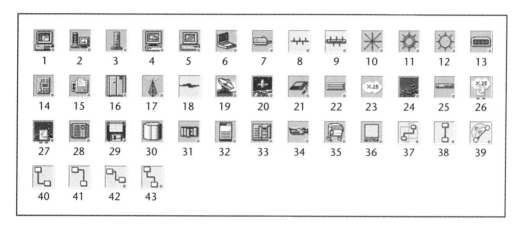

1. Desktop PC
2. Server
3. Tower box
4. Workstation
5. Macintosh
6. Laptop computer
7. Printer
8. Bus
9. Ethernet
10. Star
11. FDDI ring
12. Token ring
13. Modem
14. Telephone
15. Fax
16. Public switch
17. Radio tower
18. Comm-link
19. Satellite dish
20. Satellite
21. Pen-based computer
22. MUX/DEMUX

23. Cloud
24. City
25. Bridge
26. Cloud (sub-paging)
27. City (sub-paging)
28. Disk array
29. Removable storage
30. Database
31. Mainframe
32. Minicomputer
33. IBM AS/400
34. Video
35. Plotter
36. Custom equipment
37. Universal connector
38. Line connector
39. Line-curve connector
40. Top/bottom to side
41. Side to top/bottom
42. Side to side variable
43. Bottom to top variable

The Orgchart Stencil

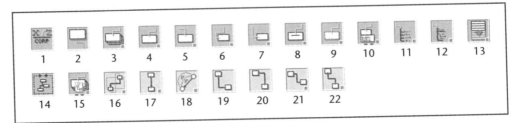

1. Title
2. Executive
3. Manager
4. Position
5. Assistant
6. Stackable position
7. Position 2
8. Position 3
9. Consultant
10. Position plus
11. Staff list
12. Team list
13. Stack of positions
14. Team
15. Department (sub-paging)
16. Universal connector
17. Line connector
18. Line-curve connector
19. Top/bottom to side
20. Side to top/bottom
21. Side to side variable
22. Bottom to top variable

The Practice Stencil

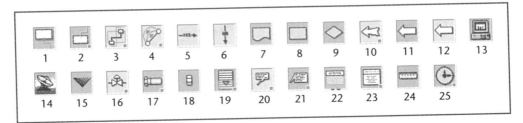

1. Executive
2. Position
3. Universal connector
4. Line-curve connector
5. YES result
6. NO result
7. Document
8. Process
9. Decision
10. Flexi-arrow
11. 2-D arrow
12. 1-D arrow
13. PC
14. Satellite dish
15. Triangle teeth
16. Valve
17. Bolt
18. Nut
19. Extendo-column
20. 1-D word balloon
21. 2-D word balloon
22. Pop-up box
23. Divided box
24. Ruler
25. Clock

The Project Management Stencil

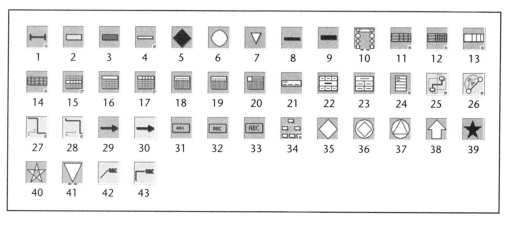

1. Solid timeline
2. Shaded timeline1
3. Shaded timeline2
4. Narrow timeline
5. Milestone
6. Circle
7. Time marker1
8. Time marker2
9. Time marker3
10. Timeline & markers
11. Wide Gantt
12. Narrow Gantt
13. Gantt chart
14. Gantt extension
15. Gantt piece

16. Title
17. Heading
18. 5 Day date block
19. 7 Day date block
20. Task label
21. Legend
22. Pert1
23. Pert2
24. Text column
25. Universal connector
26. Line-curve connector
27. Connector 1
28. Connector 2
29. 2-D arrow
30. 1-D arrow

31. Text block 8 pt
32. Text block 10 pt
33. Text block 12 pt
34. Summarization structure
35. Time marker4
36. Time marker5
37. Time marker6
38. Time marker7
39. Time marker8
40. Time marker9
41. All time markers
42. Horizontal callout
43. Right-angle horizontal

The Space Planning Stencil

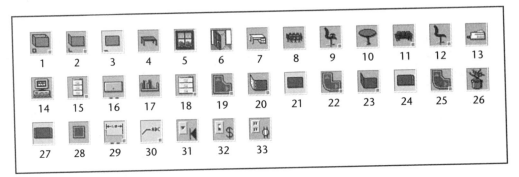

1. Wall square
2. Wall corner
3. Wall section
4. Table
5. Window
6. Door
7. Desk
8. Conference table
9. Desk chair
10. Circular table
11. Sofa
12. Chair
13. Printer
14. PC
15. File
16. Suspended lateral file
17. Bookshelf
18. Lateral file
19. Corner surface 1
20. Curved panel
21. Panel
22. Corner surface 2
23. Corner panel
24. 1 post panel
25. Corner surface 3
26. Plant
27. 2 post panel
28. Work surface
29. Dimension line
30. Bend callout
31. Telephone jack
32. Switch
33. 110 volt outlet

The States of the U.S.A. Stencil

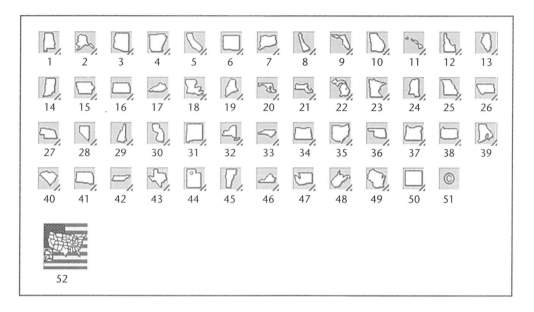

1. Alabama	19. Maine	37. Oregon
2. Alaska	20. Maryland	38. Pennsylvania
3. Arizona	21. Massachusetts	39. Rhode Island
4. Arkansas	22. Michigan	40. South Carolina
5. California	23. Minnesota	41. South Dakota
6. Colorado	24. Mississippi	42. Tennessee
7. Connecticut	25. Missouri	43. Texas
8. Delaware	26. Montana	44. Utah
9. Florida	27. Nebraska	45. Vermont
10. Georgia	28. Nevada	46. Virginia
11. Hawaii	29. New Hampshire	47. Washington
12. Idaho	30. New Jersey	48. West Virginia
13. Illinois	31. New Mexico	49. Wisconsin
14. Indiana	32. New York	50. Wyoming
15. Iowa	33. North Carolina	51. Copyright
16. Kansas	34. North Dakota	52. United States of America
17. Kentucky	35. Ohio	
18. Louisiana	36. Oklahoma	

The Symbols Stencil

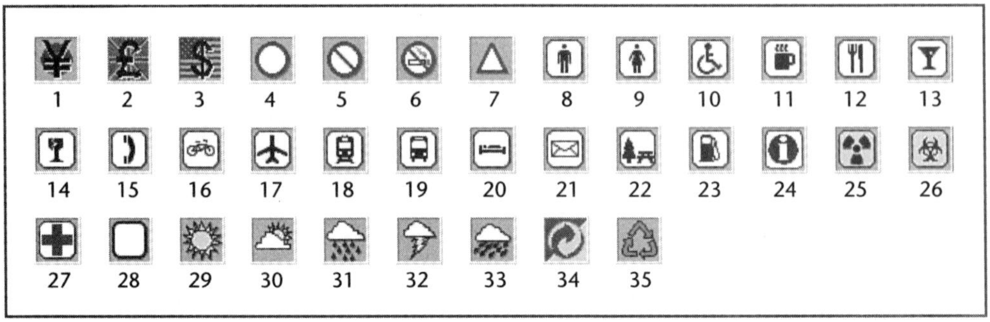

1. Yen
2. Pound
3. U.S. dollar
4. Zone
5. "NO" sign
6. No smoking
7. Warning sign
8. Men
9. Women
10. Handicap
11. Coffee
12. Dining
13. Drinks
14. Fragile
15. Telephone
16. Bicycle
17. Airport
18. Rail transportation
19. Bus station
20. Lodging
21. Post
22. Park
23. Service station
24. Information
25. Radioactive
26. Biohazard
27. First aid
28. Square box
29. Sunny
30. Partly cloudy
31. Rain
32. Lightning
33. Storm
34. Recycle 1
35. Recycle 2

The Total Quality Management Stencil

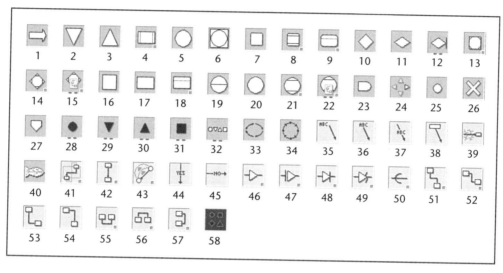

1. Transportation
2. Inbound goods
3. Storage
4. Procedure
5. Operation
6. Operation & Inspection
7. Issue
8. Organization function
9. 2-part function
10. Decision 1
11. Decision 2
12. Multi in/out decision
13. External organization
14. External process
15. Ext. proc. (sub-paging)
16. Inspection/measurement
17. Metric
18. 2-part metric
19. System database
20. System support

21. System function
22. Sys. func. (sub-paging)
23. Delay
24. Feedback arrow
25. Connector
26. Connector issues
27. Off-page connector
28. Fabrication
29. Move
30. Store
31. Inspection
32. Selectable process
33. Work flow loop 1
34. Work flow loop 2
35. Cause 1
36. Cause 2
37. Cause 3
38. Category
39. Effect

40. Fish frame
41. Universal connector
42. Line connector
43. Line-curve connector
44. Result
45. No result
46. Branch return
47. Branch no return
48. Interrupt
49. External control
50. Refinement
51. Bottom to top variable
52. Side to side variable
53. Top/bottom to side
54. Side to top/bottom
55. Bottom to bottom
56. Top to top
57. Side to same side
58. Fishbone hints

The World Map Stencil

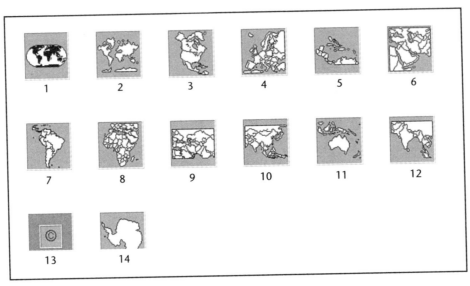

1. World 1
2. World 2
3. North America
4. Europe
5. Central America
6. Middle East
7. South America
8. Africa
9. Western Asia
10. Eastern Asia
11. Australasia
12. Southern Asia
13. Copyright
14. Antarctica

The disk that comes with this book includes the following stencils:

The Home - Appliance Stencil

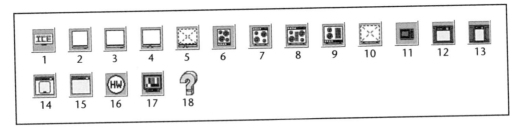

1. Chest freezer
2. Refrg 1
3. Refrg 2
4. Refrg 3
5. Built-in Refrg
6. Range 1
7. Range 2
8. Range 3
9. Range w/ grill
10. Built-in oven
11. Microwave
12. Dishwasher
13. Trash Compact
14. Washer
15. Dryer
16. Water heater
17. Television
18. Help

The Home - Bathroom Stencil

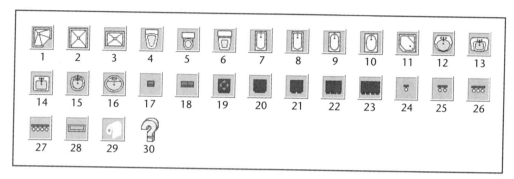

1. Corner shower
2. 36" shower
3. 48" shower
4. Bidet
5. Toilet 1
6. Toilet 2
7. Bathtub
8. 30" bathtub

9. 34" bathtub
10. Oval bathtub
11. Corner bathtub
12. Pedestal sink 1
13. Pedestal sink 2
14. Wall hung sink
15. Countertop sink 1
16. Countertop sink 2

17. Medicine cabinet 16"
18. Medicine cabinet 24"
19. Cabinet
20. 12" cabinet
21. 24" cabinet
22. 36" cabinet
23. 48" cabinet
24. Side light 6"

25. Light bar 18"
26. Light bar 24"
27. Light bar 36"
28. Towel rack
29. TP dispenser
30. Help

The Home - Electrical Stencil

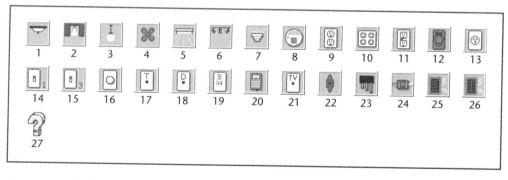

1. Surface ceiling light
2. Recessed ceiling light
3. Drop cord light
4. Ceiling fan
5. Fluorescent light
6. Track light
7. Wall light

8. Smoke Detector
9. Duplex outlet
10. Quadruplex outlet
11. GFI outlet
12. Waterproof outlet
13. 240 volt outlet
14. Single pole switch

15. 3-way switch
16. Dimmer switch
17. Telephone outlet
18. Computer data outlet
19. Stereo outlet
20. Thermostat
21. Television outlet

22. Doorbell
23. Doorbell chime
24. Doorbell transformer
25. Surface panel
26. Inset panel
27. Help

The Home - Furniture Stencil

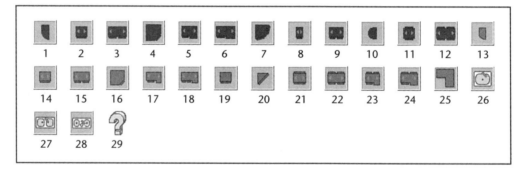

1. Love seat
2. Sofa
3. Lounge chair
4. Stool
5. Chair
6. Recliner
7. Circular dining table
8. Oval dining table
9. Square table
10. Oblong dining table
11. Circular table
12. Rectangular table
13. Bookcase
14. Large plant
15. Small plant
16. House plant
17. Grand piano
18. Spinet piano
19. Night stand
20. Double bed
21. Queen-size bed
22. King-size bed
23. Desk
24. Bunk bed
25. Twin bed
26. Chest
27. Double dresser
28. Triple dresser
29. Help

The Home - Kitchen Stencil

1. Base end-shelf
2. Base 1
3. Base 2
4. Base corner
5. Base blind corner 1
6. Base blind corner 2
7. Base and angle
8. Utility cabinet 1
9. Utility cabinet 2
10. Peninsula end-shelf
11. Base peninsula 1
12. Base peninsula 2
13. Wall end-shelf
14. Wall 1
15. Wall 2
16. Wall corner
17. Wall blind corner 1
18. Wall blind corner 2
19. Utility cabinet 3
20. Wall angle cabinet
21. Wall peninsula 1
22. Wall peninsula 2
23. Wall blind peninsula 1
24. Wall blind peninsula 2
25. L-shaped countertop
26. Sink 1
27. Sink 2
28. Sink 3
29. Help

The Home - Walls Stencil

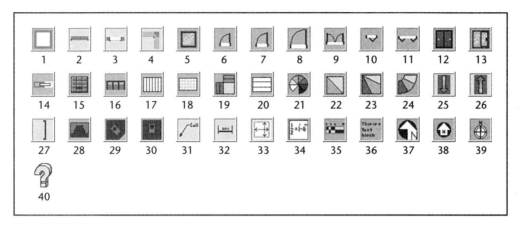

1. Premade wall
2. Wall
3. Wall opening
4. Corner
5. Window
6. Door
7. 30" door
8. 36" door
9. French doors
10. Bi-fold door
11. Double bi-fold door

12. Sliding door
13. Glass door
14. Pocket door
15. Garage door
16. Garden window
17. Deck
18. Patio 1
19. Landing
20. Stair section
21. Spiral stair
22. Corner steps 1

23. Corner steps 2
24. Corner steps 3
25. Down arrow
26. Up arrow
27. Handrail
28. Fireplace
29. Corner stove
30. Stove
31. Callout
32. Dimension line
33. Room measurements

34. Scale label
35. Scale symbol
36. Text block
37. North arrow 1
38. North arrow 2
39. North arrow 3
40. Help

The Insurance - Automobile #1 Stencil

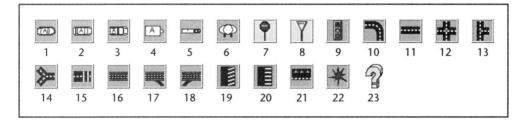

1. Sports car
2. Sedan
3. Pickup
4. Trailer
5. Truck (18-wheeler)
6. Pedestrian (top view)

7. Stop sign
8. Yield sign
9. Stop light
10. Curve
11. Straight
12. Cross

13. T-intersection
14. Y-section
15. Crosswalk
16. Freeway
17. Freeway off-ramp
18. Freeway on-ramp

19. Angle parking
20. Straight parking
21. Parallel parking
22. Crash
23. Help

The Insurance - Automobile #2 Stencil

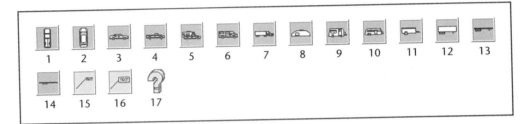

1. Detail truck
2. Detail car
3. Detail car (elevation)
4. Detail truck (elevation)
5. Camper (elevation)
6. Detail van (elevation)
7. Detail semi
8. Windshield
9. Travel trailer
10. House trailer
11. 2-wheel trailer
12. Semi-trailer
13. Flatbed (semi)
14. Flatbed (truck)
15. Callout
16. Boxed callout
17. Help

The Landscape - Plants Stencil

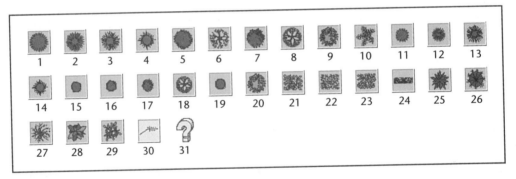

1. Conifer tree A
2. Conifer tree B
3. Conifer tree C
4. Conifer tree D
5. Decid. tree A
6. Decid. tree B
7. Decid. tree C
8. Decid. tree D
9. Broadleaf evrg. tree
10. Palm tree
11. Conifer shrub a
12. Conifer shrub b
13. Conifer shrub c
14. Conifer shrub d
15. Decid. shrub a
16. Decid. shrub b
17. Decid. shrub c
18. Decid. shrub d
19. Decid. shrub e
20. Broadleaf evrg. shrub
21. Broadleaf hedge
22. Conifer hedge
23. Groundcover
24. Perennial border
25. Succulent
26. Cactus
27. Ornamental grass
28. Potted plant 1
29. Potted plant 2
30. Plant callout
31. Help

The Landscape - Site Stencil

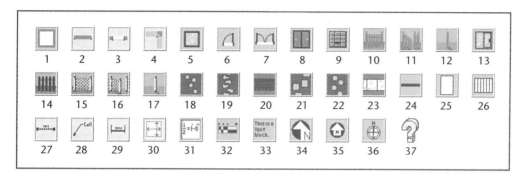

1. Premade wall	11. Wooden gate	21. Square stone	30. Room measurements
2. Wall	12. Wooden post	22. Hex stone	31. Scale label
3. Wall opening	13. Glass door	23. Concrete	32. Scale symbol
4. Corner	14. Board fence	sidewalk	33. Text block
5. Window	15. Chain link fence	24. Railroad tie	34. North arrow 1
6. Door	16. Chain link gate	25. Driveway	35. North arrow 2
7. French doors	17. Metal post	26. Deck	36. North arrow 3
8. Sliding door	18. Round stone	27. Property line	37. Help
9. Garage door	19. Flagstone	28. Callout	
10. Fence	20. Brick sidewalk	29. Dimension line	

The Landscape - Sports Stencil

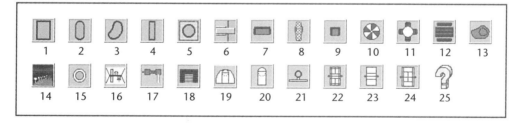

1. Rectangular pool	10. Umbrella	19. Basketball 3 pt. line
2. Oval pool	11. Table	20. Basketball key
3. Kidney-shaped pool	12. Picnic table	21. Basketball hoop
4. Lap pool	13. Boulder	22. Badminton court
5. Spa	14. Light	23. Volleyball court
6. Diving board	15. Bird bath	24. Tennis court
7. Bench	16. Swing set	25. Help
8. Lounge chair	17. Play structure	
9. Lawn chair	18. Grill	

The Kids - Dinosaurs Stencil

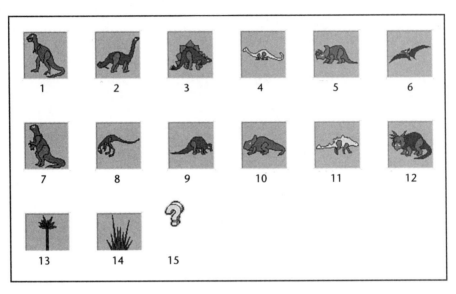

1. Tyrannosaurus	6. Pteranodon	11. Ankylosaurus
2. Apatosaurus	7. Iguanodon	12. Styracosaurus
3. Stegosaurus	8. Struthiomimus	13. Palm
4. Diplodocus	9. Anatosaurus	14. Grass
5. Triceratops	10. Protoceratops	15. Help

Visio Idea Gallery

ORDER FORM

SHIP TO:

Name:

Address:

City:

State: **Zip:** -

AVAILABLE RECORDINGS	PRICE	QTY.	
The Pirates of Penzance			
H.M.S. Pinafore			
Yeomen of the Guard			
Patience			
Princess Ida			
The Mikado			
The Gondoliers			
Shipping & handling:			
TOTAL ▶			

For office use only

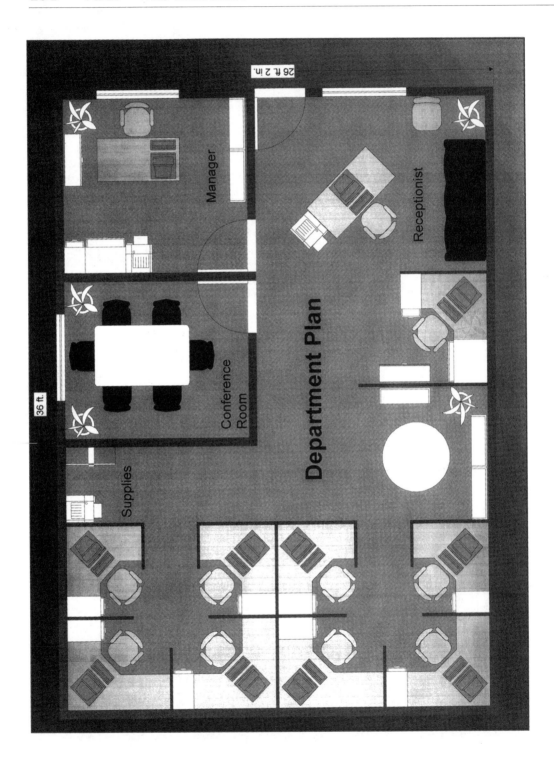

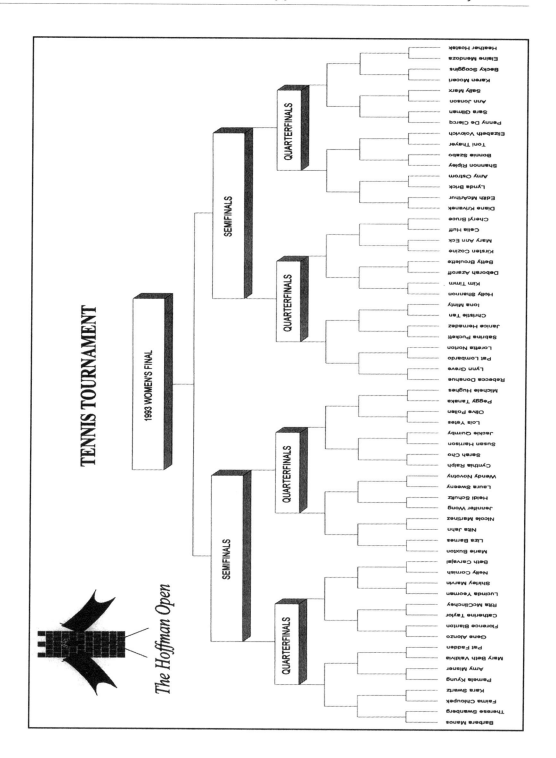

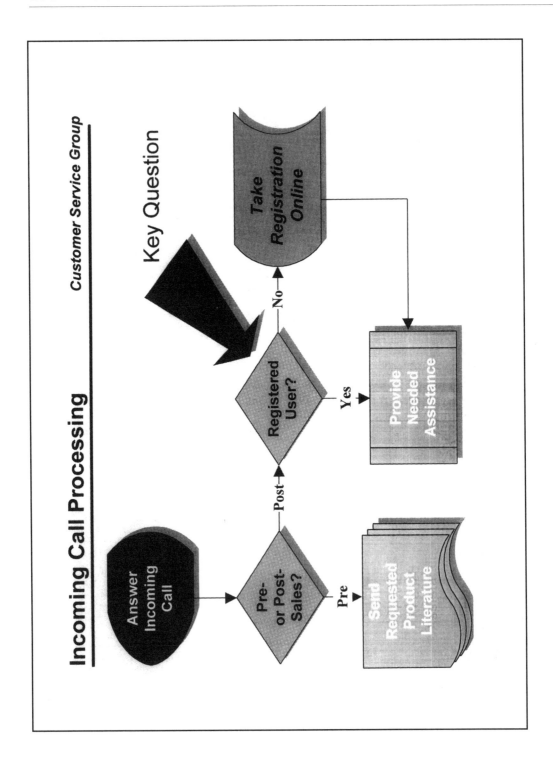

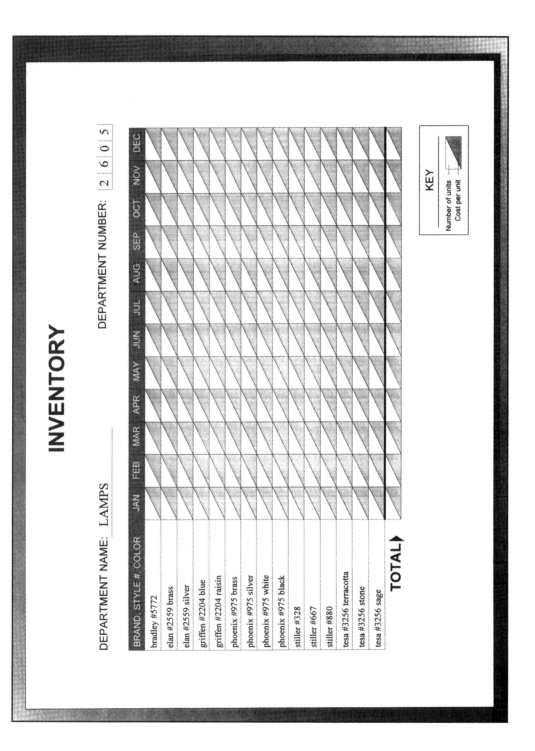

INVENTORY

DEPARTMENT NAME: LAMPS

DEPARTMENT NUMBER: 2 6 0 5

BRAND, STYLE #, COLOR	JAN	FEB	MAR	APR	MAY	JUN	JUL	AUG	SEP	OCT	NOV	DEC
bradley #5772												
elan #2559 brass												
elan #2559 silver												
griffen #2204 blue												
griffen #2204 raisin												
phoenix #975 brass												
phoenix #975 silver												
phoenix #975 white												
phoenix #975 black												
stiller #328												
stiller #667												
stiller #880												
tesa #3256 terracotta												
tesa #3256 stone												
tesa #3256 sage												
TOTAL▶												

KEY

Number of units
Cost per unit

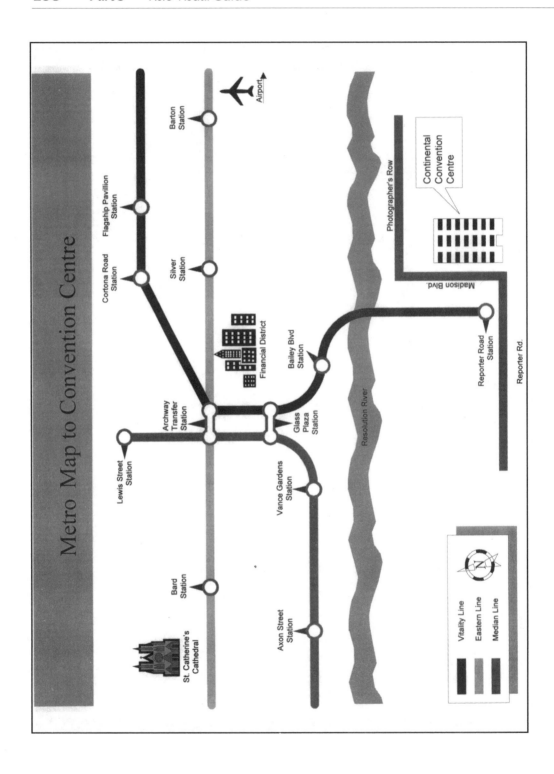

VISIO CHARTING EXAMPLES

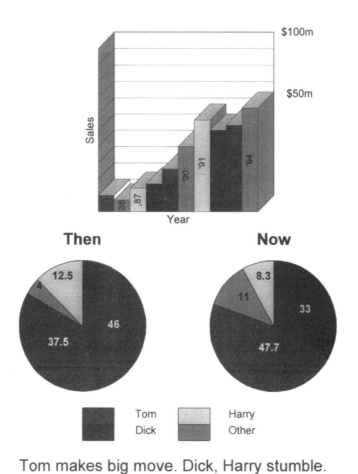

Tom makes big move. Dick, Harry stumble.

Certificate of Merit

We, the Governing Council of the Society of Visio Shape
Designers, hereby bestow this certificate upon

for meritorious service in the interests of the
Organization. Thanks again!

President

Vice President

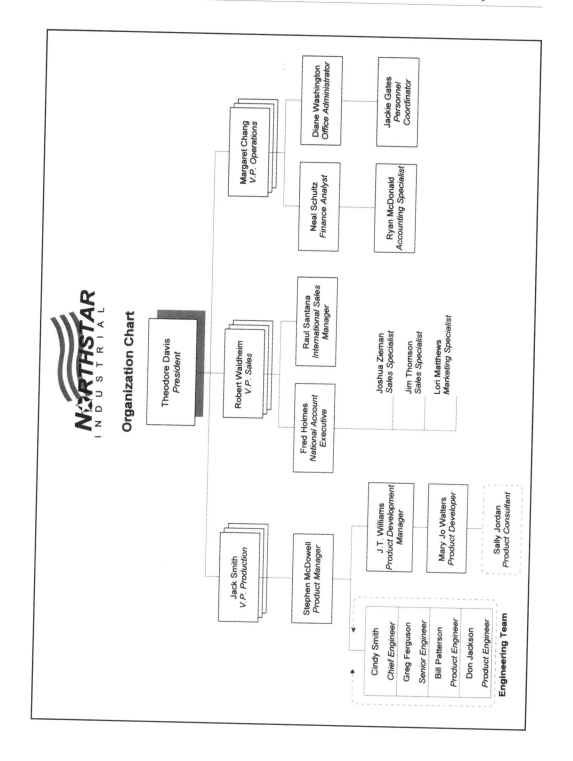

EXHIBIT B

Fig. 1

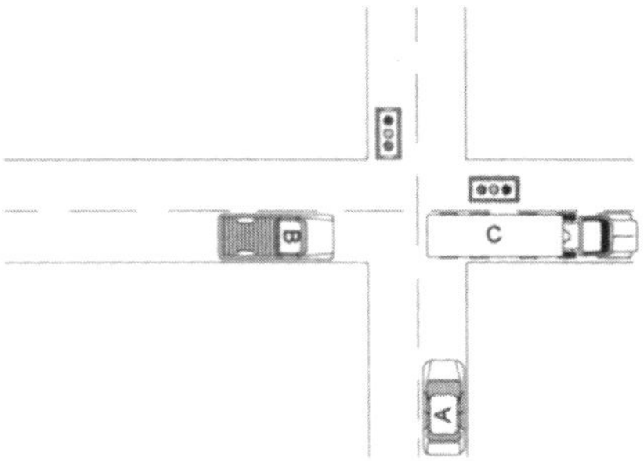
B
C
A

Fig. 2

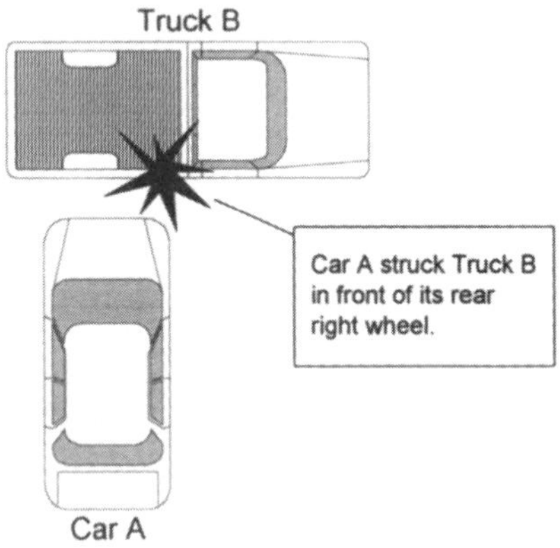
Truck B
Car A struck Truck B in front of its rear right wheel.
Car A

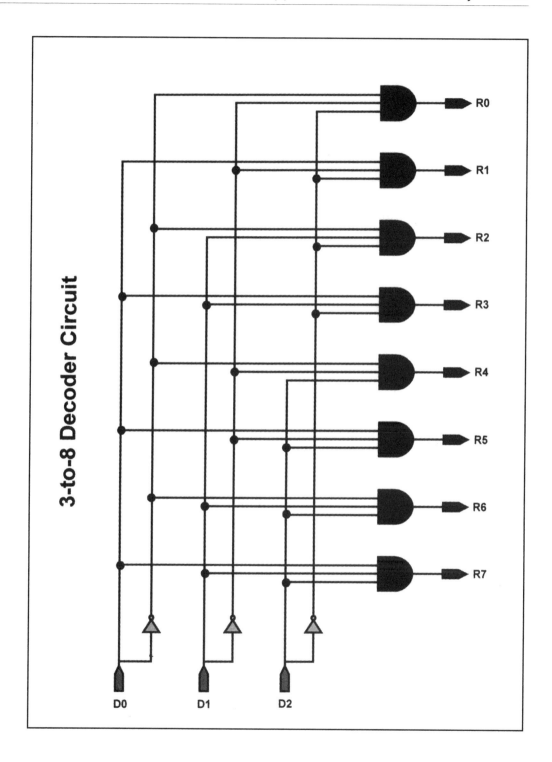

3-to-8 Decoder Circuit

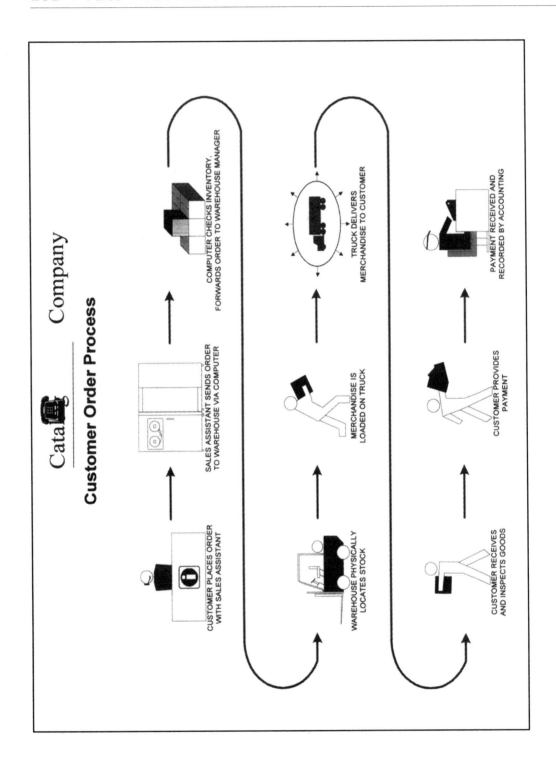

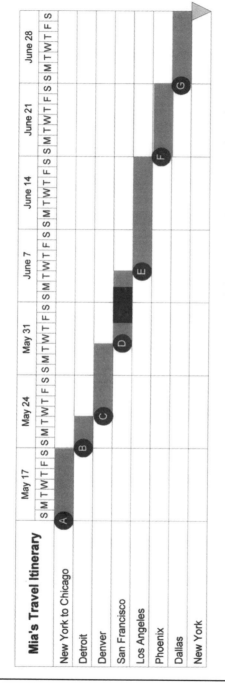

Foods from Greece Promotion

Mia's Travel Itinerary

	May 17	May 24	May 31	June 7	June 14	June 21	June 28
	S M T W T F S	S M T W T F S	S M T W T F S	S M T W T F S	S M T W T F S	S M T W T F S	S M T W T F S
New York to Chicago	A						
Detroit		B					
Denver			C				
San Francisco			D				
Los Angeles				E			
Phoenix					F		
Dallas						G	
New York							

Legend:

● AIRPORT	▶ PROMOTION ENDS
■ FOOD SHOW	

	FRONTIER AIRLINES	FLIGHT #
A	May 17: Depart 12:06 pm/Arrive 1:55 pm	1208
B	May 24: Depart 8:30 am/Arrive 9:45 am	6902
C	May 27: Depart 7:30 am/Arrive 1:20 pm	4520
D	June 2: Depart 6:45 am/Arrive 10:01 am	699
E	June 10: Depart 11:34 pm/Arrive 1:04 am	5002
F	June 21: Depart 9:09 am/Arrive 11:14 am	3222
G	June 28: Depart 2:23 pm/Arrive 10:52 pm	9898

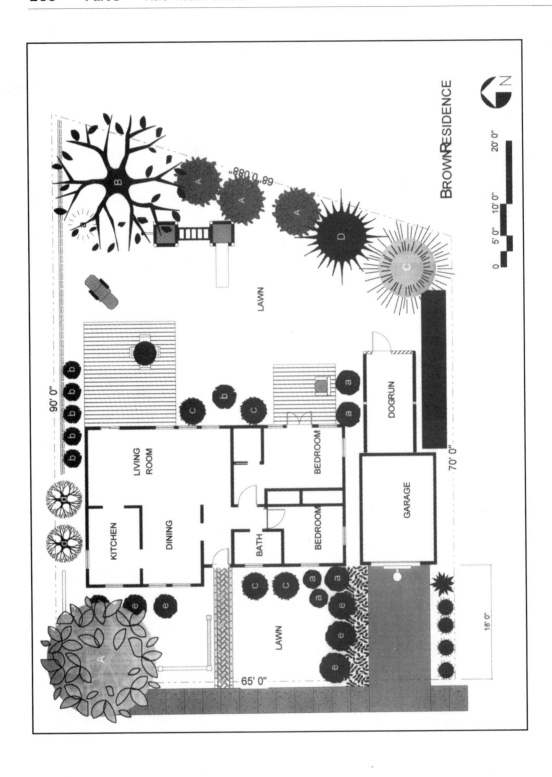

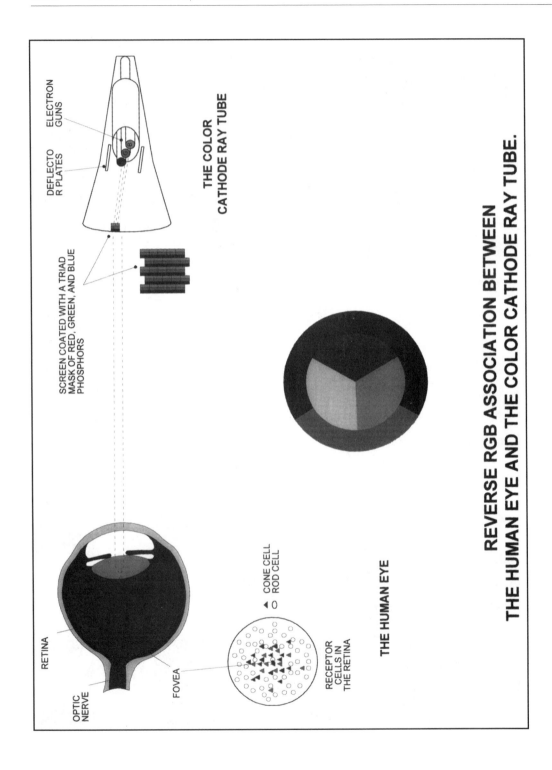

ELECTRON GUNS

DEFLECTO R PLATES

THE COLOR
CATHODE RAY TUBE

SCREEN COATED WITH A TRIAD MASK OF RED, GREEN, AND BLUE PHOSPHORS

RETINA

OPTIC NERVE

FOVEA

CONE CELL
ROD CELL

RECEPTOR CELLS IN THE RETINA

THE HUMAN EYE

REVERSE RGB ASSOCIATION BETWEEN
THE HUMAN EYE AND THE COLOR CATHODE RAY TUBE.

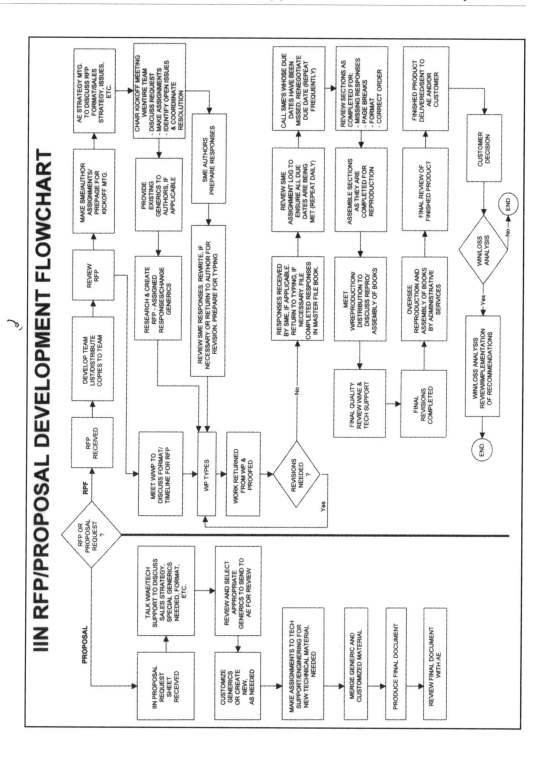

IIN RFP/PROPOSAL DEVELOPMENT FLOWCHART

THE CUSTOMER-DRIVEN ORGANIZATION

MANAGEMENT

The drawing application helps you quickly communicate ideas through the powerful medium of drawing. It is designed for business people, people in technical fields, and for the rest of us. You don't have to be a graphic artist to use Visio—you just need to know the message you want to communicate know the message you want to communicate and how to use Microsoft Windows.

STAFF

Stencils are collections of *master shapes*. When you open a stencil, you see its *master shape icons* on a gree background. When you open the drawing window, you see the drawing page—which looks like a piece of paper—on a blue background. You drag a master shape icon from the stencil to the drawing page to drop an *instance* of the master shape into your drawing.

Introduction: A new way to draw i-1

Disk directory organization chart

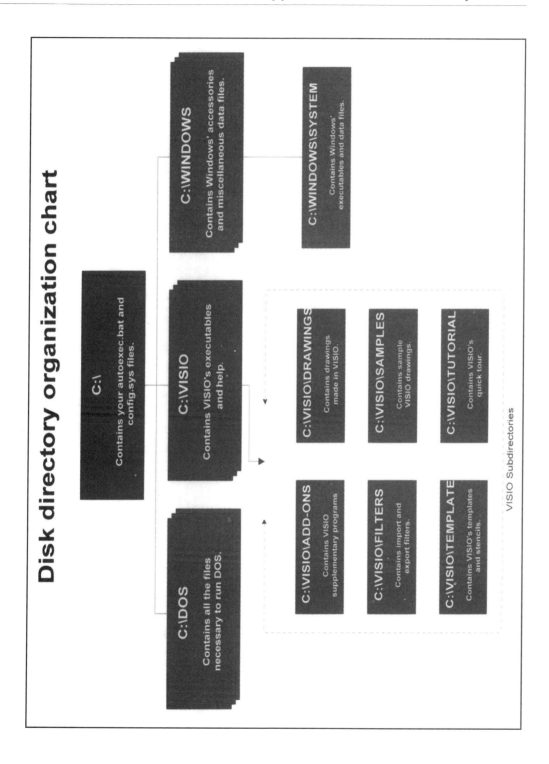

C:
Contains your autoexec.bat and config.sys files.

C:\\WINDOWS
Contains Windows' accessories and miscellaneous data files.

C:\\WINDOWS\\SYSTEM
Contains Windows' executables and data files.

C:\\VISIO
Contains VISIO's executables and help.

C:\\DOS
Contains all the files necessary to run DOS.

C:\\VISIO\\DRAWINGS
Contains drawings made in VISIO.

C:\\VISIO\\SAMPLES
Contains sample VISIO drawings.

C:\\VISIO\\TUTORIAL
Contains VISIO's quick tour.

C:\\VISIO\\ADD-ONS
Contains VISIO supplementary programs

C:\\VISIO\\FILTERS
Contains import and export filters.

C:\\VISIO\\TEMPLATE
Contains VISIO's templates and stencils.

VISIO Subdirectories

NEWELL & HOWARD CONFIDENTIAL

	JULY	AUG	SEPT	OCT
CONTRACTORS	100,000	85,000	30,000	20,000
EQUIPMENT	5,000	3,000	1,000	500
MATERIALS	15,000	15,000	15,000	11,000
TRAVEL EXPENSE	2,000	2,000	700	450
ENTERTAINING	500	400	200	150

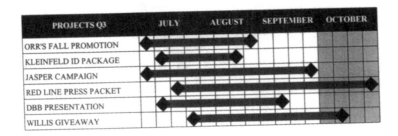

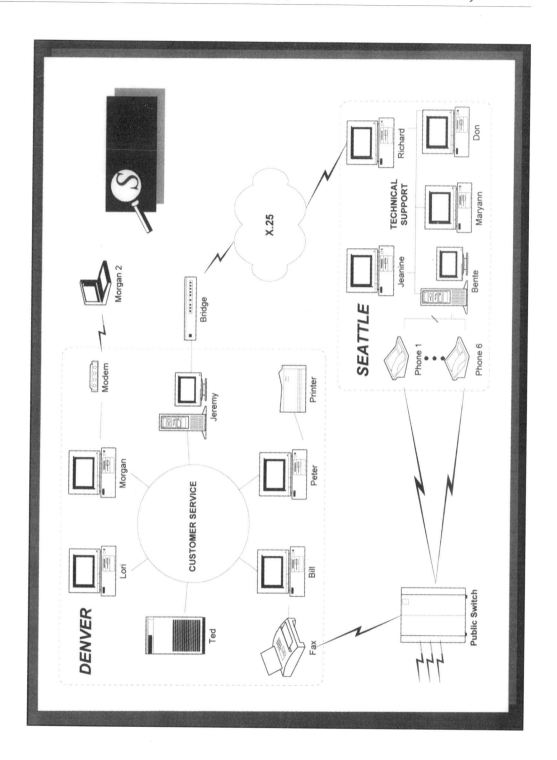

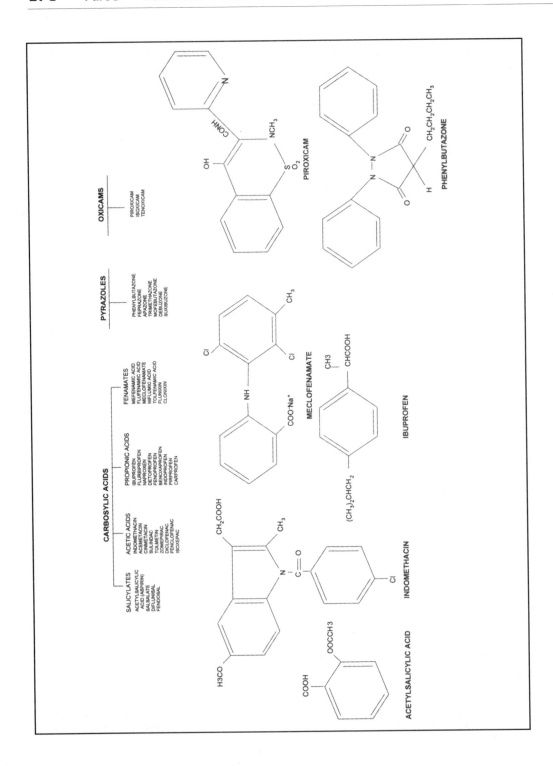

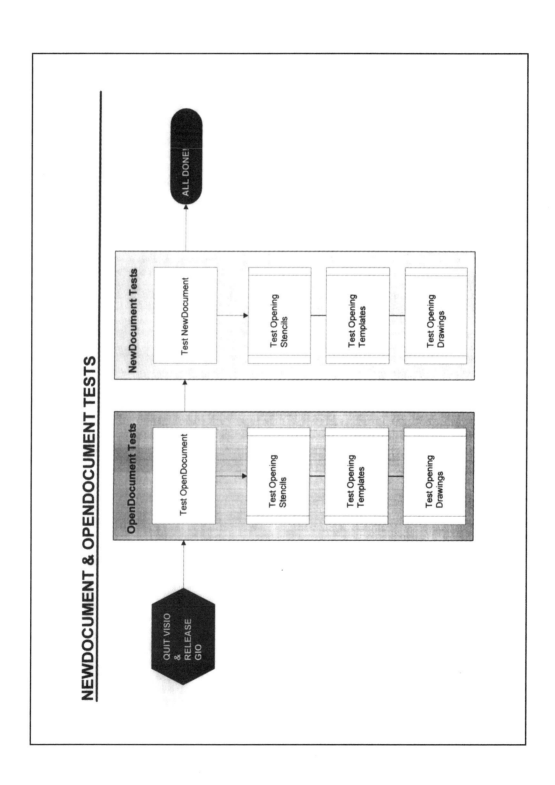

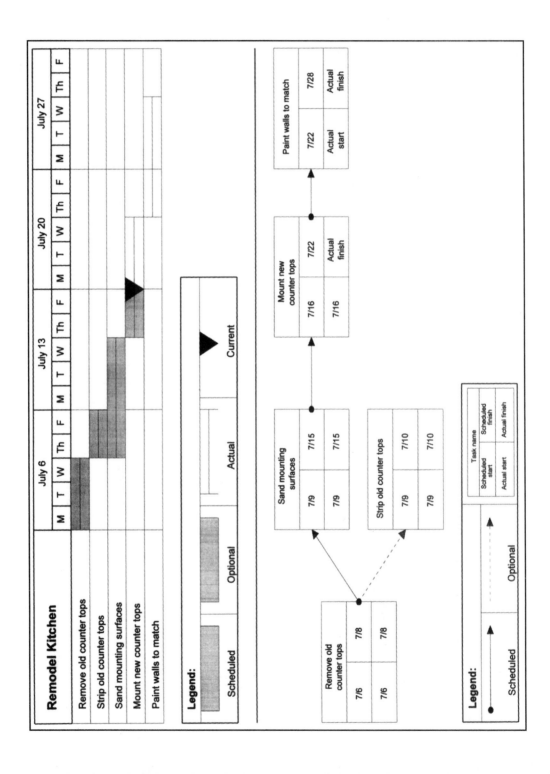

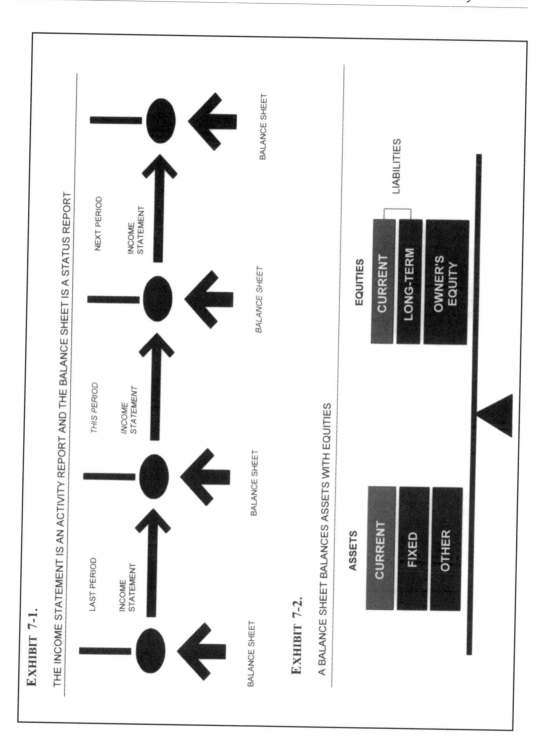

EXHIBIT 7-1.

THE INCOME STATEMENT IS AN ACTIVITY REPORT AND THE BALANCE SHEET IS A STATUS REPORT

EXHIBIT 7-2.

A BALANCE SHEET BALANCES ASSETS WITH EQUITIES

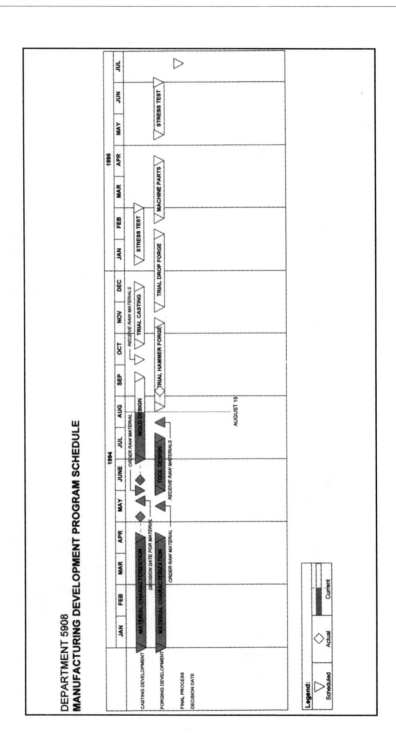

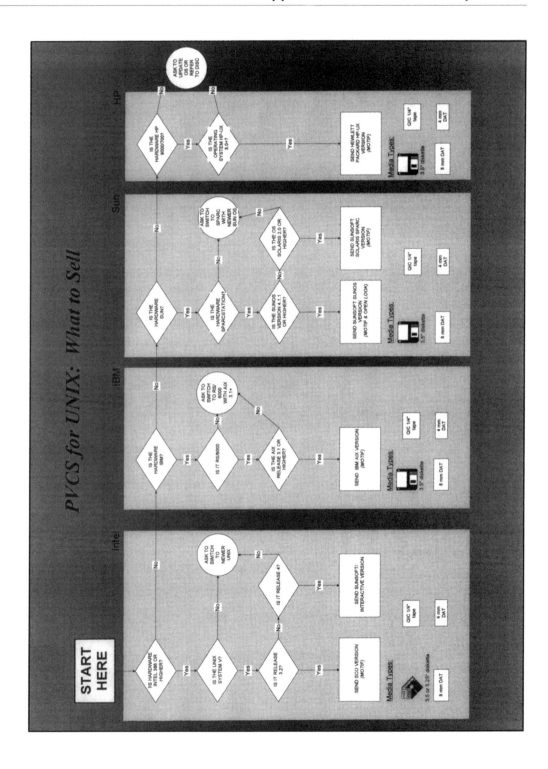

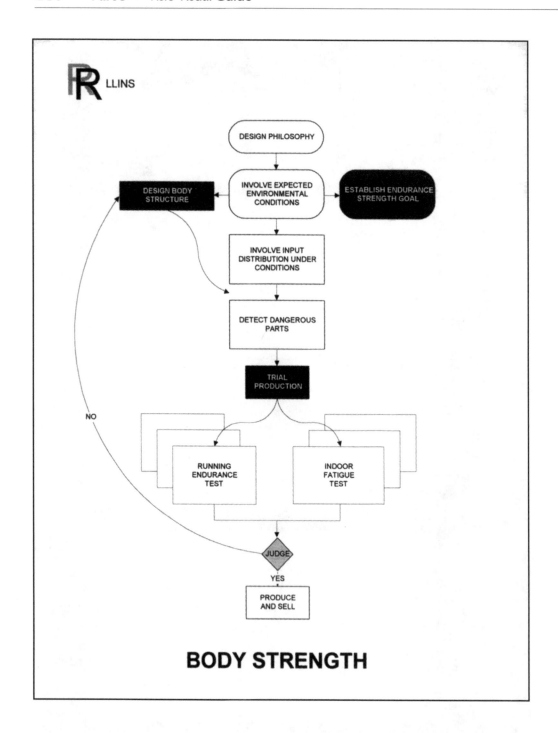

BODY STRENGTH

Power Source

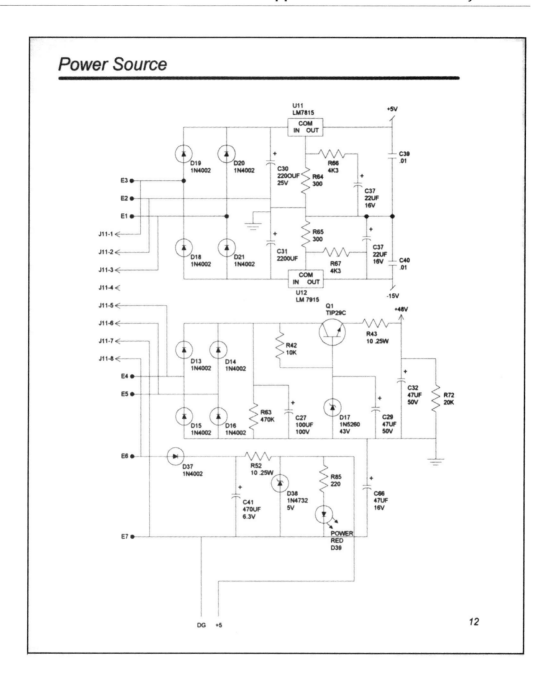

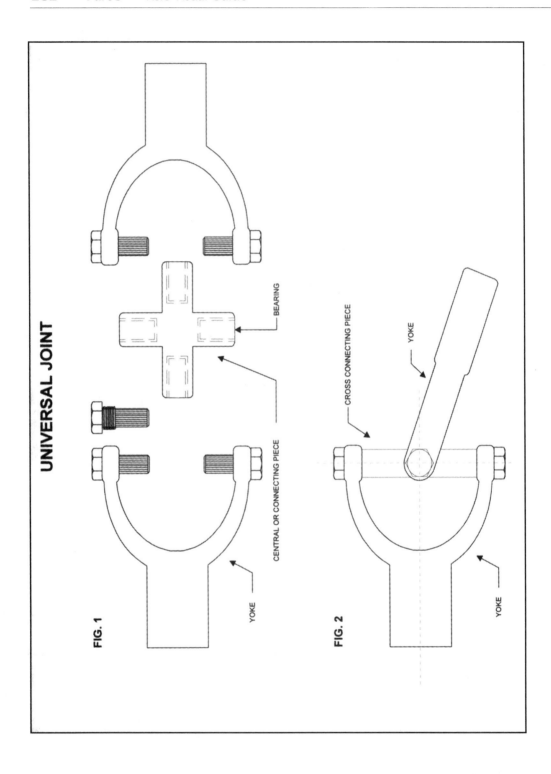

UNIVERSAL JOINT

BEARING

CENTRAL OR CONNECTING PIECE

YOKE

FIG. 1

CROSS CONNECTING PIECE

YOKE

YOKE

FIG. 2

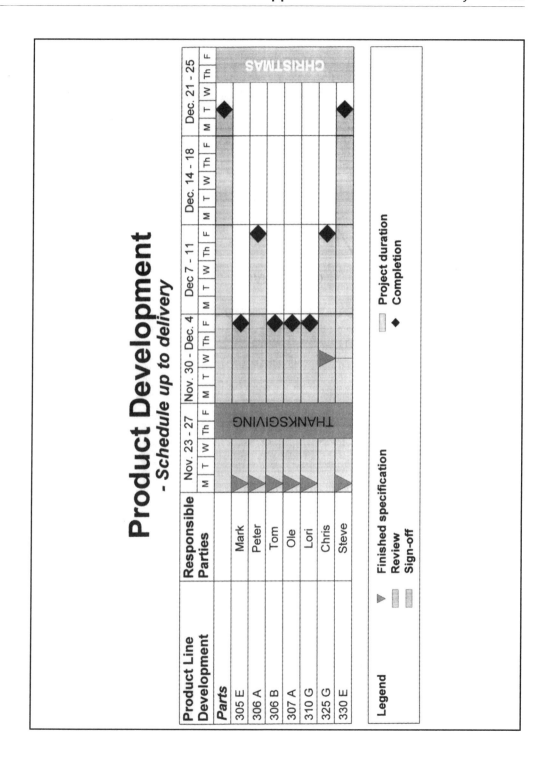

Product Development
- Schedule up to delivery

Product Line Development	Responsible Parties	Nov. 23 - 27	Nov. 30 - Dec. 4	Dec 7 - 11	Dec. 14 - 18	Dec. 21 - 25
Parts		M T W Th F	M T W Th F	M T W Th F	M T W Th F	M T W Th F
305 E	Mark					
306 A	Peter					
306 B	Tom					
307 A	Ole					
310 G	Lori					
325 G	Chris					
330 E	Steve					

Legend

▶ Finished specification
□ Review
□ Sign-off

□ Project duration
◆ Completion

TechTime

FAX Transmission

From:	Olivia Hughes	Date:	May 6, 1994
To:	Matthew Villka	Time:	1:27 PM
Company:	Hardware House	FAX#:	555-1234

Hi Matthew,
Here's to confirm our appointment on Monday at 2:30. This map will help you find our building.

I look forward to our meeting,

Olivia

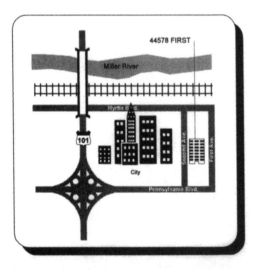

44578 First   Suite 566   Bayer   Wa   98115

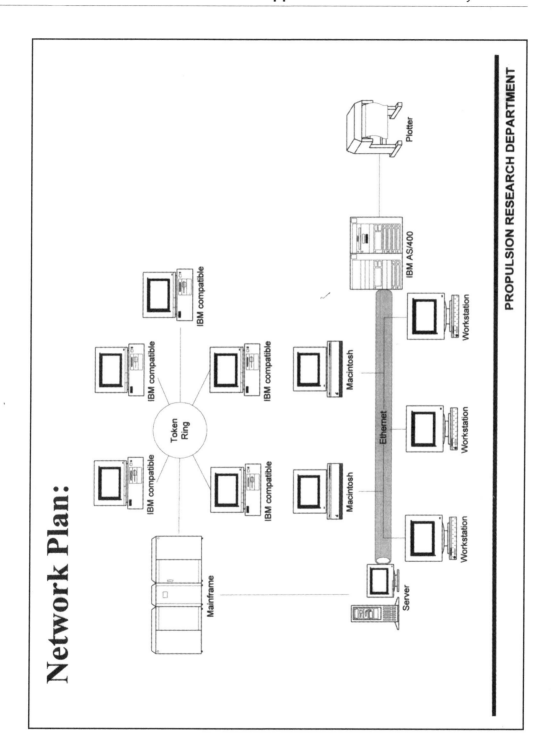

The High-Speed Data Bus

You may not be an artist, but you probably communicate through drawings every day Many people draw ideas, processes, and directions instead of writing them out pictures are often faster to create and easier to understand than the words for the same information.

The Visio™ drawing application helps you quickly communicate ideas through the powerful medium of drawing. It is designed for business people, people in technica fields, and for the rest of us. You don't have to be a graphic artist to use Visio—you jus need to know the message you want to communicate and how to use Microsof Windows.

Before you start working in Visio, it's helpful to understand the basics of drawing i Visio and how Visio differs from other drawing programs you might have used. The bi difference is this: you can create drawings without even drawing.

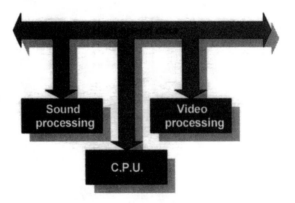

Sound Processing

The easiest way to create a drawing in Visio is by dragging shapes from a *stencil* into the drawing. This method is called drag and drop drawing.

Stencils are collections of *master shapes*. When you open a stencil, you see its *maste shape icons* on a green background. When you open the drawing window, you see the drawing page—which looks like a piece of paper—on a blue background. You drag a

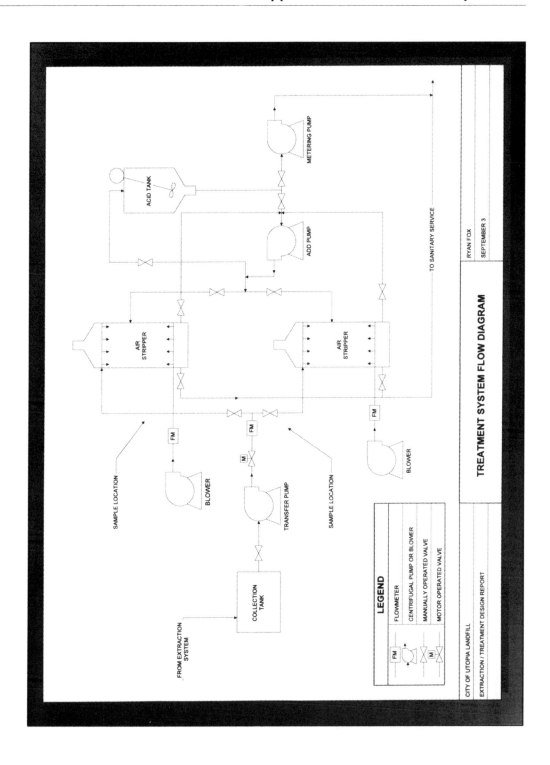

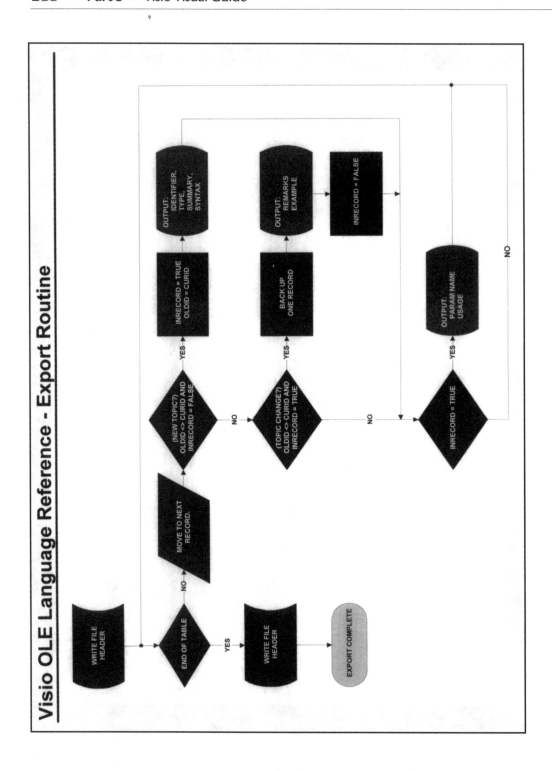

Visio OLE Language Reference - Export Routine

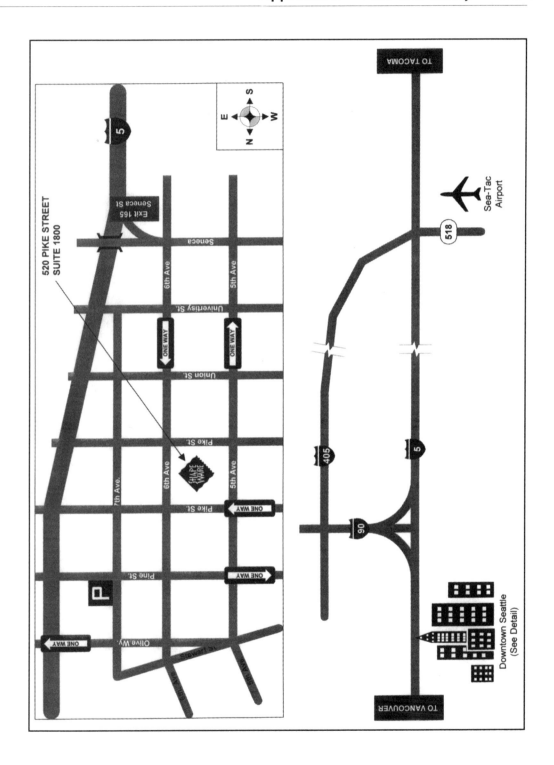

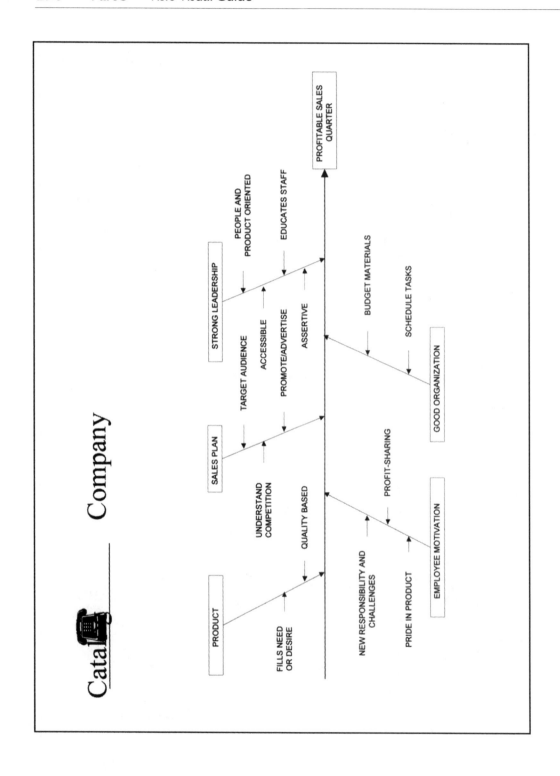

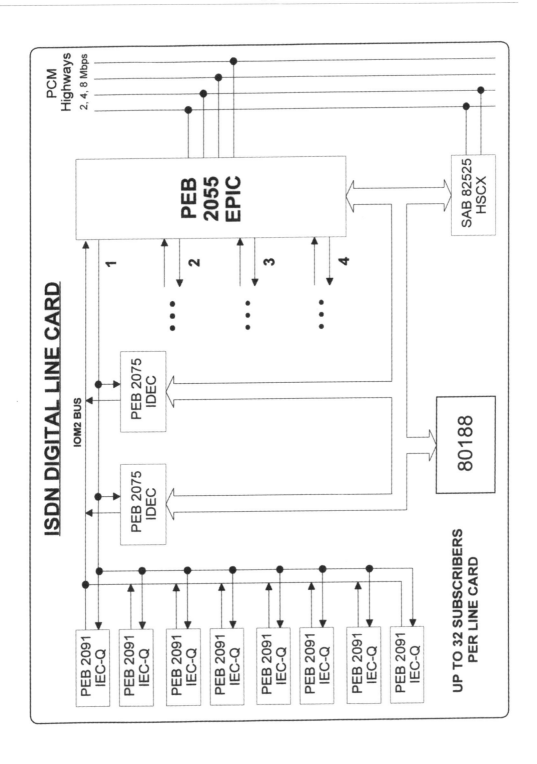

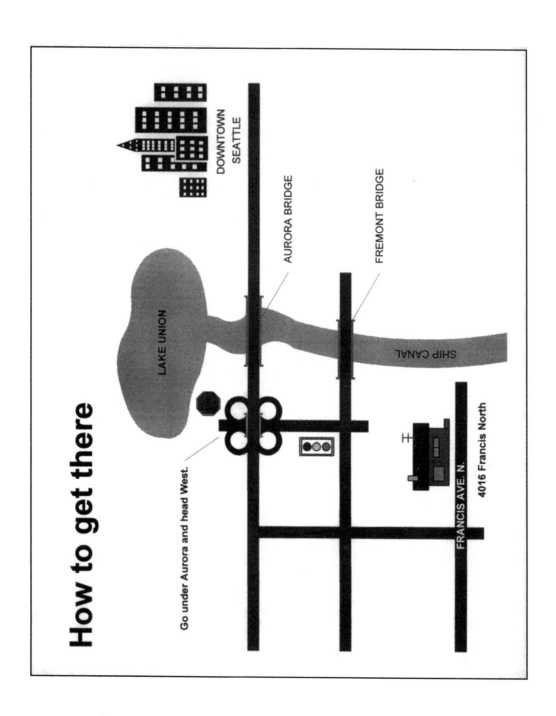

Visio Installation Instructions

Before you can run Visio, you must install the program files on your computer's hard disk. You received the program files on the five Visio disks that were in the Visio box. Follow these steps to install the program.

1. Turn on your computer and start Windows (version 3.1 or higher) by typing **WIN** at the DOS prompt (C:> or C:\>).
2. Insert the Visio disk labeled Disk1-Setup in drive A (or drive B).
3. From the Windows Program Manager window, open the File menu and select the Run command. Windows displays the Run dialog box shown below.
4. In the Command Line box, type **a:\setup** if the disk is in your A drive. If you used drive B instead of drive A, type **b:\setup**.

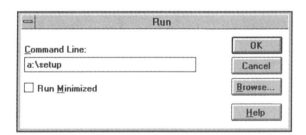

5. Click on the OK button.
6. Accept the default directory (VISIO) or change to a directory of your choice.
7. Choose Typical from the Visio Setup dialog box.

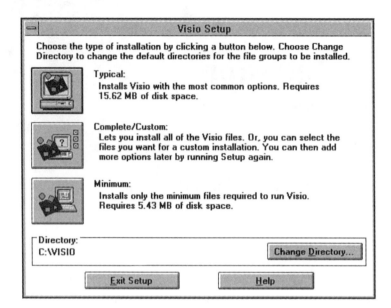

8. Follow Visio's installation instructions as they are displayed on-screen.

9. Visio Setup gives you a choice between giving the program group another name or using the default (Visio). Select OK to continue.

10. Visio Setup installs a new toolbar button for applications you have installed (such as Excel, Word for Windows, and so on). Make your choices and click OK.

11. You are given the option to Run Quick Tour Now or Skip Quick Tour and continue. Make your choice.

12. Remove the last disk when the installation is complete. You are now ready to start using Visio. See Chapter 1 for instructions on how to start Visio. You are given a phone number to call to register your copy of Visio. You should do this as soon as possible to ensure timely technical support.

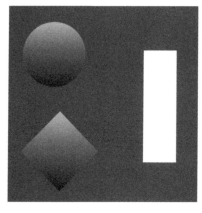

Index

Call today to order the Visio Shapes products that suit your particular drawing and diagramming needs, or call to order any of the Visio® brand products listed below.

1-800-446-3335 EXT. 84G

PRODUCT LISTING

VISIO SHAPES PRODUCTS: Additional Shapes products for more specialized drawing & diagramming

	Sugg. Retail Price	Your Price	Quantity	Cost
Advanced Flowcharts				
- expands on the flowcharting shapes that come with Visio	$ 79.00	$ 49.00	_____	_____
Advanced Software Diagrams				
- for illustrating and organizing your software project—includes several programming models	$ 79.00	$ 49.00	_____	_____
Advanced Network Diagrams				
- expands on the network equipment that comes with Visio	$ 79.00	$ 49.00	_____	_____
Marketing				
- for illustrating business, sales, and marketing concepts	$ 79.00	$ 49.00	_____	_____
Advanced Space Planning				
- expands on furniture and office equipment that come with Visio	$ 79.00	$ 49.00	_____	_____
Advanced Electrical Engineering				
- for logic, electronic schematic, and power diagrams; based on IEEE standards	$ 79.00	$ 49.00	_____	_____
Mechanical Engineering				
- for illustrating geometric dimensioning, welding, fasteners, piping, and HVAC	$ 79.00	$ 49.00	_____	_____
Biotechnology/Medicine				
- for illustrating immunology, cells, human organs, and amino acids	$ 79.00	$ 49.00	_____	_____
Chemical Engineering				
- for illustrating chemical flow diagrams	$ 79.00	$ 49.00	_____	_____
Chemistry				
- for illustrating periodic table elements, cyclic compounds, biostructures, and amino acids	$ 79.00	$ 49.00	_____	_____
Insurance/Law Enforcement				
- for auto accident reports and insurance diagrams	$ 79.00	$ 49.00	_____	_____
Petroleum Engineering				
- for chemical flow diagrams and piping specific to petroleum engineering	$ 79.00	$ 49.00	_____	_____
Home Planning				
- for home, kitchen, and bathroom design or remodeling	$ 39.00	$ 29.00	_____	_____
Landscape Planning				
- for landscape design or remodeling	$ 39.00	$ 29.00	_____	_____
Kids				
- for creating coloring books of dinosaurs, whales, castles, and more	$ 39.00	$ 29.00	_____	_____

VISIO BOOKS

	Sugg. Retail Price	Your Price	Quantity	Cost
Developing Visio Shapes (does not apply to Visio Express)				
- a book for creating your own custom shapes, written by Shapeware's Visio Shapes designers	$ 39.00	$ 29.00	_____	_____
Programming Visio (includes set of code examples)				
- information on programming add-ons and integrating Visio into a system solution using OLE Automation	$ 39.00	$ 29.00	_____	_____

VISIO:

	Sugg. Retail Price	Your Price	Quantity	Cost
VISIO 3.0				
- includes over 750 Visio SmartShapes® for business and technical drawing	$ 79.00	$ 49.00	_____	_____
VISIO EXPRESS FOR MICROSOFT OFFICE				
- general business drawing and diagramming within Microsoft Office applications	$ 79.00	$ 49.00	_____	_____
VISIO EXPRESS FOR LOTUS SMARTSUITE				
- general business drawing and diagramming within Lotus SmartSuite applications	$ 79.00	$ 49.00	_____	_____
VISIO HOME				
- easy drawing and diagramming for home, school, hobbies, sports, personal creativity and more	$ 79.00	$ 49.00	_____	_____

Name _____

Company _____
(if applicable)

Address _____
(street address required for shipping)

City _____ State/Province_____ Zip/Postal Code _____

Daytime Phone Number (_____) _____

Subtotal $ _____
Shipping & handling for first product* $ ___8.9___
Please add $3.95 shipping & handling for each additional product* $ _____
Subtotal $ _____
(CO residents add 3.8%; WA residents add 8.2%) Sales Tax $ _____
(Payment must be in U.S. dollars) **Total** $ _____

*Customers from Canada, Alaska, and Hawaii, please call Shapeware Customer Service at **1-800-446-3335 Ext. 84G** for shipping & handling information.

Offer good only in the United States and Canada. Please allow 1 to 2 weeks for delivery. 3.5" (1.44 MB) disks are standard.

☐ Check enclosed *(Make checks payable to Shapeware Corporation)*   ☐ American Express   ☐ MasterCard   ☐ VISA

Card Number _____   Exp.date _____

Signature *(required for credit card orders)* _____

Mail To:
SHAPEWARE CORPORATION
CUSTOMER SERVICE
PO BOX 22063
DENVER CO 80222-9866